The Pocket Economist

The Pocket Economist

Rupert Pennant-Rea
and
Bill Emmott

CAMBRIDGE UNIVERSITY PRESS
Cambridge London New York Rochelle Melbourne Sydney

First published by Martin Robertson & Co Ltd, Oxford
and *The Economist*, London

Published in North America by
the Press Syndicate of the University of Cambridge,
The Pitt Building, Trumpington Street, Cambridge CB2 1RP
32 East 57th Street, New York, NY 10022, USA
296 Beaconsfield Parade, Middle Park,
Melbourne 3206, Australia

First published 1983

Printed in Great Britain

Library of Congress Cataloging in Publication Data

Pennant-Rea, Rupert.
  The pocket economist.

  1. Economics – Dictionaries.   I. Emmott, William.
II. Title.
HB61.P435   1983   330′ .03′ 21   83-15054
ISBN 0-521-26070-1 (Cambridge University Press)

Contents

Preface

'Jargon', to paraphrase Bernard Shaw, 'is a conspiracy against the laity'. It is also a useful shorthand, so calling it names will not make it go away. But it can be understood and exploited by laymen, especially if they get into the subject via the front door of practical use and not the attic of high theory.

This book is a guide to the economics that affects jobs and prices and trade, that raises voices in pubs and praesidiums and that, in varying degrees, perplexes all but the truly inane. It is not a comprehensive guide to economics: that would need more space for theoretical and historical issues. Such issues do appear in these pages, but only where they shed light on the ideas, institutions and policies that shape today's economic world.

Few of the entries in this book stand entirely on their own. To understand why exchange rates change it is necessary to know something of central banks, inflation, interest rates, current accounts and so on. Wherever possible, one longer entry has sought to draw these threads together in one place. Where it is not, the links are often acknowledged by setting in small capitals words for which there is a separate but relevant entry. To do that every time, however, would be confusing, and would strain the user's eyes as well as his patience.

Many people have helped in the production of this book. Grant McIntyre had the original idea; Hugo Meynell and Christopher Hutton-Williams picked it up with enthusiasm. Several colleagues on *The Economist* lent a hand – Brenda De Fluri with statistics, Richard Natkiel with charts, Bobby Hunt with cartoons, Amanda Raymer with typing. Thanks are due to all of them.

A

Above par. A share or bond whose market value is above its face value. A fall in long-term interest rates after a bond has been issued will raise the bond's price above par (see BOND MARKET). Contrast with BELOW PAR.

Absolute advantage. The crudest way to compare efficiency. For example: in 1981, Japan produced a ton of steel with only 9.4 man-hours at a cost of only $502, compared with 16.5 man-hours and $622 in Britain. That does not tell you whether Japan should specialize in steel, because it might be even better relative to Britain at other things. The real guide to specialization and to maximizing the gains from trade is COMPARATIVE ADVANTAGE. Neither absolute nor comparative advantage are necessarily static for all time; once British steel producers were far more efficient than the Japanese.

Accepting house. One of the elite of British MERCHANT BANKS. Typically companies can raise money selling three-month bills of exchange (see COMMERCIAL BILLS) to the money markets. An accepting house buys the bill (the 'acceptance') and so lends to the creditor company in the belief that the debtor will pay up. Once 'accepted', the bill secures the bank's stamp of approval and hence has resale (DISCOUNTING) value. Originally acceptance was meant to signify that the company was a BLUE CHIP borrower, but nowadays the banks are less discriminating.

Other banks 'accept' bills, too; but accepting houses long enjoyed the special privilege that the bills they accepted would, if necessary, be bought by the BANK OF ENGLAND. All accepting houses, once specialists, now perform other banking functions: lending and taking DEPOSITS, issuing STOCKS, arranging NEW ISSUES and new investments. The seventeen top accepting houses in London form the exclusive Accepting Houses Committee which liaises with the Treasury and the Bank of England. The full list: Arbuthnot Latham; Baring Brothers; Brown, Shipley; Charterhouse Japhet; Robert Fleming; Guinness Mahon; Hambros; Hill Samuel; Kleinwort, Benson; Lazard Brothers; Samuel Montagu; Morgan Grenfell; Rea Brothers; N. M. Rothschild; J. Henry Schroder Wagg; Singer & Friedlander; S. G. Warburg. See also BANKS, DISCOUNT HOUSES.

Accounting. Recording transactions of a firm, and its assets and liabilities, to reveal (and occasionally to disguise) the financial state of the company. Until the 1970s, assets, stocks and liabilities were valued at their original cost – HISTORIC COST ACCOUNTING – but rapid inflation made this unrealistic. Now, many countries have switched to CURRENT COST ACCOUNTING.

Account period. Breathing space before share dealers have to settle their bills: the length of time varies from one country to another. See STOCK EXCHANGE.

Acid test. ACCOUNTING term for measure of a company's ability to pay immediate liabilities. The acid test is liquid ASSETS divided by CURRENT LIABILITIES. Liquid assets are cash plus money owed by debtors, normally excluding any long-term debtors. Highly liquid stocks can be included too.

Adjustment. Generically, the process by which economic variables change to some long-run equilibrium. Specifically, one of the buzz-words of the 1970s and 1980s, used to describe the painful business of countries correcting deficits in their current accounts. The INTERNATIONAL MONETARY FUND has had prime responsibility for ensuring adjustment among its members who come to it for help (and money). According to one IMF definition, 'adjustment refers to those changes in expenditure, saving and production that are needed to produce a sustainable BALANCE OF PAYMENTS situation — namely, one where any deficit on current account can be financed by normal capital inflows'. To achieve this happy state, the IMF usually advocates DEVALUATION of the EXCHANGE RATE, plus tighter FISCAL POLICY and MONETARY CONTROL.

Administered interest rates, prices. See PRICE CONTROLS.

Ad valorem. An indirect tax that is levied as a percentage of the price of a good or service. The revenue raised then increases with the value of the good. Examples are VALUE ADDED TAX and most SALES TAXES. Contrast with SPECIFIC DUTIES, which are a fixed amount regardless of value — for example, £1.00 on a bottle of whisky whether it is the cheapest or the finest.

Advance. Bankers' word for a loan. Normally fairly short term, two or three years, in the form of an overdraft to a company or individual.

Agricultural policy. Most industrial countries cosset their farmers, for four reasons: (1) to insulate farmers from the volatility of the food market and the unpredictability of the weather; (2) to slow down rural depopulation and preserve the character of the countryside; (3) to soothe the effects of ENGEL'S LAW, that demand for food does not rise in step with rising incomes; and (4) to keep farmers' lobbies quiet. They do this in one of two ways, plus some frills:
• By handing farmers money to top up their income. This was accompanied in the United States in the 1930s by requirements that, in return, farmers must stop using part of their land (a scheme known

as 'set aside'). In Britain, before joining the EUROPEAN ECONOMIC COMMUNITY (EEC) in 1973, direct top-ups were known as 'deficiency payments'.

● By guaranteeing stable (and often high) prices, whatever the state of the market or the weather. This is the EEC's choice; if the price falls below a predetermined level, all goods offered for sale are bought up by the authorities at that price and stored, to be either sold later or destroyed. To support these high prices, import levies have to be imposed, and exports need subsidies to compete on world markets.

The United States now uses a blend of these two methods. The federal government spent $14 billion on farm support in 1981–82. The EEC's COMMON AGRICULTURAL POLICY opts chiefly for high guaranteed prices, and spent $13 billion on its farmers in 1981. Even Japan props up its agriculture – for instance, by guaranteeing prices for rice that are six times American levels.

Amortization. Running down, or depreciation of a loan by instalments. Mortgages for house purchase, for instance, are 'amortized' by making regular payments over time plus INTEREST. With loans that are not 'amortized', the borrower pays only interest during the period of the loan, and then repays the sum in full.

Animal spirits. Entrepreneurial zeal, the term was coined by KEYNES but emphasized by many economists as a major influence on GROWTH and the level of economic activity. Economists' models on the determinants of INVESTMENT can judge accurately the impact of measurable variables such as the costs of CREDIT, materials and so on, but their most arbitrary assumption is of ENTREPRENEURS' moods. If entrepreneurs begin to expect good markets, economists' forecasts may be upset. Governments have often believed they could talk the economy

into growth (see INDICATIVE PLANNING and JAW-BONING) or into lower INFLATION, by raising animal spirits and expectations. Unfortunately, few businessmen believe politicians.

Anti-trust. Monopoly bashing by governments. Anti-trust laws aim to regulate abuses by big companies and, in some cases, to prevent mergers or take-overs that create dominant firms. The trust-busters' mecca has been:

The United States. The Sherman Anti-trust Act of 1890 provides for fines or imprisonment for contracts or 'conspiracies' that restrain trade, or people that 'monopolize' commerce. After Sherman, the courts took the power to break up big companies. In the early 1900s, the heyday of trust-busting, the Du Pont chemicals firm was split into three, railroad companies were split up and, in 1911, Standard Oil was broken up. Since then the rate of trust-busting has slowed, and, especially in the 1930s, many companies were given trust exemption.

A government agency, the FEDERAL TRADE COMMISSION, was set up in 1914 to police free COMPETITION, and has the power, enforceable in the courts, to issue 'cease and desist' orders against unfair practices, against CARTELS and against mergers and take-overs. The Sherman Act has been reinforced by the Clayton Act (1914), which banned exclusive dealing arrangements (allowing only a restricted set of licences to sell a product), interlocking directorships between competitors, price discrimination for big purchasers, and buying shares in a competitor. The Clayton Act's provisions against price discrimination were strengthened by the Robinson-Paxman Act (1936), and its ban on buying shares in competitors by the Celler-Kefauver Act (1950).

American anti-trust law – and practice – is still the most powerful. In 1982 two important decisions were taken: to break up the telephone networks of American Telephone and Telegraph (AT & T –

known as Ma Bell), set up dozens of 'Baby Bells' in competition, and allow AT & T and International Business Machines (IBM) to compete in telecommunications; and to drop a thirteen-year-old anti-trust action against IBM.

Other countries have anti-trust laws, though none have gone as far as the United States.

● In Britain, the Office of Fair Trading (set up in 1973) has the power to refer trading practices and potentially monopolistic mergers and take-overs to the MONOPOLIES AND MERGERS COMMISSION. This quasi-legal body (set up in 1948) can investigate markets and prevent mergers.

● In West Germany, the Bundeskartellamt (Federal cartel office) can ban RESTRICTIVE PRACTICES and mergers that threaten to produce an overly dominant firm.

● EUROPEAN ECONOMIC COMMUNITY competition law is the closest to American. Under Articles 85 and 86 of the Treaty of Rome, the EEC commission can ban all price fixing, market sharing or other restrictive practices that restrain trade, and impose fines for 'abuse of dominant position'. Exclusive dealing arrangements are also banned, though exemptions can be granted. The EEC's toughest action has been against firms like National Panasonic and Hoffman-La Roche that tried to block trade between EEC member states in order to charge widely different prices. As yet, the EEC has no powers to vet or block mergers.

Arbitrage. Dealing to exploit price differences between CURRENCIES, COMMODITIES or financial ASSETS in different markets. Certain types of arbitrage are riskless. If, for instance, D-marks are slightly cheaper in London than in New York, foreign exchange dealers can make a profit by buying D-marks for dollars in London and selling D-marks simultaneously in New York. The trade will tend to close the gap between the two markets.

Riskless arbitrage opportunities also exist in the EUROMARKETS. If, for instance, EURODOLLAR holders see higher interest rates being offered in New York, they will shift their dollar deposits there. This will raise interest rates in Europe (by reducing the supply of dollars) and reduce them in New York (by increasing the supply of dollars), thereby bringing domestic and Eurodollar interest rates into line. This simple process is undermined by EXCHANGE CONTROLS, which restrict the flow of currency, prevent arbitrage and allow interest rates to diverge.

Another form of riskless arbitrage – in bills – arose from the BANK OF ENGLAND's own operations in 1981–82. The Bank bought large numbers of COMMERCIAL BILLS from companies, via banks, at a favourable rate. Smart company treasurers sold a bill, then on-lent the money at a higher rate of interest in the London INTERBANK MARKET.

One American usage of the term 'arbitrage' involves big risks. In the stock market, somebody may buy shares in a company on the expectation that the company is going to be taken over by another. If that happens, its shares will typically rise in price and the arbitrageur will sell at a profit.

Asset. Anything owned by a company or an individual that can be given a money value. A business's BALANCE SHEET is split between assets and liabilities, which are always equal by definition. Assets come in various forms.

Financial assets. These include CASH, bank DEPOSITS, marketable SECURITIES, other items that can easily be made LIQUID, such as STOCKS, bills owed to the company, work in progress (that can be stopped, or will shortly be paid for). These are also known as current assets.

Fixed assets. These include buildings, land, machinery, heavy plant, and vehicles, valued (under HISTORIC COST ACCOUNTING) at cost of purchase minus DEPRECIATION.

Investments in other companies or in subsidiaries are assets too; some assets, known as intangibles, cannot be entered on a balance sheet, such as patents, skills, reputation, good will and so on. Assets can be hard to value. Fixed assets are usually valued by the saleable value, or the number of years of useful production left in them.

Asset stripping. Profitable practice of buying up quoted companies cheaply and selling off their ASSETS. Fairly common motive for take-overs, but made fashionable (and controversial) by the press attention given to it in the 1970s. Only profitable when the share price and so purchase price of the firm is below the realizable value of its assets. In theory, share prices reflect asset values – but a BEAR market or poor company performance can drive prices well below them. Most famous British asset stripper of the 1970s was Jim Slater, of Slater Walker.

Autarky. Utopian aim of self-sufficiency. An autarkic country tries to substitute domestic products for IMPORTS from other countries to gain independence from the vagaries of trade. However, no country is able to produce the whole range of goods demanded at competitive prices, so autarky condemns its disciples to inefficiency and relative poverty.

B

Backwardation. COMMODITY markets term for state when FUTURES prices are lower than spot prices (see SPOT MARKETS). If a commodity moves into backwardation, the markets are expecting prices to fall. Contrast with CONTANGO.

Bagehot, Walter (1826–77). British sage on the operations of the CITY OF LONDON and on the British constitution. Banker turned economic commentator, Bagehot combined editing *The Economist* (a post he assumed from his father-in-law, James Wilson, in 1860 and held until 1877) with writing numerous tomes on ECONOMICS, including *Universal Money* (1869), *Lombard Street: A Description of the Money Market* (1878) and *Postulates of English Political Economy* (1876). Famous in his lifetime for his economic expertise and his encouragement (in *Lombard Street*) to the BANK OF ENGLAND to act as LENDER OF LAST RESORT, Bagehot has, after his death, come to be best known for *The English Constitution* (1867). There he made a distinction between the 'dignified' aspects of the constitution (for example the monarchy) and the 'efficient' aspects (government, prime minister, cabinet, the House of Commons). Since then, many commentators have argued that the Commons and the cabinet have also ceased to be efficient and have turned dignified.

Balance of payments. Politically sensitive record of a country's transactions in goods, services and money with other countries and with international institutions. A country's balance of payments has two accounts, current and capital: by definition, the two must balance. The most widely quoted is the current account.
Current account. On the current account appear:
● 'VISIBLE' TRADE – known, in the United States, as merchandise trade – imports and exports of goods.
● 'INVISIBLE' TRADE – payments and receipts for services, such as shipping, insurance, banking, tourism, plus dividend and interest payments. A large item on the deficit side of West Germany's current account is tourism, the money spent by sun-seeking Germans on Mediterranean beaches, worth a net DM26.2 billion ($11.6 billion) in 1981. The United States and Britain, by contrast, have long experienced a large deficit on visible trade balanced by a surplus on invisibles.
● Private transfers – such as remittances from migrant workers, for example, Turks, Greeks and Yugoslavs working in West Germany.
● Official transfers – such as debt interest or payments to international organizations (for example contributions from Britain to the EEC budget). Sometimes, however, the current account is shown net of official transfers.

A current account deficit sets alarm bells ringing and hits headlines because it has to be paid for by capital inflows.

Capital account. On the capital account appear:

● Long-term capital flows – for INVESTMENT, for instance. These, plus the current account balance, are sometimes known as the basic balance.

● Short-term 'autonomous' capital flows (that is, excluding government transactions for balance of payment purposes). These are typically flows of HOT MONEY searching for currencies that will appreciate in value, or chasing the highest nominal interest rates on deposits. These flows consisting of, for example, the liquid assets of companies and countries, can have a very destabilizing effect on EXCHANGE RATES.

Balance. The balance on capital account plus the balance on current account make the balance for official financing or settlement. That is where the trouble starts. Bills must be paid, so the accounts must be balanced. The identity (inflows and outflows must sum to zero) is completed by:

● Changes in FOREIGN EXCHANGE reserves;

● Borrowing from (or lending to) international institutions such as the IMF or the EEC;

● Foreign currency borrowing (or lending) by the PUBLIC SECTOR;

● Balancing item. A purely statistical entry to cover lags and inconsistencies in any one year's accounts.

If a country is in chronic deficit, money to balance the books cannot be found indefinitely: reserves run out, lenders insist on repayment and charge hefty interest on their loans. So the economy must adjust (see ADJUSTMENT) by FISCAL POLICY and MONETARY CONTROL and/or by EXCHANGE RATE changes. Often the INTERNATIONAL MONETARY FUND insists on policy changes to enforce adjustment as a condition for its loans.

World-wide, all surpluses are matched by deficits. So the counterparts of a vast OPEC current account surplus in the 1970s were huge deficits in the rest of the world. As the OPEC surplus has shrunk (because OPEC countries have bought more imports and sold less oil) so too has the aggregate non-OPEC deficit. However, statisticians have found it impossible to make the world balance of payments sum to zero, probably because of delays in recording transactions and the different conventions used for doing so. As a result, the world has apparently been running a large (almost $100 billion) deficit in recent years.

Balance sheet. A snapshot of a company's financial position at any one moment, it measures wealth, but not INCOME; profit and loss are measured in a separate account (see ACCOUNTING.) Normally published once a year in the annual report, or quarterly if national law requires it.

A balance sheet has two columns – on the left are liabilities and on the right assets.

● Liabilities normally include: issued share (see EQUITIES) capital (that is, money provided by shareholders); mortgages, loan capital, DEBENTURE stock; capital reserves; current liabilities including bank overdrafts, unpaid taxes, debts owed to suppliers.

● ASSETS are fixed (factories, buildings, machinery and so on) or financial (cash in hand, office items such as stocks, work in progress and short-term loans that can be quickly turned into cash, and money owed by customers). By definition the two sides balance.

Bank. Home of DEPOSITS, source of loans, banks come in all shapes and sizes, with different name tags applied in different countries, often quite loosely. Banks make most of their money from the difference between interest rates paid to depositors and charged to borrowers. For banks, deposits are LIABILITIES (since they have to be repaid), while loans are ASSETS.

Here is a guide to the main name tags:

Commercial banks. The standard High Street banks, also known as RETAIL BANKS, publicly quoted and profit oriented. They deal directly with the public, taking deposits, making loans and providing a range of financial services from foreign exchange to investment advice. Most countries have settled for between four and ten; the main ones in Britain are known as the BIG FOUR BANKS, or CLEARING BANKS (because they run a common centralized system of clearing cheques).

The United States is very different, boasting some 14,700 commercial banks. This proliferation is due to banking laws that have prevented banks operating in more than one state, and in different types of business (see GLASS-STEAGALL ACT). Most of the 14,700 are small banks; banking is dominated by a dozen 'money-centre' banks with household names like Chase Manhattan and Bank of America.

Merchant banks/investment banks. Often privately owned, with names recalling their founding fathers, investment banks live on their wits, advising companies, governments and central banks how to manage their money or to raise more. In Britain, elite merchant banks are also called ACCEPTING HOUSES.

Savings banks. Institutions aimed at encouraging the small saver, especially in continental Europe. Gradually they have become more like commercial banks.

Mortgage banks or building societies. These attract deposits to finance very-long-term loans for home ownership. (Known in the United States as SAVINGS & LOANS ASSOCIATIONS.)

Co-operative banks or credit unions. These are small local institutions organized by a group of individuals with a common bond – for example, they all work for the Ford Motor Company or are all farmers. They give members easier and cheaper access to credit. Most powerful example: France's Crédit Agricole, an umbrella organization for a large number of agricultural co-operative banks, which is now the largest bank in the country (and, by certain definitions, the world).

Universal banks. Jacks of all trades – and masters of all of them, in Switzerland and West Germany, where the big banks take on all the above functions.

Bank for International Settlements (BIS). The central bankers' CENTRAL BANK, it was founded in Basle in 1930 and now occupies a suitably opulent, gold-tinted building in the Centralbahnplatz. Its members are the GROUP OF TEN, plus Switzerland. The BIS has three main functions.

• As banker, accepting deposits from its member central banks (which it then holds in short-dated paper), and making loans on their behalf. One recent example: through the BIS, the leading industrial countries lent the INTERNATIONAL MONETARY FUND $1 billion in May 1981 to supplement the IMF's lending capacity. The BIS also lent money to Hungary, Mexico and Brazil in 1982, when they were unable to borrow what they needed from commercial banks.

• As clearing house on questions such as the supervision of the EUROMARKETS. By pooling information on banks operating in their countries, members build up a world-wide picture of banks' lending and deposit practices and can then try to ensure that they stick to prudential guidelines.

• As pressure group, promoting the central banks' view on both domestic and international questions. This is usually done discreetly (the BIS has a deserved reputation for being one of the world's most tight-lipped organizations). However, it uses its annual report to analyse the world economy and make policy reccomendations. The BIS president (chosen by his peers for a five-year term) also makes speeches that reveal some of its principal concerns: EXCHANGE RATE stability, fiscal and monetary rectitude (see FISCAL POLICY and MONE-TARY CONTROL), prudent bank lending. The BIS has hád a lot to worry about in the 1970s and 1980s.

Bank of England. 'Bulls goaded by Old Lady' was a recent headline in a British newspaper. No septuagenarian female matador this, but

Britain's CENTRAL BANK. Founded in 1694 (pipped at the post by Sweden's bank in 1668 as the world's first) and known jocularly as the 'Old Lady of Threadneedle Street', or simply 'the Bank', it has five main functions:

• As the government's bank manager, taking in taxes (see TAXATION), making payments and managing the NATIONAL DEBT. It floats new loans for the government and lends money directly to the government.

• In consultation with the British Treasury, the Bank carries out the monetary policy (see MONETARY CONTROL) of the government. The Bank issues all bank notes and coins; it keeps the country's foreign reserves (see RESERVE CURRENCIES); it influences the money market by changes in the INTEREST rates at which it deals with the CITY OF LONDON and by sales or purchases of GILT-EDGED STOCK and COMMERCIAL BILLS (see OPEN MARKET OPERATIONS); and, in the past, it controlled bank lending by setting rules about the size of reserves that banks must deposit at the Bank. Since 1981, banks and certain other financial institutions have been required to hold $\frac{1}{2}$ per cent of their eligible liabilities at the Bank, in the form of a cash ratio.

• As the bankers' bank, holding on deposit some of the commercial banks' reserves, and acting as LENDER OF LAST RESORT to the financial system.

• As supervisor, the Bank is responsible for ensuring that the financial institutions act in a responsible way and do not endanger their depositors' money.

• As pressure group, promoting the Bank's and the City's view on economic and monetary questions. The governor of the Bank of England (chosen by the government for a five-year term) makes speeches, and the Bank publishes a quarterly bulletin that reveals its views and *post hoc* explanation of its behaviour.

The Bank is obliged by law to carry out orders from the Treasury. It has been criticised by some politicians and commentators for not making a noisy protest when it disagrees with the orders – and by others for undermining the intentions of the elected government.

Bankruptcy. When a firm or individual goes bust. That simple definition becomes complicated in practice: at what point should bankruptcy be declared, how are creditors paid off, can a bankrupt company continue operating, how long should an individual bankrupt be penalized for his past? The British answer to these questions has traditionally been more extreme than the American or continental European approach.

In the United States, companies can file for 'Chapter 11 bankruptcy': by presenting the court with an acceptable plan for recovery, they can be protected from their creditors for a specified period. In Britain, a firm or its creditors can apply for a bankruptcy order. If granted, the company's assets come under the control of an official receiver, who appoints a liquidator to sell them and distribute the proceeds.

Barrier (to entry or exit). Big firms' ways of keeping out COMPETITION. If a MONOPOLY is producing a large volume of output and benefiting from ECONOMIES OF SCALE, aspiring competitors find it tough initially to match the monopoly's pricing. The monopoly can cut prices right down to its low-cost levels, or even run for a short time at a loss to drive out rivals. Cash-rich giants can also step up advertising to maintain their market share, or even take over competitors. ANTI-TRUST laws seek to outlaw abuses of size or dominant position that raise barriers. Barriers can, however, be legal – for example (until recently) the Post Office's monopoly in Britain – or can consist of patents and copyrights to an invention or innovation. Generally, barriers result in mediocre service and beggar consumers. The three best vigilantes against barriers: TRUST-BUSTING, shifting demand and fast technological change. (For international trade barriers, see PRO-TECTIONISM.)

Barter. Cabbages for chemicals. Also known as counter-trade, the payment of bills by a direct swap of goods has become an increasingly important form of trading between east and west, circumventing eastern block countries' shortage of foreign exchange. Snag: how many West German machine tools can be bought with 10,000 pairs of Polish trousers?

Base-point pricing. Way of presenting a uniform price list when a bulky product has to be transported over distances of varying length from factory to customer. In the steel industry, firms draw up a 'base-point price' for steel from standard mills. This is a 'factory-gate' price, so for any given customer freight charges must be added for delivery from the 'base'. In iron and steel, a common base-point pricing system has been used in Europe to cartelize the industry, by ensuring that all buyers faced the same prices from different producers. TRUST-BUSTING, competition from outsiders such as Brazil and South Korea, and heavy discounting by troubled steel firms broke up Europe's base-point cartel in the 1970s. The EUROPEAN ECONOMIC COMMUNITY's industry commissioner, Viscount Etienne Davignon, effectively restored the system in 1980 by setting up a legal cartel under the European Coal and Steel treaty.

Basis point. A convenient shorthand for describing one hundredth of a unit of one hundred. Example: if the pound sterling falls against the dollar from, say \$1.5700 to \$1.5650, then it has fallen by 50 basis points. The fall is only half a cent, but, because by common agreement each cent is divided into 100 basis points, this fall is measured as 50 points. As for interest rates, a change of one tenth of one per cent (from 10 per cent to 10.1 per cent, say) is called 10 basis points.

Bear. A pessimist, who expects share prices (see EQUITIES), CURRENCY values or COMMODITY prices to fall. Some bears make money from their gloom; the system of account periods (see STOCK EXCHANGE), whereby no money or shares change hands until the end of the period, means that a bear speculator can sell securities he does not actually possess, buying them later at a lower price. He then passes the shares to his original high-price customer. The same result can be achieved by selling a commodity or currency in the FORWARD MARKETS. When the time comes to deliver on the contract, a successful bear will buy more cheaply in the SPOT MARKETS.

Beggar-my-neighbour. Trading policies guaranteed ultimately to beggar yourself. Beggar-my-neighbour comes in two forms:
● Trade PROTECTIONISM. If one country protects its domestic industry from foreign competition, whether by TARIFFS, SUBSIDIES, technical rules, QUOTAS or other jiggery-pokery, then this protection is always at another's expense and simply exports UNEMPLOYMENT.
● Competitive DEVALUATION, where countries devalue their EXCHANGE RATES in rapid succession in order to make EXPORT prices more competitive. This was prevalent in the 1930s. Sweden's devaluation of the krona on 8 October 1982 was attacked as a competitive devaluation.
  Beggar-my-neighbour policies can work for a short time to boost the domestic economy; but (1) the protected industry is inefficient, so consumers have to pay higher prices; (2) trading partners are forced

to retaliate with their own protectionist policies; and (3) they earn less foreign exchange, so buy less of the first country's exports. Result: everyone is beggared. This happened in the 1920s and 1930s, but was partly outlawed in the GENERAL AGREEMENT ON TARIFFS AND TRADE (GATT) after 1947. The slump-ridden 1970s have rekindled beggar-my-neighbour instincts. Moral for all governments: love thy trading neighbour.

Below par. Description of a share or bond whose market value is below its face value. In the BOND MARKET this happens when interest rates are higher than they were at the time the bond was issued. It can also happen if the investors change their view of the creditworthiness of the company or government that issues the bond. Contrast with ABOVE PAR.

Big four banks. The four biggest British COMMERCIAL BANKS – National Westminster, Barclays, Lloyds and the Midland. Once five, but in 1968 the Westminster Bank merged with the National Provincial Bank – and then there were four. These banks handle roughly four out of every five personal bank accounts in Britain, have branches on every High Street, and handle about 90 per cent of company accounts. The only other commercial banks of any size in England are Coutts and Williams & Glyn's, and in Scotland the Royal Bank of Scotland and the National & Commercial banking group. Despite their rivalry, the big four operate a sophisticated centralized system for clearing cheques. Since 1980, they have diversified into the home mortgage market, competing with the BUILDING SOCIETIES. Barclays has the reputation of being the most aggressive of the big four – and the other three resent it. See BANK, COMMERCIAL BANKS, RETAIL BANKING.

Bill of exchange. See COMMERCIAL BILLS, LETTER OF CREDIT.

Black economy. Psst . . . want your car mended/house painted/dinner cooked – and all cheap, provided you pay in cash? This is the black economy: transactions for goods and services that are not declared to the tax man and do not show up in the figures for GROSS NATIONAL PRODUCT (GNP). The black economy may mean the country is actually richer than the figures suggest. 'Black' work can be moonlighting (work done in spare time without paying tax), outright crime, and (probably the biggest single item) the fruits of tax evasion by companies and individuals working a normal working day but understating their income. One way of measuring the size of the black economy is by taking the difference between gross national product and gross national expenditure. As undeclared money is spent, it should turn up in the expenditure figures. Snag: this misses money stashed away by individuals or companies, for instance in offshore tax havens.

Studies of the black economy suggest that in Britain in the 1970s it was worth 1.5–2 per cent of GNP and in the United States 1.5–3 per cent. In Italy, it could represent 14 per cent – this fund of initiative and hard work may be the engine-room of Italian GROWTH. Some optimists argue that black work keeps the unemployed above the breadline. However, it seems more likely that black work is performed by those already in employment and so possessing the necessary tools, equipment and contacts.

Blue chip. Term originally used for the highest value gambling chip, now used for top notch companies whose shares (see EQUITIES) or CREDIT are thought to be of low RISK and high quality. Blue chip companies' shares command high prices and yield steady earnings, and they can obtain loans and overdrafts at the cheapest rates. Blueness is in the eye of the beholder, however: BANKS and STOCK EXCHANGES often continue to regard companies as blue chips long after the firms have ceased to deserve the label. Rolls-Royce, for instance, still held blue chip status right up to its collapse in 1971. And West Germany's AEG-Telefunken continued to be treated as a safe company after its financial troubles started in 1973. AEG finally had to file for partial bankruptcy in 1982, forcing banks to write off 60 per cent of their 'blue chip' loans. Chrysler and Continental Illinois bank are two American examples of blue chip companies getting into trouble – and both have made some progress in getting out of it.

Bond market. A place where bonds and SECURITIES are sold by governments, companies, banks and other institutions to raise CAPITAL. The bond normally carries a fixed rate of INTEREST, and is repaid after a fixed period (known as maturing); long-term government bonds are called gilts (GILT-EDGED STOCK) in Britain. In America, public bonds are issued by federal, state and local governments.

Most bonds can be bought and sold in a secondary market – the bond market – between the time they are issued (first sold in the primary market) and the time they mature. This gives them the important feature, for a buyer, of LIQUIDITY. But bond prices fluctuate in secondary markets, depending on how competitive the bond's fixed rate of interest is to other interest rates. Example: a bond paying £10 of interest a year is sold for £100, at a time when interest rates are 10 per cent. Suppose interest rates then halve, to 5 per cent. The £10 of interest now provides a 5 per cent return on £200, so the bond's price doubles. The combination of interest plus capital changes is calculated by the gross redemption yield. Note that some bonds carry little or no interest (see DEEP DISCOUNT BONDS and ZERO COUPON BONDS).

Interest rates on bonds also vary according to 'maturity' – the bond's length of life. Differing interest rates on differing maturities are expressed by the YIELD CURVE.

Bourse. Name of Paris stock exchange; also generic title for all STOCK EXCHANGES.

Bretton Woods. The deal that shaped the INTERNATIONAL MONETARY SYSTEM for twenty-five years after the Second World War, and set up the INTERNATIONAL MONETARY FUND (IMF) and the WORLD BANK. In 1944, officials from forty-five non-communist nations met at Bretton Woods in New Hampshire, USA, and agreed on a system of international liquidity and EXCHANGE RATE management, to be administered by the IMF. This was the first time that a formal world agreement had laid down rules for the international monetary system.

Under Bretton Woods, exchange rates of IMF members were fixed in terms of gold, or the dollar; but only the dollar was actually CONVERTIBLE into gold, at a fixed price of $35 an ounce. Members guaranteed to maintain their CURRENCIES' value (by buying and selling them) within 1 per cent either side of parity, and were required to inform the IMF of any parity changes, and needed IMF permission for changes of more than 10 per cent. The IMF rules required that changes should only be made if a country's BALANCE OF PAYMENTS was in 'fundamental disequilibrium'.

For governments in payments difficulty, the Bretton Woods agreement envisaged two kinds of international reserves:

● Holdings at the IMF. These were (and still are) relatively small. IMF members deposit a 'quota' of national currency (and also, until 1976, gold) with the IMF, the quota being set according to the country's importance. The IMF then uses these deposits to lend to countries in balance of payments difficulties.

● National currencies. Principally the dollar though, for large parts of the old British empire, also sterling (see STERLING AREA). Because of the dollar's convertibility into gold, the dollar increasingly became the world's RESERVE CURRENCY. The dollar had all the qualities that money requires: a stable value, convenience, and widespread acceptability for transactions.

At first, the dollar's foreign obligations were fully backed by gold, but during the 1960s America's debt overtook its gold stocks. The stability of international money then depended on faith in the dollar itself. In August 1971 this faith was shattered: America's domestic economic troubles and problems paying for the Vietnam war led President Richard Nixon to devalue the dollar against gold (to $38 an ounce) and hence against other major currencies. At a stroke, central banks' reserves were reduced in value. After several months of instability, confusion and American arm-twisting, the leading industrial countries agreed in December 1971 to a new set of exchange rate parities under the SMITHSONIAN AGREEMENT. Bretton Woods – the fixed exchange rate part of it, anyway – was on its last legs. By 1973, all the main currencies were floating.

Broker. A middleman trader. Brokers deal in STOCKS and shares (see EQUITIES), COMMODITIES, FOREIGN EXCHANGE, INSURANCE and bullion, for instance, on behalf of their clients, charging a commission for the service and for advice. In Britain STOCKBROKERS have a virtual monopoly, holding the right to act as middlemen in all deals, and providing their clients with a variety of advice and information services in return for their cut. Other brokers trade only on their specialist knowledge of the market, against competition from individuals and larger direct sales organizations such as BANKS, insurance companies and BUILDING SOCIETIES.

Bucket shop. Term originally applied to any agent offering a DISCOUNT, especially unwanted share issues. Now, the most common usage is for travel agents offering ultra-cheap air tickets, to the travellers' joy and airline cartel's horror. Airlines set air fares in an international CARTEL, the International Air Transport Association (IATA) and offer carefully regulated discounts only for purchase well ahead of departure (APEX) and for tickets on selected flights, though with penalties for cancellation. But airline seats are one of the most perishable of all commodities; once a plane has taken off, an empty seat is a complete loss. Moments before take-off, an airline could reduce that loss by selling off empty seats at ultra-cheap prices. Almost any money taken in would represent a gain compared with the empty seat: hence the airlines' willingness to offer 'standby' fares.

While standby fares are accepted under IATA, bucket shop sales are not. During the 1970s airlines started selling surplus tickets surreptitiously at a big discount to bucket shops. These agents buy up empty seats, sometimes well ahead of flight day, and sell tickets cheaply (perhaps at half-price) to customers determined enough to shop around and to accept awkward flight times. Business passengers, the core of airlines' revenues, are generally put off by the potential inconvenience, and still pay full fares. Gradually, however, airlines have sold more and more tickets to bucket shops, undermining their main tariffs.

Budget. Annual rigmarole to decide how to finance PUBLIC EXPENDITURE for the year ahead and how to slant FISCAL POLICY – through changes in taxes, borrowing or expenditure. The presentation and approval of a budget is shrouded in national ritual. Two examples:
● In the United States, the President announces his proposed budget in the February before the fiscal year concerned (so in February 1983 for the 1983–84 budget), which begins on 1 October. Though the President proposes, Congress disposes; the budget passes through lengthy consideration and, often, a complete rewrite by the House and Senate budget committees before the 'final budget resolution' is passed – normally by 15 September.
● In Britain, the government controls the budget reins. There, the Chancellor of·the EXCHEQUER (finance minister) presents his finance bill in a long speech, usually at the beginning of March, for the fiscal year beginning on 5 April (that is, just a month later). Parliament then debates it, in Select Committee and in several full sessions. Many tax changes are imposed at midnight on the date of announcement (to be revoked if rejected by parliament). Britain's more obedient parliament normally lets the budget through with few changes.
See also DEFICIT FINANCING, FINE TUNING.

Buffer stock. Method of stabilizing commodity prices. When a commodity's price falls, buffer stock managers buy up large quantities in order to steady prices. Purchases are stored, and then sold off once the price is high again. Snags abound: see COMMODITIES.

Building society. A non-profit-making institution, peculiar to Britain, that specializes in loans for house purchase, served by mortgages. Building societies attract DEPOSITS with a variety of rates of interest depending on the rules for withdrawal, and also give preferences in their allocation of mortgages to their own depositors. Deposits are used to make loans to house purchasers that are usually repaid by regular monthly instalments of capital and interest over 20–25 years. In a 'repayment mortgage' both interest and capital are repaid, the capital reducing during the duration of the mortgage. In an 'endowment mortgage', the borrower pays regular interest on the sum borrowed but repays no capital during the life of the mortgage. Instead he makes insurance payments; at the end of the period, the insurance policy repays the mortgage. Interest paid on mortgages gains tax relief – but only on one house and only on interest on the first £30,000 worth of a mortgage. This ceiling was raised in March, 1983 from £25,000, its level since 1974.

Building societies compete with other institutions for depositors, and since 1980 have competed with the BIG FOUR BANKS on loans for house purchases too. The Building Societies Association meets regularly to set recommended mortgage rates of interest. Rough equivalents abroad include the Bausparkassen and Hypothekenbanken in West Germany, and the SAVINGS AND LOAN ASSOCIATIONS (S & Ls) in the United States.

Bull. An optimist who buys shares (see EQUITIES) (or CURRENCY, COMMODITIES, or any other marketed item) expecting the value to rise, so that he can sell later at a profit. In STOCK EXCHANGES, bulls take advantage of the ACCOUNT PERIOD to anticipate price rises. In currency and commodity markets, a bull buys forward (see FORWARD MARKETS), expecting the purchase to be worth more once exchange takes place because prices rise. In a bull market, optimistic buyers push the price up by their purchases, thus fulfilling their expectations. Contrast with BEAR.

Bundesbank. West Germany's CENTRAL BANK, perhaps the most independent of all from government. Housed in a dull, grey skyscraper just outside Frankfurt, the Bundesbank's powers and duties are vested in the federal constitution: first to safeguard the CURRENCY by fighting off INFLATION and, only second, to support the economic policy of the government. The memory of HYPERINFLATION in the Weimar republic of the 1920s is engraved not only on German minds but in the Bundesbank's terms of reference. So its hallmark is tight money, achieved (see MONETARY CONTROL) through INTEREST rates (see LOMBARD RATE, DISCOUNT RATE), OPEN MARKET OPERATIONS, SPECIAL DEPOSITS and targeting the central bank money stock (see MONEY SUPPLY, MEASURES OF). The Bundesbank has a president appointed by the bank's council on government advice (the incumbent in 1983: Karl-Otto Poehl). Its council consists of representatives from *Land* (regional) central banks, the government and Bundesbank directors.

Business cycle. Wave in economic activity between boom and slump. See KONDRATIEFF CYCLE.

Buyback deal. Wheeze common in the oil industry (among others) to give governments control over the destination of output, and its price. Example: the British National Oil Corporation (BNOC), a nationalized body, has a deal with the oil companies producing in the North Sea that it will 'buy' 51 per cent of their output. It then sells it back to the companies (that is, it is just a paper transaction; no oil actually moves). BNOC sets the North Sea price, and the government knows what the companies were paid for the oil – and how much tax they should pay.

C

Call money. Money on call is deposited or borrowed, carries an INTEREST RATE, but has no fixed maturity date – so it can be 'called' or withdrawn at any time.

Call option. STOCK EXCHANGE jargon meaning the right to buy a particular SECURITY at the current price, within a specified period, normally three months. An 'option' is the contractual right to buy or sell within the period; a 'call' option refers to a right to buy, and a 'put' option is the right to sell. See also OPTION DEALING.

Capacity. The amount a factory can produce using its present stock of equipment, manpower and buildings at full tilt. Companies normally operate 15–20 per cent below peak capacity, because some machinery will always need repair and servicing. In the slump of the 1970s and early 1980s, many firms were operating at 50–65 per cent of capacity – a sure recipe for BANKRUPTCY. Unless they become a NATIONALIZED INDUSTRY, that is.

Capital. Stuff used to produce things. Popularly capital means money or wealth; to economists capital is the third FACTOR OF PRODUCTION (the others are labour and land), which are combined to produce goods and services. The proportions of capital and labour used to make a car, for example, depend on two things:
- Their relative prices, that is, labour costs and the rate of INTEREST, which is one measure of the cost of capital;
- The state of technology.

Processes that use a lot of capital relative to labour are called capital intensive; big labour users are called LABOUR INTENSIVE. Although capital goods are normally taken as being machinery, buildings, plant and so on – anything used to make something else – capital is further divided into:
- Fixed capital, that is, machinery, buildings and plant.
- Working or circulating capital, that is, stocks of raw materials and semi-finished goods, components and, crucially, money, that are used up quickly in the production process. For other uses of the term, see CAPITAL MARKETS, HUMAN CAPITAL and CAPITAL–OUTPUT RATIO.

Capitalism. An 'ism' that serves variously as a term of approval and abuse. It is the system of free enterprise where individual profit seekers invest their CAPITAL and employ labour. According to devotees of market economics, this self-seeking behaviour is the best way to ensure prosperity for all (see INVISIBLE HAND). Abuses abound – for example, slavery in America, apartheid in South Africa, MONOPOLIES everywhere – because the system has not proved as individualistic as devotees would like. Nevertheless it has proved able to reform itself, refuting (so far) Karl MARX's proposition that capitalism contains the seeds of its own destruction. Contrast with COMMUNISM.

Capital markets. These are markets in long-term SECURITIES — company bonds (see BOND MARKET), DEBENTURES and so on — where companies and governments raise money from long-term investors, like pension funds and insurance companies. See MONEY MARKET and INTERBANK MARKET, which are essentially short-term.

Capital–output ratio. The amount of CAPITAL involved in producing some level of output, and as such a measure of the efficiency with which capital is used. Sometimes the ratio is expressed as the incremental capital–output ratio (ICOR), which measures the increase in the stock of capital of a firm, industry or economy over a given period, as a ratio of the increase in output over the same period. The lower the ICOR, the more efficient the firm or economy. See INPUT–OUTPUT ANALYSIS.

Cartel. An agreement, written or unwritten, between producers to fix prices, share out markets or set their production levels, in order to restrain COMPETITION and to raise profits. The temptation is so great that Adam SMITH viewed all business contracts with the deepest suspicion: 'People of the same trade seldom meet together, even for merriment and diversion, but the conversation ends in a conspiracy against the public or in some contrivance to raise prices.'

Cartels became especially popular during the depression years of the 1920s and 1930s. In Germany, for instance, several steel companies formed the Ruhrstahl cartel and the three biggest chemical firms in the world at the time, Bayer, BASF and Hoechst, merged into a notorious holding company called I. G. Farben. The enemy of cartels is ANTI-TRUST law. Co-operation between oligopolists has also been called collusion.

Cash. Money that can easily be spent at short notice: actual notes and coins, or quickly realizable deposits and SECURITIES, known as 'money at call or short notice'. Cash flow is the amount of money arising at a firm from sales and repaid debts, and net of the amount being spent. 'Cash flow problems' mean that there is not enough money, possibly because customers are not paying up quickly. Often 'cash flow problems' is a euphemism for 'about to go bust'.

Cash limits. British way to control the spending of taxpayers' money. Until 1976, PUBLIC EXPENDITURE plans were detailed in advance, in volume terms — that is, the number of nurses to be employed, schools built and so on, their cost being calculated at 'survey' prices prevailing about 18 months before the financial year began. INFLATION made this system highly inaccurate: worse, it also meant that ministries had no reason for trying to control costs. In 1976 the system was changed. Departments were allocated actual cash, and had to provide goods and services out of these budgets.

Cash limits now apply to about 60 per cent of all British public spending. Their record has been mixed. Limits have generally been observed (so overshooting of spending targets has been reduced). When the limits loom, however, ministries have been inclined to cut the volume of their spending rather than finding more economical ways of achieving a given volume of spending. In 1982, to overcome this weakness, cash limits were combined with volume planning to form cash planning. Each programme now has a specific budget to which guesstimated inflation rates will be applied. This is intended to give more incentive to provide efficiency and value for money. NATIONALIZED INDUSTRIES are subject to EXTERNAL FINANCING LIMITS which dictate the maximum they can obtain in loans and grants from all sources.

Central bank. Repair man cum policeman for the monetary system. Every country has one, or shares one (for example, in the French African Community). America's is the FEDERAL RESERVE, Britain's is the BANK OF ENGLAND, West Germany's is the BUNDESBANK. Central banks stand uncomfortably at the point where FISCAL POLICY and MONETARY CONTROL meet, ensuring the government has the finances to meet its bills, and servicing the public debt that results. Central banks have little or no control on fiscal policy; but they do operate monetary policy and oversee the financial system. Routine maintenance and police work involves central banks in four ways:

● As banker to the government. PUBLIC EXPENDITURE on goods and services typically accounts for 20–40 per cent of GROSS DOMESTIC PRODUCT (and more if TRANSFER PAYMENTS are included). A government deposits its revenues and RESERVE CURRENCIES with the central bank and pays its bills with central bank cheques. The central bank typically charges the government a fee for acting as its bank: this is one of its major sources of revenue.

● As banker to the BANKS. The central bank takes deposits from banks, and lends to them. This function helps the central bank to control the supply of money (see MONETARY CONTROL and OPEN MARKET OPERATIONS), but also helps it to maintain the stability of the financial system. The central bank acts as LENDER OF LAST RESORT – that is, it stands ready to provide any bank with cash should it be in difficulty, or if its customers want to withdraw their deposits. This safety net enables banks to borrow short and lend long, without losing sleep over it. Often central banks control bank lending by setting a fixed proportion of deposits that must be deposited at the central bank (see LIQUIDITY RATIO).

• As supervisor to the banks. Central banks usually have a big say over who can operate as a bank or take the public's deposits. They regularly check the banks' balance sheets and, either by law or by gentle arm-twisting, can force financial institutions to toe the line.

• Issuing CURRENCY, and offering a guiding hand in FOREIGN EXCHANGE markets. Designing, printing, issuing and withdrawing notes (and often coins as well) is the job of the central bank. In consultation with the government, and with other central banks, the central bank intervenes in currency markets to smooth fluctuations or to protect a target value. Central banks can also nudge currencies either way by shifting INTEREST rates up or down relative to those prevailing in other countries.

Centrally planned economies. Rule of man over mammon, according to COMMUNISM, over market forces, according to CAPITALISM. In most communist economies, including the Soviet Union and China, bureaucrats make all price, output and resource allocation decisions. In theory, central planning could be more rational and equitable than the market-place; in practice it has always yielded inefficiency, a slothful bureaucracy and little incentive to work hard or innovate. Central planning's drawbacks have led Yugoslavia, Rumania and Hungary to experiment with free market dilutions. See MARKET SOCIALISM.

Certificate of deposit. SECURITY first introduced by New York's biggest bank, Citibank, in 1961. A similar sterling instrument was created in London in 1968. Certificates of deposit (CDs) are ordinary fixed-term INTEREST-bearing DEPOSITS with one extraordinary feature – like bonds and shares they can be bought and sold in a secondary market. CDs are only available in big denominations, but their growth has been spectacular – from nothing in 1961 to over $140 billion in America alone, and to £8.6 billion in Britain.

City of London. Known as the City, this is the set of private financial institutions, dominated by men in grey suits, that make up the square mile of historic, windy streets in the east end of London – MERCHANT BANKS, STOCKBROKERS, INSURANCE companies, DISCOUNT HOUSES, finance houses, COMMODITY brokers and so on. The City is normally quoted as the collective view of the financial institutions.

The City earns millions in INVISIBLE (TRADE) exports every year (a surplus of £1.95 billion in 1981), but the gratitude of the nation is mixed with suspicion. Although the City was pronounced more or less clean and efficient by a committee headed by a former Labour prime minister, Sir Harold Wilson (Cmnd 7937, HMSO, 1980) Labour party opinion still believes that it does not invest enough in British industry.

Classical economics. The dominant theory of ECONOMICS from the eighteenth century until it was refined in the twentieth century into NEO-CLASSICAL ECONOMICS. Big names included Adam SMITH, David RICARDO and John Stuart MILL. Classical economists held that the pursuit of individual self-interest produced the greatest collective benefits (see INVISIBLE HAND).

The classical school believed that an economy is always either in EQUILIBRIUM or moving towards it. Equilibrium, the theory went, is ensured by movements in wages (the price of labour) and the rate of INTEREST (the price of CAPITAL).

The rate of interest moves to ensure equality between SAVINGS and INVESTMENT. If, for instance, entrepreneurs suddenly decide (perhaps because of technological improvements) that they want to invest more, then firms boost their borrowings, and so bid up interest rates. Higher interest rates have two effects:
• Households are prepared to save more, and so, indirectly, lend to the investing firms;
• Some firms gradually go off the idea of investing more, because of the higher cost of borrowing.

This theory is founded on two assumptions: first, that investment is highly sensitive to interest rates; and second, that the rate of interest is perfectly free to vary, so that saving and investment are quickly equalized.

As for wages, they adjust to ensure that the equilibrium level of national income is that which produces full employment. If there is unemployment, then wages would fall and so the demand for labour would increase to mop up the unemployed. Conversely, wages would rise to choke off the demand for labour if an economy was heading for unsustainable growth in national income. This belief in the inevitability of full employment equilibrium produced a (probably apocryphal) scene at the London School of Economics. During the early 1930s, as Britain's unemployment rate headed towards 20 per cent, a professor of firmly classical views began his lecture on national income with the words 'Assume full employment'.

The classical and neo-classical schools were eclipsed between the mid 1930s and the mid 1970s by the followers of Maynard KEYNES. Keynes attacked the two main classical tenets, arguing that (1) the rate of interest is determined or influenced by the speculative actions of bondholders; and (2) that wages are inflexible downwards, so national income may be in apparent equilibrium at a point below full employment. Recently, attention has turned back towards some of the logic of classical and neo-classical economics (see also MONETARISM).

Clean floating. Movement of a CURRENCY freely on the FOREIGN EXCHANGE market without any government or CENTRAL BANK intervention. Contrast with DIRTY FLOATING. See EXCHANGE RATE, OVERSHOOTING.

Clearing banks. British term for commercial banks that deal direct with the public, and 'clear' ordinary cheques. See BANK, RETAIL BANKING, BIG FOUR BANKS.

Closed shop. TRADE UNIONS' method of increasing their power, and subscriptions. A closed shop is an agreement between a union and the management that only union members may be employed, either in a particular factory or office, or in particular jobs. New recruits must join the union, or lose their jobs. The result is that the union is able to negotiate for all the workers, so no non-union members can benefit from union bargaining without paying their dues. Some employers favour closed shops in order to avoid negotiating with more than one group. But closed shops can also mean that wages are higher because the union has a monopoly of supply of labour, that hiring and firing is impossible, that restrictive practices are prevalent, and that the individual's freedom to choose membership or non-membership is violated.

Closed shops can be divided into pre-entry and post-entry ones: in a pre-entry shop, a worker must have satisfied requirements before being given a job (see RESTRICTIVE PRACTICES for the ridiculous requirements for practising as a barrister in Britain); in a post-entry shop the union is joined after getting the job.

Cobweb theorem. Often known as the hog cycle, this describes how time lags in adjusting production affect the way supply and demand are balanced — and how some markets can therefore be highly unstable. Pigs take a long time to breed and fatten, so farmers set output for next year in relation to the price this year. Say pigs get the porcine version of myxomatosis, and the quantity produced falls to Q1 in Figure 1. Then the price will rise to P1. That high price (and a wonder cure for the disease) will induce farmers to produce more in year 2. With that number of pigs on the market, the price falls to P2. This triggers lower output in year 3 of Q3, raising the price to P3, and so on. In this example, the swings get smaller and the price and quantity eventually converge.

But this benign outcome does not always occur, because of the relative ELASTICITY of demand and supply. If demand is less elastic

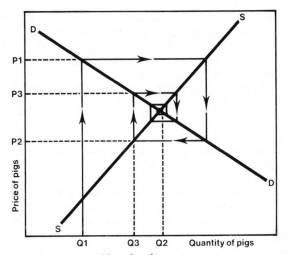

Figure 1 *A stable cobweb*

than supply (that is, less responsive to changes in price, so the slope of its curve is steeper), the cobweb can diverge, causing ever larger swings in supply and price. In Figure 2 the disease reduces quantity to Q1, setting in train an unstable series of swings. This instability is one reason why most rich countries use AGRICULTURAL POLICIES to support farmers and to steady the market. The problem applies to other markets with inflexible supply, such as housing.

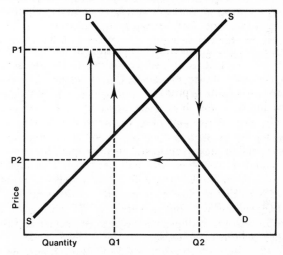

Figure 2 *An unstable cobweb*

Collective bargaining. The main job of TRADE UNIONS. Union committees, or officials, negotiate with management at shop floor, branch, and company or industry level on the wages, benefits and working conditions of their members as a whole. 'Free' collective bargaining means with no interference from the government or the law (for example, by an INCOMES POLICY). The ultimate weapon of collective bargainers is to strike.

Collusion. See CARTEL.

Comecon. The communist world's version of the EUROPEAN ECONOMIC COMMUNITY, except that in Comecon one member of the trading block calls the tune: the Soviet Union. Comecon – full title the Council for Mutual Economic Assistance – was set up in 1949. Its members are mainly Eastern European communist countries, but also include Vietnam, Cuba and Mongolia. Comecon members trade with one another on special terms, often by BARTER – for example, Russian oil for Cuban sugar.

Command economies. Economies where decisions on output, investment, jobs etc. are made by bureaucrats rather than by markets. Another term for CENTRALLY PLANNED ECONOMIES.

Commercial banks. See BANK, RETAIL BANKING, BIG FOUR BANKS.

Commercial bills. Also known as bills of exchange. Bills of exchange are DEBTS between companies due to be paid at some future date, usually in three months' time. BANKS 'accept' bills of exchange (see ACCEPTING HOUSES) and lend to the creditor company in the belief that the debtor will pay up when the bill is due.

Committee on public accounts. Gladstonian parliamentary watchdog in Britain. The PAC is a select committee of the House of Commons, currently with fourteen members, that monitors spending by all British government ministries and agencies. It has power to interrogate ministers and their civil servants, and produces reports on spending and on economic issues. Until 1979 the PAC was the only parliamentary committee with any real clout; then fourteen new select committees were set up alongside.

Commodity. Usually refers to a raw material or primary product that is relatively homogeneous, and is traded on a free market. Examples are tin, coffee, tea, sugar, wool, cotton, rubber, silver, cocoa. Commodities are bought and sold on a commodities exchange by dealers and commodity brokers or traders. The materials' homogeneity, fast communications and an efficient system of quality grading and control mean that commodities can be traded without an actual transfer of the goods. SPECULATORS, HEDGERS and traders buy and sell rights of ownership in SPOT or FORWARD (also known as FUTURES) MARKETS.

Commodity prices swing more violently than prices of manufactured goods. A small surplus of supply over demand can cause a dramatic slump in prices; floods or frost in a producing country can send a crop price soaring.

Commodities can be crucial for the welfare of developing countries dependent on one or two EXPORTS for most of their FOREIGN EXCHANGE earnings – Zambia with copper, for instance, or Ivory Coast with coffee and cocoa. CONSUMERS would prefer more stable prices, too. So two ways have been tried of stabilizing commodity prices, both with faults.

International commodity agreements. These agreements between producers and consumers try to stabilize prices using BUFFER STOCKS and export or production QUOTAS. They were in vogue in 1977 when the United Nations conference on trade and development (UNCTAD) recommended eighteen commodities for agreements. But, so far, the only existing agreements are for sugar, cocoa, tin, rubber and coffee. The trouble with the deals is that often the biggest producer or consumer does not join in (for instance, neither the Ivory Coast nor the United States are privy to the cocoa deal). Also, when prices rise sharply, producers try to slither out of the agreement; when prices slump, consumers do likewise. No buffer stock has yet proved big enough to steady prices. Only the tin agreement has managed to keep prices relatively stable, mainly by enforcing export or production quotas. (See Figure 3.) These benefit established (often high-cost) producers at the expense of expanding (lower-cost) producers.

Long-term contracts. They offer producers stable prices, but are nego-

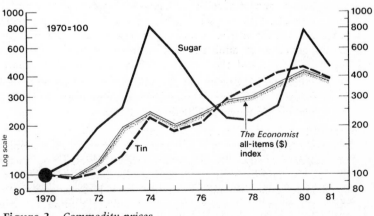

Figure 3 *Commodity prices*

tiated with an eye to market prices; the more long-term contracts there are, the more marginal (and erratic) spot prices become. This has happened in the sugar market.

These attempts to stabilize prices have not worked well – especially because commodity prices in 1980–82 all slumped at the same time, so swamping the money available, for example, for buffer stocks. So the INTERNATIONAL MONETARY FUND and EUROPEAN ECONOMIC COMMUNITY have tried to stabilize producers' export earnings too by compensatory financing – making grants or loans to top up income. Here, too, the earnings slump in 1980–82 overstretched the cash on offer.

Common agricultural policy (CAP). The EUROPEAN ECONOMIC COMMUNITY's proudest achievement, but also its prodigal son. When the EEC was set up in 1957 the strong farming interests of France were squared with West Germany's industrial needs by swapping trade liberalization for a generous common policy to support farmers. A common policy with common prices for farm goods also had the attraction of ensuring free trade – and hence, it was hoped, growing trade – in farm produce between the members.

Now, about 90 per cent of EEC farm output is covered by the CAP; the only major outsiders are potatoes and agricultural alcohol. The CAP's farm fund, known as FEOGA from its French initials, helps out farmers in five ways:

● High support prices. More than 70 per cent of farm output – chiefly cereals, dairy products, sugar, beef, veal, pork, some fruits and vegetables and wine – benefits from high prices fixed each spring by the EEC members' farm ministers. If prices fall below these levels, the EEC intervention boards buy up produce and store it, ideally for sale at a later date when prices recover. These common prices are expressed in EUROPEAN CURRENCY UNITS (ECUs) and converted into national currencies by the EEC's complicated GREEN MONEY system.

● Import levies, to raise IMPORT prices to EEC levels. All CAP produce benefits from these: about a quarter of community farm output (flowers, some cereals, good wine, some fruits and vegetables) relies solely on TARIFF protection, with no market intervention system.

● EXPORT subsidies, that bridge the gap between EEC and world prices to enable farmers to sell on world markets. As EEC output has grown, so export subsidies have expanded to swallow up half of all CAP spending.

● Supplementary and fixed rate aids. For durum wheat, olive oil, some tobaccos and some oilseeds (2.5 per cent of total EEC farm output) support prices are kept low, but producers get direct subsidies in proportion to their output. For a tiny group of products – like cotton, hemp, silkworms and seeds – fixed rate subsidies are paid per hectare or per quantity produced, and no market intervention takes place.

● Aid for farm modernization, from FEOGA's guidance section.

In 1981 the CAP spent 11.5 billion ECUs (around $11 billion), taking about 65 per cent of all EEC spending. The policy's high prices, backed by an open-ended guarantee, have encouraged farmers to produce more and more, and have accelerated the introduction of new, more productive technology. The result: fast-rising spending;

Table 1 *Importance of agriculture in EEC economies.*

| | Agriculture's share in | | Country's share in |
	Employment % (1981)	GNP % (1981)	EEC farm output % (1981)
Britain	2.8	2.3	12.2
Holland	4.9	3.5*	7.9
Luxembourg	5.6	2.0*	0.1
Belgium	2.9	2.9*	3.4
France	8.4	3.8	26.6
Italy	13.0	6.7	20.8
West Germany	5.9	2.2	18.8
Ireland	18.9*	12.0*	2.1
Denmark	8.4	6.0	3.7
Greece	30.0*	14.2	4.4

* 1980

fast-rising production that, especially for meats, dairy products and cereals, has to be sold off on world markets using export subsidies; and infuriated trading partners, such as the United States, Australia and New Zealand, that see markets being whittled away and world prices depressed.

The strength of farm lobbies, especially in France, has so far ruled out any major reforms of the CAP. The EEC commission has tried freezing prices (ministers accepted this for only two years, 1978 and 1979) and tinkering with quotas and other controls on production. The CAP is still enormously costly to taxpayers and consumers, yet (see Table 1) agriculture plays a relatively insignificant role in most member states' economies. See also AGRICULTURAL POLICY and ENGEL'S LAW.

Common stock. American term for ordinary EQUITIES.

Communism. The final stage of the dialectic described by MARX: feudalism, CAPITALISM, the dictatorship of the proletariat, communism. In this nirvana the state will 'wither away', and economic life will be organized to achieve 'from each according to his abilities, to each according to his needs'. So far the nuclear family has got closest to this idea, which is not what Marx had in mind.

Comparative advantage. This principle, first described by RICARDO, demonstrates how countries can gain from trading with each other even if one of them is more efficient − has an ABSOLUTE ADVANTAGE − in every activity. The main qualification is that, domestically, the ratio of their production costs must differ.
- *Example*: two countries, A and B, can produce two goods, C and D, in the following maximum quantities:

  A: 10 of C, or 8 of D, or some combination of C and D.

  B: 4 of C, or 6 of D, or a combination.
- *Assertion*: although A has an absolute advantage in both goods, it is comparatively better at producing C, selling what it does not need to country B and buying D in return.
- *Proof*: if neither specializes, instead dividing their time between each product, their combined output will be 7C and 7D. But if A concentrates on C, and B on D, their combined output will be 10C and 6D. They have lost 1D, but gained 3C − a net gain, because 1D is worth 3C/2 in B and 4C/5 in A.

Comparative statics. Basic (and unrealistic) form of economic analysis. It isolates one part of an economy (a consumer, a firm, or a market, for example) and describes when it will be in EQUILIBRIUM. A market for cowboy hats, for instance, is in equilibrium when the supply of hats equals the demand for those hats. Comparative statics then compares this equilibrium to another, new equilibrium which results when some exogenous determinant of the equilibrium changes. Demand for cowboy hats at a given price may alter because, for example, the Dallas TV programme produces a once-for-all change in consumer preference.

Comparison of the two equilibria reveals little about the behaviour of the economic system during the move from one to the other – a bad weakness, as economies are rarely (perhaps never) in equilibrium. To study this, economists use more complex 'dynamic analysis', building ECONOMETRIC models describing how the economy reacts to exogenous shocks. (See also PARTIAL EQUILIBRIUM.)

Competition. The more the merrier, for lower prices and more efficient firms. Competition is not black and white; there are shades between pure competition and pure MONOPOLY. Most economic textbooks identify three broad categories and depict them in diagrams plotting their marginal and average costs and revenues (see MARGINAL ANALYSIS):

Perfect competition. This is an idyllic state with a large number of sellers and buyers, a homogeneous good and free entry to the market. No buyer or seller is big enough to affect the price through his purchases or sales, so all are price takers. If firms make SUPERNORMAL PROFITS (that is, more than the minimum needed to keep them in business) more firms enter, competing down the price. In long-run equilibrium, perfectly competitive firms operate as in Figure 4. In this figure MC is marginal costs, ATC is average costs, AR is average revenue and MR marginal revenue. Firms are assumed to maximize

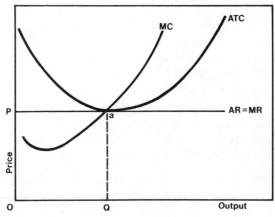

Figure 4 *Little-Mr-Perfect Inc.*

profits by raising output to the level where the marginal revenue from an extra unit equals the marginal cost of making it.

This is, however, pure fantasy – or at least, pure theory. In the real world there are few perfectly competitive markets. Most exhibit some form of

Monopolistic competition. Here there may be fewer firms, and all can differentiate their products from the rest somewhat, perhaps by advertising or differences of design. As a result, all face a downward sloping demand curve, and operate roughly as in Figure 5.

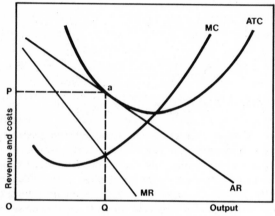

Figure 5   *Zappo-Washes-Whiter Inc.*

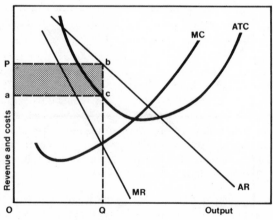

Figure 6   *Big Bucks Inc.*

Most real markets and firms are like this, though the textbook model would mystify many a manager. When one firm grows (perhaps by virtue of success) to swallow up the whole of a market, there is a

Monopoly. Here the firm can charge whatever price it likes for the product as it is the sole producer. The absence of competition means that average total costs need not be forced down to the most efficient point, and that the firm earns supernormal profits – represented by the shading in Figure 6.

Although firms in all three models are seeking to maximise profits (at MR equals MC), under monopolistic competition and monopoly they produce less – and at a higher price – than under perfect competition.

Compound interest. If a DEPOSIT (ACCOUNT) of £100 earns a rate of INTEREST of 10 per cent a year, then at the end of the year the account will contain £110. If all the principal (original sum) and interest are left in the account, then the 10 per cent rate of interest will then be levied on £110, so at the end of the second year £11 interest will be added, making £121 in all. And so on. Simple interest just pays 10 per cent on the original sum lent or borrowed.

Comptroller of the Currency. Shares, with the SECURITIES AND EXCHANGE COMMISSION and the FEDERAL RESERVE Board, the job of regulating America's commercial banking and financial system. Investors wishing to set up a bank in the United States must obtain permission either from the banking authorities of an individual state or from the Comptroller of the Currency. If they choose the second course, they have to join the Federal Reserve System. They must also have their deposits insured by the Federal Deposit Insurance Corporation.

Concentration. The tendency of industrial economies to become dominated by larger and larger firms that have swallowed the minnows. Karl MARX predicted that concentration, by creating a small capitalist elite and a vast exploited mass, would sow the seeds of CAPITALISM's destruction. So far, it hasn't – partly because the birth of new small businesses, and technological innovation, constantly undermine the giants. Still, all industrial economies have experienced concentration. In steel, for instance, the West German giants Krupp and Thyssen in the Ruhr area gradually took over small steel-makers in the 1950s and 1960s. When concentration means monopoly, trust-busters act. See ANTI-TRUST, COUNTERVAILING POWER.

Conglomerate. Company that owns firms producing widely different products, often with the aim of diversifying its operations and sources of income. Tobacco companies have generally become conglomerates (so that a medical report on smoking and health does not halve their profits). Even Coca Cola has gone that way, buying Columbia Pictures. The British company, Grand Metropolitan Hotels, owns leisure industries, brewing, shops and much else besides hotels. Conglomerates are often owned by holding companies – which produce nothing themselves, but are the umbrella organization in which all shares are vested.

Consols. British government SECURITIES carrying a fixed INTEREST rate of 2.5 per cent, and unredeemable. Shorthand for 'consolidated funds' or 'consolidated annuities', consols were first issued in 1751. But their contemporary title came after various types of government securities were consolidated in 1887. Like all fixed interest bonds, their price varies inversely with interest rates (see BOND MARKET).

Constant prices. If a shop's sales or a factory's production have risen from £1 million last year to £1.1 million this, is that proof of expansion – or simply INFLATION? The answer can be found by using the same set of prices in both periods, to remove the froth of inflation. In constant prices, our example may show sales or output rising from £1 million to £1.04 million: so volume has expanded by 4 per cent, with price rises accounting for the remaining 6 per cent of the 10 per cent boost to sales. See INDEX NUMBERS for how constant prices can be computed.

Consumer durables. Goods that (supposedly) last a long time. Examples are washing machines, bicycles, refrigerators or record players. Because a CONSUMER buys a washing machine only once every five years, say, his demand may not be very sensitive to price (see ELASTICITY). Quality may count more. In the trade, household appliances such as washing machines or dishwashers are known as 'white goods', appliances like televisions or hi-fi are 'brown goods'.

Consumer price index. American version of RETAIL PRICE INDEX.

Consumers. An oppressed majority. As private individuals, consumers are in constant danger of being exploited by big companies' sharp selling practices – for example, advertising that might claim that aspirins prevent heart disease – and by trade PROTECTIONISM that stops them buying from the cheapest suppliers. As a result, consumers need (and get) protection by the law. In America, Ralph Nader has been the chief lobbyist for the consumer case; in Britain the Consumers' Association plays a similar, if weaker role.

Consumers' surplus. A creature of NEO-CLASSICAL ECONOMIC theory propounded by Alfred MARSHALL. Simply, consumer surplus is the amount a consumer is willing to pay for a good minus the amount he actually pays for it. The point of this is that consumers gain UTILITY (usefulness) from goods, but utility diminishes as they buy more of the same good. A banana-loving consumer might be willing to pay £1.50 for his first banana, because of high utility, then £1.00 for his second and so on, down to the actual price of 30p. Since all the bananas he buys actually cost 30p, consumers' surplus measures the extra utility gained on the first few bananas. He will keep buying bananas, the theory goes, until 30p exactly measures the utility gained from the marginal banana (see MARGINAL ANALYSIS).

Consumption. What CONSUMERS do. Consumption can be subdivided into private and public consumption (see PUBLIC SECTOR, PUBLIC EXPENDITURE). Arithmetically, the more resources a society consumes the less it has to invest. Complications: investment ultimately yields goods for consumption; consumption, by expressing demand, encourages investment. Nevertheless, forgoing consumption now (by saving and investing more) yields greater consumption possibilities in the future. See PERMANENT INCOME HYPOTHESIS, RELATIVE INCOME HYPOTHESIS.

Contango. Term used in COMMODITY markets to describe when spot prices (see SPOT MARKETS) are lower than FUTURES prices. This relation indicates that dealers expect prices to rise or remain stable; with stable prices, futures prices will always be slightly higher than spot ones to cover INTEREST costs. Contrast with BACKWARDATION.

In STOCK EXCHANGES, it takes two to contango. Here, the term is used for the charge made by a STOCKBROKER for carrying over a deal from one ACCOUNT PERIOD to another – a manoeuvre that removes the artificial deadline for a share deal.

Conversion. Issue of a fresh STOCK to replace another. This can be when a stock matures, or when a firm wishes to convert, for example, DEBENTURES into EQUITY.

Convertibility. CURRENCIES are convertible if they can be readily swapped for gold, or for another currency. The major currencies – the dollar, the Deutschmark, the pound and so on – are fully convertible, the last vestiges of non-convertibility having been abandoned in 1958. This oils the wheels of international trade, because countries can pay for their IMPORTS in any convertible currency, not one that is specified by the CENTRAL BANK.

Minor currencies in beleaguered economies – such as the Mexican peso – may be convertible only under strictly regulated circumstances. Withdrawing convertibility, as happened in Mexico in September 1982, is one way to halt a run of SPECULATION on a currency. To allow convertibility, a country must have sufficient reserves (see RESERVE CURRENCIES) of FOREIGN EXCHANGE or gold to back likely demands on the currency, or must have trust from the money markets. Mexico had neither.

Convertible. Loans, preference shares or DEBENTURES, for example, that carry the option of CONVERSION at a predetermined future date into CASH, in the case of a loan, or ordinary shares, in the case of preferences or debentures.

Corporation tax. Tax on company profits. Taxable profits are, however, far removed from accountants' definitions; the taxman allows many and various tax reliefs for capital DEPRECIATION and STOCK appreciation, for example, before arriving at his slice. Although companies pay the tax, CONSUMERS bear the eventual brunt as the tax is passed on, at least partially, in prices.

In Britain, companies pay two kinds of profits' tax:
● Advance corporation tax (ACT), which they pay on behalf of their shareholders for the dividends they pay out.
● 'Mainstream' corporation tax, levied at 52 per cent of taxable profits, whether distributed or not. Because companies receive generous tax-free allowances for their investment spending (and also on stock appreciation), the total received from mainstream tax in 1981–82 was only £2.2 billion, barely 3 per cent of all tax receipts.

Corset. Neat CITY (OF LONDON) slang for the BANK OF ENGLAND's 'supplementary special deposits scheme' introduced as an instrument of MONETARY CONTROL in December 1973, and finally abolished in June 1981. The corset placed quantitative restrictions on the growth of COMMERCIAL BANKS' 'interest-bearing eligible liabilities'. The corset's innovation was to control the liabilities side of banks' BALANCE SHEETS, while most monetary controls are aimed at ASSETS (for example, setting a sum of bank reserves to be deposited at the central bank, and then limiting bank lending to a fixed ratio – perhaps five times – those of reserves).

Under the corset, 'eligible liabilities' meant sterling DEPOSITS from both British and foreign residents, and foreign CURRENCY deposits lent out in sterling. The corset applied only to the banks, not the DIS-COUNT HOUSES, and the banks could deduct from the eligible lia-bilities figure their net holdings of claims on the rest of the banking system. A limit was placed on the growth of banks' eligible lia-bilities; any excess was penalized by the erring bank having to lodge special deposits at the Bank of England, where they earned no inter-est. These special deposits got progressively tougher for bigger trans-gressions.

The corset was resented by the banks because it encouraged DISIN-TERMEDIATION (companies lending to each other directly instead of through the banking system). When it was finally removed in June 1981 it was followed by monetary disaster: the government's target for the sterling M3 measure of the MONEY SUPPLY was growth of 7–11 per cent, but in July 1981 alone sterling M3 jumped by 5 per cent, busting the target. The reason? Money diverted from the banks by the corset flooded back into the official measures.

Cost. The price paid to buy, produce, keep or achieve something. Nor-mally related to firms, costs are divided into two groups:
- Fixed costs, also known as overheads, are big, unavoidable expenses like buildings, rent, machinery, that must be paid irrespec-tive of the amount produced.
- VARIABLE COSTS, or running costs, are raw materials, wages, main-tenance, electricity, postal charges – anything that varies according to the amount of goods produced.

In basic economic theory about how firms work, measures of cost are further divided into marginal and average **cost** (see MARGINAL ANALYSIS). Marginal cost is the cost of producing one extra unit of production; a firm, if it wants to maximize its profit, will produce the number of units at which marginal cost is equal to marginal revenue. Average cost is the total cost (fixed and variable) divided by the number of units produced.

In reality, many firms set their prices by working out average cost and adding desired profit. This is known as cost-plus pricing, and is made easier if the market is not very competitive. An ENTREPRENEUR or self-employed businessman will calculate costs (also for tax purposes) to include an element for his own salary; this is an imputed cost.

Costs are an important source of price INFLATION. Fast rising wages, or materials costs rising perhaps because of DEVALUATION (which raises import prices) or a shift in the TERMS OF TRADE, can fuel a spiral of inflation. When costs are thought to be the driving force behind price increases, 'cost-push inflation' is said to result. This contrasts with 'demand-pull inflation', which pins the blame on excessive demand, causing companies to raise prices as a way of cutting back demand to manageable levels. Snag with this distinction: all costs – wages, raw materials, INTEREST rates – are themselves formed in markets where demand plays a role. Excess demand there will raise costs, giving the impression of cost-push but in reality being affected by demand.

Cost–benefit analysis. Standard accounting of income and costs, but with a difference. Cost–benefit analysis tries to measure things for which no obvious market price exists – like clean versus dirty air, saving or losing lives, and noise versus peace and quiet. It is most commonly used in assessing public investment projects: a motorway will cost more than an ordinary road, but it will save motorists' time, spoil more countryside, preserve more old villages, and so on.

Perhaps the most thorough cost–benefit analysis ever undertaken in Britain was for the Roskill commission, which appraised possible sites for London's third airport. It made heroic efforts to quantify, for example, the social cost of destroying the breeding ground for a rare species of goose. After four years of work, it concluded that the best site was Maplin. In five minutes in parliament, the government of the day rejected that conclusion and chose an alternative. After months of protest, local pressure groups succeeded in killing that plan as well.

Cost, insurance, freight (CIF). For computing trade figures, the full cost of IMPORTS to a country is understated if only the price of the goods is recorded. The cost of transporting the goods and insuring their passage must be paid by the purchaser, and hence affects that country's BALANCE OF PAYMENTS, too. Trade statistics normally record imports on a CIF basis. (See FREE ON BOARD.)

Cost of living. Vague idea made precise by compiling a weighted basket of goods and services commonly purchased, and then registering changes in the basket's overall cost over time. In America the official basket index is the consumer price index (CPI); in Britain it is the retail price index (RPI). See INDEX NUMBERS, REAL VALUES.

Council of Economic Advisers. Three-man team that advises the president of the United States on economic policy. Can get shirty if its advice is not taken: of President Ronald Reagan's original three (Murray Weidenbaum, Jerry Jordan and William Niskanen) only

William Niskanen remained by the end of 1982. He was joined by two new recruits: Martin Feldstein (the chairman) and William Poole.

In West Germany, the federal government has a five-man team, also called the Council of Economic Advisers (more popularly the 'five wise men') which is required by law to produce a report twice a year on the economy.

Counter-trade. Another term for BARTER.

Coupon. The actual amount of INTEREST payable on a bond (see BOND MARKET) or DEBENTURE, expressed in pounds or dollars per unit. Originally the coupon was attached to a bond certificate, cut off when payment was due, and sent to claim the interest.

Countervailing power. Concentration of economic power in the hands of small groups, for example, multinational corporations, can be neutralized (countervailed) by clout in the hands of an opposing group, for example TRADE UNIONS or government. Countervailing power, exerted by unions, by the law or by large customers (for example, car hire companies buying large fleets of Ford cars) can make the CAPITALIST system more stable and fair than it would seem at first sight. The idea was first developed by the American economist J. K. Galbraith in his book *American Capitalism: The Concept of Countervailing Power* (1952).

Crawling peg. Method of adjusting EXCHANGE RATES by small, frequent changes to an officially determined rate.

Credit. Tick. Either a straight loan, or permission to delay payment of a bill. The firm, individual or bank giving the loan or permitting delayed payment is a CREDITOR; the recipient of the loan or payment breathing space is a debtor (see DEBT). Confusing point: in a BALANCE SHEET definitions are different. Credits mean money possessed, or due from debtors, while debits mean money owed, or lost. See MONETARY CONTROL, BANK.

Credit cards. Examples are Barclaycard and its American uncle, Visa: they enable the holder to sign for goods and services, and to pay later when the bill arrives. He can then still delay payment but will be charged a heavy interest rate. Contrast with the so-called travel and entertainment cards like Diners and American Express: they provide convenience, not credit, so any member who tries to delay payment will be ticked off.

Creditors. Lucky lenders or suppliers owed money by debtors (see DEBT); unlucky if the debtor declares default, or goes bankrupt. For sharing out the remains after a bankruptcy has happened, creditors are ranked as senior creditors and JUNIOR CREDITORS. Pity the juniors.

Crowding out. Idea that government borrowing to finance a BUDGET deficit elbows private borrowers out of the market. Common sense suggests that if, by borrowing, the government increases the demand for a given supply of credit, then the cost of CREDIT (INTEREST rates) will increase, pricing some marginal borrowers out of the market. But the effects are not clear cut: nobody can say how much private borrowing has been crowded out, since that depends on the state of actual and potential demand for credit. In a recession, government 'crowding out' may have a negligible or non-existent effect if nobody else wants to borrow. Crowding out is shouted loudest by opponents of Keynesian DEFICIT FINANCING.

Cum dividend. Literally, 'with dividend'. Simply means that the purchaser of 'cum div' shares or stocks is entitled to a DIVIDEND on the appointed day. Most shares (see EQUITIES) and STOCKS are sold 'cum dividend': but some go 'ex div', meaning that new buyers have got in too late for that year's dividend.

Currency. Pounds, dollars, Deutschmarks . . . just MONEY. Any medium of exchange, though originally currency referred to paper money or coins rather than the gold or silver backing the money. See EXCHANGE RATE.

Currency basket. Several currencies combined to produce a common unit, their values weighted according to, for example, their importance in a country's trade (see EFFECTIVE EXCHANGE RATE). Weights may also be determined by the countries' gross national products, or importance in world trade – as in the EUROPEAN CURRENCY UNIT and the SPECIAL DRAWING RIGHT.

Current account (bank). The standard bank account in a RETAIL BANK into which money is deposited but from which (usually) no interest is received. Using cheques, current account balances can be withdrawn immediately on demand. In the United States, this is known as a 'checking account'.

Current account (external trade). See BALANCE OF PAYMENTS.

Current cost accounting. Method of correcting for the distorting effect of INFLATION on company accounts. Under HISTORIC COST ACCOUNTING, STOCKS and ASSETS increase in nominal value because of inflation and so add artificially to profits. In general, this effect has been accommodated by pricing assets and stocks in current prices rather than historic ones. The specific methods used are:

● In Britain, the Statement of Standard Accounting Practice (SSAP) 16 laid down in 1980 three adjustments to be made to the historical cost profit before interest and taxation: (1) a DEPRECIATION adjustment to allow for the higher cost of replacing fixed assets; (2) a cost of sales adjustment to allow for the higher cost of replacing stock; and (3) a monetary working capital adjustment to allow for the effect of the movement of prices on trade debtors and creditors. This provides a current cost operating profit.

● In the United States, inflation accounting was made part of the reporting requirement for some large public companies by the Statement of Financial Accounting Standards 33 at the end of 1979. This adjusts values for changes in the general level of prices rather than costs.

In other countries, inflation accounting has been introduced only where there has been high inflation – so in West Germany, for instance, accounting is still based on historic cost, but in France a price adjustment is made.

Current liabilities. In accounting, liabilities due to be paid within 12 months of the BALANCE SHEET date, for example DIVIDENDS, TAXATION, payments to suppliers.

Customs union. Free trade area inside a PROTECTIONIST fortress. A customs union involves countries that gradually abolish TARIFFS and other BARRIERS for trade between themselves, and set up a common external tariff wall around them. The best example is the EUROPEAN ECONOMIC COMMUNITY. In a free trade area, by contrast, .intra-area tariffs are abolished, but there is no common external tariff.

D

Dawn raid. Mass grab for a company's shares (see EQUITIES) at the stockbroker's equivalent of dawn, that is, between 9 and 10 a.m. A company wishing to take over another firm organizes swift buying of shares, usually by several different agents, that is completed before the victim (or other possible buyers) has finished his first cup of coffee. These became a popular method in London in the early 1980s. Since the buyer was only aiming to scoop a controlling interest in the company, he did not offer the same (high) price to all the company's shareholders. This was deemed unfair, so the STOCK EXCHANGE stepped in to regulate dawn raids.

Debenture. Form of company DEBT (Latin *debeo*, I owe), a bond (see BOND MARKET) bearing a fixed rate of INTEREST payable whether the firm makes any profit or not (unlike EQUITIES), and giving the right to part of the ASSETS of the company. Debenture holders get priority treatment in BANKRUPTCY pay-outs. Debentures can normally be bought and sold on a STOCK EXCHANGE.

Debt. Charles Dickens's character Mr Micawber had a dictum: 'Annual income twenty pounds, annual expenditure nineteen nineteen six, result happiness. Annual income twenty pounds, annual expenditure twenty pounds ought and six, result misery.' Debt is Micawber's unhappiness. But note another aphorism, from J. M. KEYNES: 'If you owe a bank £100, you have a problem. If you owe it £1m, it has a problem.'

Keynes is the more apt for CAPITALIST economies, for debt is the essential lubricant for GROWTH. Companies borrow in expectation of future profits greater than the INTEREST paid on the borrowing (see DISCOUNTED CASH FLOW). Individuals borrow to buy now, pay later. When a country cannot repay a debt it declares DEFAULT. Then the bank (and, perhaps, the world economy) has a problem.

Debt ratio. A company's long-term liabilities (DEBT) divided by total long-term CAPITAL employed, that is, by debt plus EQUITY. Another way is to divide long-term debt by SHAREHOLDERS' FUNDS – which is called the debt/equity ratio. Both provide a guide to a firm's viability and how deep in debt it is. See GEARING.

Debt servicing. The payment of INTEREST on money borrowed, and, if necessary, repayment of the sum borrowed (known as the principal). For countries, the debt/service ratio – one criterion of credit-worthiness – is defined as interest plus CAPITAL repayments in a particular year as a percentage of EXPORT earnings.

Deep discount bonds. Children of the 1970s, born out of companies desparate to maximize immediate CASH flow, and investors keen to avoid TAXATION. These are bonds (see BOND MARKET) that carry little or no INTEREST, but are instead sold by the issuing company at a price well below their face (that is, redemption) value. For example, a £1.00 bond might be sold for 50p and be redeemable in five years' time for £1.00. The investor gets a capital gain on redemption of 50 per cent, worth, therefore, 10 per cent a year; as most countries tax capital gains at a lower rate than investors' marginal rates of income tax, the buyer also pays less tax than for an ordinary bond. The issuer gets an immediate cash injection and little or no interest burden until the redemption date. Tax authorities have however wised up to deep discount bonds and their more brazen sisters, ZERO-COUPON BONDS (which never carry interest – deep discount bonds may bear some combination of interest and discount) and have altered tax laws in response.

Default. Refusing to pay DEBTS. A company unable to repay or service its debts declares itself BANKRUPT, and creditors have some claim on its ASSETS. A country unable (or unwilling) to pay declares default. No country has openly defaulted since the Cuban and Chinese revolutions (both nationalized banks and ignored debts); fearing a collapse of confidence, bankers have turned head over heels to prevent troubled debtors actually defaulting. In 1982, the spectre of a major debtor nation, for example, Mexico ($80 billion worth of debts) or Brazil ($90 billion), calling default loomed large, giving bankers sleepless nights. For how they cured their insomnia, see RESCHEDULING.

Deficit. In the red; a shortfall. For instance, a BUDGET deficit occurs when PUBLIC EXPENDITURE exceeds government revenues (see DEFICIT FINANCING); a current account deficit (see BALANCE OF PAYMENTS) when VISIBLE and INVISIBLE (TRADE) exports, plus inflows from private and official transfers, are worth less than IMPORTS and transfer outflows.

Deficit financing. Deliberately running a BUDGET DEFICIT (see FISCAL POLICY) in order to pump money into an economy and thereby to expand aggregate DEMAND. It is possible for a government to run a deficit without this objective. It may choose to fund its deficit by borrowing from private lenders rather than expanding the money supply.

Deflation. Popping the bubble of DEMAND. By raising TAXATION and/or cutting government spending, purchasing power can be taken out of the economy (see FISCAL POLICY). This is normally for one (or both) of two reasons: (1) To slow down price inflation. (2) To reduce demand for imports, and domestic demand for exportable goods, in order to cure a current account DEFICIT.

Demand. Aggregate demand is the total demand expressed through spending in an economy. KEYNESIANS attempt to manage employment and productive activity by altering demand through FISCAL POLICY. In theory, demand can be FINE TUNED to ensure FULL EMPLOYMENT. However, this has never been performed fully successfully. See STOP-GO.

A demand curve can be used to plot the amount of a good that a CONSUMER (or all consumers) is willing to buy at different prices. Consumers typically buy more as the price falls, so the curve slopes downwards from left to right (the price being on the vertical axis and quantity on the horizontal axis). The slope of the curve depends on the ELASTICITY of demand.

Demography. People, and the statistical study of them. See MALTHUS for how demography was brought into economics in the nineteenth century by apocalyptic – and, so far, wrong – predictions of permanent world food shortages. Demography does matter, however: the effects of the baby bulge of the early 1960s in western Europe came home to roost in the 1980s when the 'babies' expanded the labour forces. At a time of world recession, that meant one thing: rising UNEMPLOYMENT.

Deposit (account). BANK account that offers interest in return for restrictions on speed of withdrawal. DEMAND deposits offer almost immediate withdrawal; TIME DEPOSITS require money to be deposited for a fixed period (or fixed notice to be given before withdrawal), usually for a higher rate of interest. In the United States these are known generically as savings accounts.

Depreciation. Wearing out. As ASSETS get older and rustier, they are worth less and become less useful. Depreciation is a genuine COST to a company as it measures the need eventually to replace the machine with a new one, so it can be included in costs for tax purposes. Normally rates of depreciation for tax purposes are fixed – one form of special grant given by governments to industries in poor regions is to allow higher rates of depreciation (allowances) to be put against tax.

Depreciation is also used to describe falling EXCHANGE RATES.

Depression. A long-lasting RECESSION in economic activity. Companies close, DEMAND falls, dole queues lengthen, people get poorer. People will always spend their last penny on a newspaper to find out why.

Devaluation. Sudden adjustment of an EXCHANGE RATE by a government making it worth less in terms of other CURRENCIES. Devaluation only occurs with fixed exchange rates. Floating rates DEPRECIATE.

Developing countries. Euphemism for the poor of the Third World, also known as less developed countries (LDCs). Most LDCs' GROSS DOMESTIC PRODUCTS grew tolerably during the 1970s, on average by 5.1 per cent a year, getting slightly less poor in the process but still miles behind the rich world. The exception was black Africa where, in countries without the luck to find oil (most), GDP per head was stagnant or actually fell. See GROWTH for a chart (Figure 13) comparing LDCs' performance with that of the industrialized countries.

Diminishing returns. Common-sense idea that as more CAPITAL is poured into a factory, say, so the resulting increases in output (see MARGINAL ANALYSIS) get smaller after some peak point of efficiency. Eventually this leads to the average return on the capital getting smaller as well. Clearly there is some optimal combination of FACTORS OF PRODUCTION for a given state of technology and relative prices; beyond that returns diminish, to the point where the operation may become unprofitable. Diminishing returns are sometimes known as diseconomies of scale (compare with ECONOMIES OF SCALE).

Dirty float. Managing an allegedly floating EXCHANGE RATE by intervention (buying or selling by the central bank). In a 'clean' float, no intervention is used. America under President Reagan has followed a 'clean float', intervening only in 'exceptional circumstances' – such as when President Reagan was shot and wounded early in 1981.

Discount. A reduction. Popularly, a cheaper price for offering a special favour; for example, a discount for cash can be offered to reward customers for not paying by credit cards, a system in which payment is slower and which costs the seller the card company's commission. In the financial markets, a discount is the amount of deduction given for immediate payment of a bill not yet due – effectively the same as INTEREST, except paid now rather than periodically in the future.

When a banker discounts a bill, he buys it for less than its face value. The difference is the banker's payment, or interest, for holding the bill until it is due. In the City of London, discounting is mainly performed by the DISCOUNT HOUSES. See also DEEP DISCOUNT BONDS.

Discounted cash flow. Method of evaluating INVESTMENTS and the likely profits from them in terms of OPPORTUNITY COST. The real present value of future profits depends on when (that is, how soon) they are earned, because the money invested could be earning INTEREST instead. So an investment of £1,000 could, if the interest rate is 10 per cent, be worth £1,100 in a year's time, £1,210 in two years' time, if the money is deposited in a bank instead of being used to buy machines.

There are two ways of calculating discounted cash flow: see RATE OF RETURN.

Discount houses. Lubricants of the CITY (OF LONDON). The twelve members of the London Discount Market Association make their money by borrowing money at call (a short period of uncertain length; see CALL MONEY) by DISCOUNTING bills, mainly TREASURY BILLS, and then investing the cash for three months or longer. Borrowing at call and lending on is a risky business, but discount houses, such as Alexanders or Smith, St Aubyn enjoy the privilege of knowing that the BANK OF ENGLAND will always act as LENDER OF LAST RESORT. Every day, indeed, the Bank ensures that the market is not perilously short of money by injecting funds (or removing them if there is a surplus). In return, the discount houses underwrite the weekly tender of Treasury bills, that is, they guarantee to buy any bills not bid for by other big buyers. The discount houses' success depends on judging INTEREST rates and the value of their investments correctly.

Discount rate. Generic term for the rate charged by CENTRAL BANKS for lending to BANKS and other financial institutions. In Britain, this was the old term for (also now obsolete) bank rate – the rate at which the Bank of England lends to the DISCOUNT HOUSES. This, and its later variants, MINIMUM LENDING RATE and, now, dealing rates, set a practical and psychological lead for other money market rates. Similarly, in America, the discount rate is the rate the FEDERAL RESERVE charges banks that borrow from it.

Disinflation. Cutting out INFLATION. Has never been achieved without pain – a loss of potential output, rising BANKRUPTCIES and UNEMPLOYMENT. Those are also the consequences of DEFLATION: the difference between the two is not entirely semantic, partly because deflationary policies may be adopted for reasons other than disinflating (for example, improving the BALANCE OF PAYMENTS), and partly because deflation may not persist long enough to achieve disinflation.

Disintermediation. Doing without the middleman and escaping the monetary policemen (see MONETARY CONTROL). Disintermediation is a way of evading official control of BANK lending (like the CORSET) by circumventing the banking system as an intermediary – so lenders deal directly with borrowers, for example by lending between companies. Through disintermediation, lenders can exploit unusually big differences between market INTEREST rates and bank deposit rates. The other principal escape route has been parallel markets. The opposite of disintermediation is reintermediation.

Disposable income. Cash to spend or save, after the taxman has had his fill. EARNINGS are a poor method of evaluating spending power because tax, and alternative sources of income such as TRANSFER PAYMENTS, complicate the picture.

Diversification. Putting eggs in more than one basket. Firms diversify by providing a new good without stopping production of existing ones; for example a soap powder firm like Proctor & Gamble has diversified into disposable nappies (diapers). Often the new product has something in common with existing ones; in this case, marketing techniques. Diversification spreads sources of profit and gives an escape route into new, faster expanding markets. CONGLOMERATES diversify simply by buying up companies in other markets, providing a wider profit base. Caveat: diversification can land the company with heavy losses if it backs a loser – for example, the German firm AEG-Telefunken was sunk by trying to stay in consumer electronics as well as high-tech electrical engineering.

Dividend. Slice of company profits paid out to shareholders. The dividend may be expressed as a percentage of the nominal (face) value of the share, say 8 per cent on a £1 share; 8p per share will be paid whether the share is now valued at 30p or £20. Dividends are announced at company annual general meetings, but interim dividends are also common. Oddly, British shareholders can vote only to reduce the dividend, not to raise it. Irate shareholders have just one recourse: to sack the board.

Dividend cover. Ratio of profits to DIVIDENDS. So, if profits are £200,000 and £20,000 is paid in dividends, a firm's dividend cover is 10.

Division of labour. The basis of modern economics, first developed into a theory by Adam SMITH. Instead of individuals, firms or countries trying to be jacks of all trades but masters of none, they have specialized. As a result, skills are fully developed, production is more efficient, and therefore output is maximized. See COMPARATIVE ADVANTAGE.

Domestic credit expansion (DCE). Gauge of MONEY growth adjusted for BALANCE OF PAYMENTS and foreign CURRENCY finance. DCE is defined as (1) BANK lending in domestic currency to the PRIVATE SECTOR and overseas; plus (2) the PUBLIC SECTOR BORROWING REQUIREMENT; minus (3) sales of public sector DEBT to the non-bank private sector.

As such, DCE provides a better guide to the external consequences of financial policy than does monetary growth. A wide measure of the MONEY SUPPLY can be expanding quite slowly at the same time as DCE is rapid: the difference is that some domestic credit is being spent abroad, hence contributing to a current account deficit. Since the INTERNATIONAL MONETARY FUND is concerned with the causes of current deficits, it pays close attention to DCE in all its lending programmes.

Dow Jones index. Barometer of the New York STOCK EXCHANGE. The main index takes the share prices of thirty 'typical' industrial companies and measures their movements. Note for the statisticians: the Dow is not actually an index, but is calculated by simply adding the New York closing prices of the thirty shares and adjusting them by a 'current average divisor' – an adjustable figure calculated to preserve the continuity of the Dow over time amid changes in its component parts. Contrast with FINANCIAL TIMES INDEX, which really is an index in the technical sense. There are other Dow Jones indices for specialist groups of shares like transport (twenty companies) and utilities (fifteen companies) and bonds.

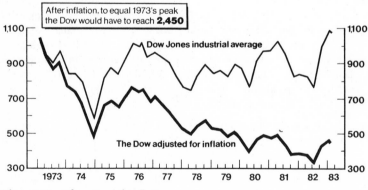

Figure 7 *The price of inflation*

Note for BULLS: beware of reports that the Dow has reached new record 'highs'. Although the index shows the direction of movement, it is not adjusted for inflation; Figure 7 shows the Dow's real and nominal movement during the 1970s.

Dumping. Selling below cost. Can be done by a firm simply to offload stocks or cut its losses on uncompetitive products, or to act as a loss leader to gain market share. More often, the culprit is a state subsidized industry, such as steel, which can absorb losses because of government hand-outs. Under the GATT International Dumping Code, countries can retaliate by slapping on anti-dumping duties or stopping trade altogether. Disputes go before GATT panels for adjudication. They have had a lot to adjudicate in the 1970s and early 1980s. In American law, the Anti-Dumping Act of 1921 empowers the US International Trade Commission, after protest by domestic producers, to slap on an anti-dumping duty.

Dutch auction. An upside-down sale. Goods are offered for sale at a price well above their true value, and the price lowered until they find a buyer. First to lose his nerve gets the goods.

E

Earned income. Taxman's definition. INCOME from work as opposed to INTEREST, DIVIDENDS or profits gained from financial investment or RENT from land, known as UNEARNED INCOME. In some countries, unearned income is taxed at a higher rate.

Earnings. Full fruits of toil. Statistics for earnings include overtime and bonuses, and so are a better measure of pay than figures for wage rates or settlements.

Figure 8 shows changes in real hourly earnings in manufacturing in the 1970s for various countries.

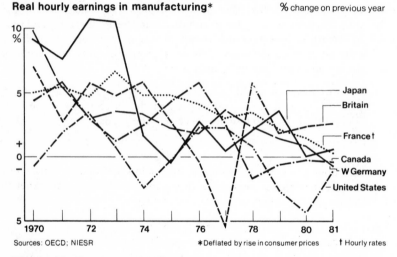

Figure 8 *Earnings and inflation*

Earnings per share. Measures a company's total net return earned on ordinary share capital. It is calculated by first deducting TAXATION, DEPRECIATION, INTEREST, and payments to preference shareholders and other minority interests from gross income, and then dividing by the number of ordinary shares.

Econometrics. Mathematical and computer wizardry applied to economics. The econometrician's best-known activity is building mathematical 'models' of the relationships in the economy, using equations that embody those relationships between, for example, INVESTMENT, INTEREST rates and economic GROWTH. Once built, the model can be used (with a computer) to forecast the economic future.

Econometrics clearly has a valuable role to play in quantifying economic relationships; a computer can now handle such quantities of data that econometric analysis has become practical and accessible.

It has its critics, none the less. One of the most venerable of twentieth-century economists, Joan Robinson of Cambridge (England) put it this way: 'I don't know any mathematics. I have to think.' Unless econometric seeds are sown on soil that has been thoroughly and thoughtfully prepared, they will spring up only to wither from the lack of coherence and relevance.

Economic rent. See RENT.

Economics. Like an elephant, economics is hard to define, but most people recognize it when they see it. Vaguely, it is the study of how the world makes a living; more specifically, how scarce resources are used to produce and distribute goods and services to meet human wants. Because one of its early practitioners, MALTHUS, believed that scarcity was so acute as to put the world permanently on the edge of famine, economics came to be known as the 'dismal science'.

The subject is normally divided into MICROECONOMICS and MACRO-ECONOMICS. In both branches, certain operating standards obtain: theorizing, collecting facts, analysing them, and then re-examining theory in the light of them. Throughout this (never-ending) process, economics is concerned to develop general propositions that can be applied in a variety of countries, periods, and circumstances – and still hold good. That is why it has claims to be a 'science', even though it is almost impossible to set up a laboratory experiment in the way that physical scientists can arrange every day.

Economies of scale. The benefits of MASS PRODUCTION. In many industries, big is beautiful (or anyway cheaper) because unit costs of production fall. Examples: mass production of cars; giant shipbuild-ing yards; steel works, where initial investment costs are heavy and can be lightened only if output is expanded (see RETURNS TO SCALE).

All processes have an optimal level of output beyond which effi-ciency falls, however, often because of managerial problems. Large-scale production can become inflexible, and can be slow to innovate because of heavy investment costs. Giant steel furnaces, for instance, are now being hit by competition from small, flexible, mini-arc fur-naces.

Effective exchange rate. Way of gauging a currency's movement in terms of its trade, rather than just against, say, the dollar or the Deutschmark. Effective exchange rates are calculated in the form of an INDEX (NUMBER) with a base period (often 15 December 1971, the date of the SMITHSONIAN AGREEMENT).

For example, the index for currency A is usually computed by weighting other currencies according to their importance in country

A's trade, and then summing the movement of currency A against each of the others. This is also known as TRADE WEIGHTING.

Effective protection. TARIFF levels provide the simplest measure of the protection against imports given to an industry (see PROTECTIONISM), but may not tell the whole story. If tariffs are also levied on an industry's inputs (that is, raw materials, components and so on), this raises its costs at the same time as increasing the level of protection against outsiders.

To take account of this, and to measure the true level of protection, economists calculate the effective rate of protection: this is defined as the percentage by which the entire set of a country's trade barriers raises an industry's VALUE ADDED per unit of output. Take a simple example where there is a 10 per cent tariff on clocks, and a 5 per cent tariff on imports of the materials from which clocks are made. With free trade, a clock costs £20, of which the inputs cost £14, so the value added is £6. The 10 per cent tariff raises clock prices to £22, and the 5 per cent tariff on inputs raises input prices to £14.70; so the value added per unit rises from £6 to £7.30 (£22 minus £14.70). To calculate the effective rate of protection, the following formula is used:

$$\frac{£7.30 - £6}{£6} = 21.7\%,$$

that is the increase in valued added per unit resulting from protection.

Note that the effective protection (21.7%) is higher than the apparent protection (10%), because the tariff on outputs is higher than the tariff on inputs. If the reverse were true, the effective rate of protection on the final product would actually be negative. Most tariff structures apply higher tariffs to final outputs than to inputs. However, examples have been found in Pakistan and in 19th century Europe where inputs received higher protection, so giving manufacturing industries less protection than they would have had under perfectly free trade.

Elasticity. Responsiveness of one variable to changes in another. Usually measured in four categories:

● Price elasticity of, for example, DEMAND. This measures how much the quantity of a good demanded changes if its price changes. Formally, this becomes

$$PE_D = \frac{\%\Delta Q_D}{\%\Delta P}$$

If the figure is greater than 1, demand is 'elastic'; if less than 1, 'inelastic'. Similarly, price elasticity of supply tests the response of supply to price changes.

● Income elasticity of demand tests the response of demand to changes in income:

$$YE_D = \frac{\%\Delta Q_D}{\%\Delta Y}$$

● Cross-elasticity, which shows how the demand for one good (A) changes when the price of another one (B) changes. Formally this becomes

$$\frac{\%\Delta Q_{DA}}{\%\Delta P_B}$$

If the goods are substitutes (for example, tea and coffee), the cross-elasticity will be positive: for example, if the price of tea rises, people will switch to coffee, raising the demand for it. If the goods are complements (for example, video recorders and televisions), then cross-elasticity will be negative. If they are unrelated − air travel and soap − then a change in the price of one will have no effect on sales of another, so the cross-elasticity will be zero.

● Elasticity of substitution measures the ease with which one input in a productive process can be substituted for another, for a given technology. Example: if wages rise relative to the cost of machinery, some companies will be able to use more machines and fewer people. For them,

$$\frac{\%\Delta \text{ in capital/labour ratio}}{\%\Delta \text{ in price of labour relative to price of capital}}$$

will be positive. For others, no substitution will be possible; the elasticity is therefore zero.

Engel's law. Notion first formulated by a Russian statistician, Ernst Engel, in 1857 that the proportion of INCOME spent on food shrinks as income rises. Food is a necessity − but something on which rich people will spend less than poorer people as a proportion of their income. Engel's law forms part of the argument for the COMMON AGRICULTURAL POLICY, and other schemes of farm support.

Enterprise zones. Britain's latest form of REGIONAL POLICY, a bid by the Conservative government elected in May 1979 to attract new industries to depressed areas, especially inner city areas like London's docklands or Clydebank near Glasgow.

Firms setting up inside a zone − a small area of 100–900 acres − do not have to pay RATES for up to ten years, and are freed from many bureaucratic regulations so that plant can be built more quickly. Trouble is that areas immediately around the zone – generally pretty depressed, too – now look unattractive to firms, so non-zone local councils have complained. Like all regional policies, it is hard to tell how many new firms have simply been diverted from other areas. By December 1982 twenty-two zones had been created. Other countries have started to copy the idea – Belgium in 1982, for example.

Entrepôt. Literally, between places. A port, like Rotterdam or Singapore, which receives goods for shipment on to somewhere else, often after transferring them into smaller ships or barges, is an entrepôt port. Any temporary depository for goods is an entrepôt.

Entrepreneur. The life and soul of the capitalist party. An entrepreneur has a smart business idea, invests his (or somebody else's) CAPITAL and takes risks, with an eagle eye on likely profits. An entrepreneur owns his firm; modern companies – run by salaried managers and owned by inert shareholders – at one stage threatened to make the entrepreneur extinct. But the small-is-beautiful fashion, generous tax breaks and adaptable technology have since combined to give him a new lease of life. However, few large businesses are headed by entrepreneurs; when they are, they can rise high – or fall with a bump, like Sir Freddie Laker in 1982.

Equilibrium. Sacred balance – on which much of economics, especially CLASSICAL ECONOMICS, hinges. To chart the course of economic variables, the classicists assumed that economies always tended towards equilibrium, a settled state where supply and demand are in balance, whether of goods (through changes in price), of labour (through wage changes), or SAVINGS and INVESTMENT (through INTEREST rate changes). Equilibrium would be general (of the whole economy) or PARTIAL (of just one pair of variables, for example the demand and supply of hats). KEYNES, too, believed in equilibrium, but rejected the classicists' assumption that economies always moved towards equilibrium at FULL EMPLOYMENT in the long run. Equilibrium is a useful tool of analysis and does accurately mirror events in many markets (see TATONNEMENT). Snag: economies contain so many variables, including exogenous and psychologically determined ones, that the path to equilibrium may not be easily identifiable; and, after all, no economy is ever actually in equilibrium, just tending towards it. In a bid for self-improvement, economists have tried ECONOMETRICS and analysis of disequilibrium, the state (clearly more common) when economies are not in a cosy balance.

Equity. CAPITAL of a firm, after deducting outside liabilities, except those to shareholders. In a typical public company this capital is roughly equivalent to the value of ordinary shares. Those shareholders have a prior claim to this 'equity' and so shares are popularly known as equities on the British STOCK EXCHANGE. See DEBT RATIO.

Eurobond. A long-term, fixed INTEREST loan raised in the EUROMARKETS by top-notch borrowers (for example, multinational companies, banks, countries) and provided by long-term investors like insurance companies and pension funds.

Eurocredits. Bank loans denominated in a CURRENCY held outside its country of origin (see EUROMARKETS). Example: a borrower goes to his bank in London, wanting to borrow \$1 billion. The loan may be spread — 'syndicated' — among several dozen banks. It will typically run for up to eight years; its interest rate will vary, being set at some margin ('spread') of perhaps $\frac{1}{2}$ per cent above a market rate. The latter is usually the LONDON INTERBANK OFFER RATE (LIBOR — the six-month Eurodollar rate) or the prime rate charged by American banks.

Eurocurrency. A CURRENCY deposited and lent outside its country of origin. The predominant Eurocurrency is the dollar (which has always accounted for more than 70 per cent of the total market), but there are also EuroDeutschmarks, Euroyen, Eurosterling and so on. See EUROMARKETS.

Eurodollar. A buck placed in a bank outside America. See EUROMARKETS and EUROCURRENCY.

Euromarkets. Markets in CURRENCIES held outside their country of origin — for example, dollars held in Europe (the first formal market, hence its name), but sometimes taken to include, for example, D-Marks in Singapore. The Euromarkets have grown spectacularly in the 1970s (See Figure 9):

Note, though, that the bulk of Euromarket transactions are between BANKS. By the end of 1980, only 26 per cent of the banks' outstanding loans were to final users, like countries or companies; the rest were in the INTERBANK MARKET. For the way that Eurocurrencies are lent, see EUROBOND and EUROCREDITS.

Dollars have, of course, been deposited outside America for years. But the Euromarkets only started to flourish in the mid-1950s when banks began to open offices all over the world to borrow and lend dollars. Why then? Nobody really knows, but everyone has a pet theory:

● Because Russia (via the Moscow Narodny Bank) wanted to hold its large dollar earnings outside America for fear of sequestration;

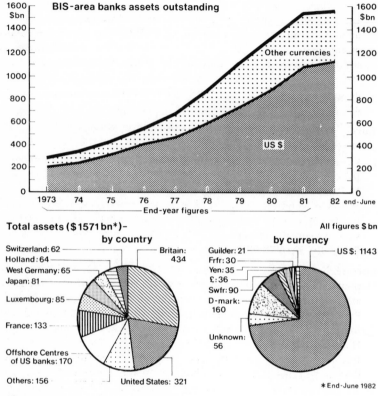

Figure 9 *Growth in Euromarkets*

● Because controls on American banks made it attractive for them to hold dollars abroad (see REGULATION Q).

The Euromarkets have grown fast because they are free from the reserve requirements that are so costly to the domestic bankers. This means that depositors can be offered a higher rate of INTEREST, and borrowers a cheaper rate than elsewhere. Spates of regulation in America have been associated with fast growth in the Euromarkets. Euromarket business takes place in 'offshore banking centres', so-called because of the lack of domestic control, such as London, Singapore, Nassau, Hong Kong and Luxembourg.

Since 1974 the Euromarket has been expanded by flows of oil money. OPEC countries were paid in dollars for their oil, deposited them short term in the high-interest Euromarkets, and the banks lent them on to other countries. Big drawback of this highly efficient recycling operation: huge sums are now owed by politically and economically unstable LDCs, like Mexico, Argentina, Brazil, the Philippines, South Korea and Turkey. Apart from general observation and guidance by the BANK FOR INTERNATIONAL SETTLEMENTS, little attempt was made to monitor and control Eurolending. CENTRAL BANKS have recently made greater efforts to co-ordinate their supervision, largely by trying to make banks produce 'consolidated' accounts of their lending world-wide. But the process is a slow one, and is still incomplete.

European currency unit (ECU). Basket of CURRENCIES used by the EUROPEAN MONETARY SYSTEM to set values for its parity grid and for some CENTRAL BANK transactions. Gradually the ECU, which contains snippets of all EMS currency plus sterling, is becoming used for COMMERCIAL BANK transactions, too. Like its big, elder brother, the SPECIAL DRAWING RIGHT, the ECU is a more stable way for companies to borrow, price export contracts, hold bank deposits and so on. Yet, even in the sophisticated world of finance and trade, the ECU has been slow to catch on.

European Economic Community (EEC). Trade, aid, agricultural and political club for western Europeans that occupies many of the largest and ugliest office blocks in Brussels, Luxembourg and Strasbourg. Popularly known as the common market, the EEC was founded on 25 March 1957, when six countries – France, West Germany, Belgium, Holland, Luxembourg and Italy – signed the Treaty of Rome. The EEC was a direct development from the European Coal and Steel Community, founded by the above six at the Treaty of Paris in 1951, which still exists as an adjunct to the EEC. In 1973, three more members joined the club – Britain, Ireland and Denmark – and in 1981 Greece joined too, making ten in all. Spain and Portugal have both applied to join, but are still waiting in the wings.

The Rome treaty, and subsequent policies built upon it, have established:
● A CUSTOMS UNION. Inside the ten members all quota and TARIFF BARRIERS to trade have been abolished, and there is a common external tariff for IMPORTS from non-EEC members. The bulk of those enter largely unhindered by virtue of a plethora of trade deals between the EEC and its trading partners, and aid deals like the LOMÉ CONVENTION. Agricultural imports are, however, subject to hefty tariffs under the
● COMMON AGRICULTURAL POLICY. This is the EEC's only major common policy for an economic sector. See separate entry for details.
● EEC law superior to national law. A pile of EEC directives and regulations aim to harmonize national laws, especially those relating to technical standards for goods, in order to remove NON-TARIFF

BARRIERS TO TRADE, and to raise legal standards for, for instance, working conditions, company law or pollution control.
- Freedom of movement and work throughout the EEC for citizens of the member states.
- The EUROPEAN MONETARY SYSTEM. See separate entry for details.
- Competition policy. See ANTI-TRUST.

The EEC has a small bureaucracy, called the Commission, to administer its affairs and make proposals for new policies. This is headed by fourteen commissioners (politicians cum bureaucrats) appointed by the member governments. Decisions are however made by the Council of Ministers – meetings of ministers from the member states competent for the particular area in question, for example finance, agriculture, fisheries and so on. Before it makes a decision, and for approval of its $20 billion budget, the Council must consult the European Parliament. This body of politicians from the member states was first elected directly in 1979 and has been struggling to boost its powers ever since. As yet, however, it is purely consultative, with scant powers of decision.

In the early 1980s the pressures of recession, and the difficulties of decision-making by ten countries with often divergent interests, has meant that progress in economic fields has largely stagnated. More encouraging is the development of joint foreign policy positions on, for instance, the Middle East.

European Free Trade Association (EFTA). Free trade club for Europe's outer circle. Set up at Stockholm in 1959, EFTA's members now are Norway, Sweden, Austria, Iceland, Portugal and Switzerland. Finland has stayed out in order to appear neutral between east and west, but is, in effect, a full member. TARIFFS and QUOTAS on industrial goods between EFTA members have been phased out, and part of agricultural trade is free of duty. EFTA is not a CUSTOMS UNION, as it has no common external tariff, so it has elaborate rules on the flow of non-EFTA goods inside the area, and on processing for outward trade.

Originally Denmark and Britain were members, but they both deserted in 1973 to join the EUROPEAN ECONOMIC COMMUNITY. Then, EFTA signed a series of free trade deals with the EEC that now ensure virtual free trade in industrial goods between the seventeen EEC and EFTA countries.

European monetary system (EMS). Snake that wanted to be a prince. Born in March 1979, the EMS is a mechanism of EXCHANGE RATE management between European CURRENCIES, and a direct descendant of the so-called 'snake' system born in 1972.

The snake was hatched in response to the SMITHSONIAN AGREEMENT of December 1971, which allowed currencies the freedom to move by

$2\frac{1}{4}$ per cent either side of their dollar parity. This meant that, against each other, European currencies could 'swing' by 9 per cent in the worst of circumstances; that is, if the D-Mark was $2\frac{1}{4}$ per cent above its dollar parity and the French franc was $2\frac{1}{4}$ per cent below, the gap between the two was $4\frac{1}{2}$ per cent. If they swapped positions, they would open up a $4\frac{1}{2}$ per cent gap the other way, making a 9 per cent swing.

The Europeans, keen to steady rates in order to facilitate intra-EEC trade, thought this swing excessive. The Basle agreement of April 1972 set up narrower limits: the six founding members of the EEC, plus the trio soon to join (Britain, Denmark and Ireland), plus Norway, agreed to let their currencies move against each other by a maximum of only $2\frac{1}{4}$ per cent. This band was to be maintained within the $4\frac{1}{2}$ per cent limits against the dollar: hence the name of the 'snake in the tunnel'.

But the snake soon started to rattle. Turbulent exchange markets forced Britain and Ireland to withdraw within six weeks; Italy followed at the beginning of 1973. The dollar itself was highly unstable and, after a spell in March 1973 when all foreign exchange markets had to be closed for a few days, the Europeans abandoned limits against the dollar.

So with floating against the dollar, the 'tunnel' disappeared, though the snake survived – but uncertainly. France pulled out in January 1974, rejoined in July 1975, and finally quit in March 1976, leaving the snake as a primarily West German block.

The instability of the dollar in 1977–79, enthusiasm from the EEC Commission, and the close relationship between France's President Valéry Giscard d'Estaing and West Germany's Helmut Schmidt, brought snakery back to the fore in 1978. The nine EEC members agreed to devise 'a scheme for the creation of closer monetary co-operation leading to a zone of monetary stability in Europe'. After some falterings, the scheme was born on 13 March 1979.

The new EMS was, in many ways, similar to the old snake; membership is voluntary – Britain opted not to join, but Ireland did, and when Greece entered the EEC on 1 January 1981 it stayed out of the EMS. But in the eyes of its architects, the EMS was a higher creature than the snake: it was to involve closer collaboration between CENTRAL BANKS, more specific arrangements on exchange rate intervention, and efforts to align domestic policies in order to keep exchange rates steady. It contained two significant innovations; a new kind of money, the EUROPEAN CURRENCY UNIT (ECU), and a two-pronged approach to stabilizing exchange rates.

The ECU is a basket of European currencies that now forms part of the foreign exchange reserves of European central banks. They obtain

ECUs in return for depositing 20 per cent of their dollars and gold with the European monetary co-operation fund, known as FECOM by its French initials. Central banks use the ECU to denominate their debts and credits with each other. And each currency's central rate in the EMS is set in ECUs, in two forms:

The parity grid. Each currency has a central rate against the ECU, which is then translated into cross-rates for each pair of currencies. Each currency can move by $\pm 2\frac{1}{4}$ per cent (the same limit as in the snake) against its cross-parity – except the lira which was allowed limits of 6 per cent. Once, say, the Belgian franc falls to its bilateral limit against another currency, say the D-Mark, then both Belgium's

central bank and Germany's Bundesbank have to intervene (buying francs, selling D-Marks) to prevent any further widening. To avoid frequent (and sometimes fruitless) intervention, however, the EMS designers added an early warning system,

The divergence indicator. Each currency has a divergence threshold set at three-quarters of the 'maximum permissible difference' between its actual ECU rate and its ECU central rate. This is separate from the $2\frac{1}{4}$ per cent of the parity grid, and varies from currency to currency because the ECU's value is itself changed when its component currencies change. A move by the D-Mark (35 per cent of the ECU basket) will pull the ECU along far more than a move by the Irish punt (1 per cent of the ECU) – so the divergence indicators are adjusted to equalize this effect.

Once a currency hits this indicator, it is assumed that its government will take remedial action – that is, altering interest rates, fiscal policy and so on. Then, it was thought inflation rates and trade performance would converge, making the EEC resemble a single economy. Currencies can be realigned to new central and cross-rates if the market pressure is too great. This takes place at a weekend meeting of EEC finance ministers in Brussels, when the foreign exchange markets are closed.

At the outset, the EMS's future looked secure chiefly because the economic policies and performance of the biggest members – France and West Germany – were fairly similar. But it was born into a turbulent world – only months before the second oil shock sent the world into recession and rising inflation. Against this pressure the EMS has provided only short-term defence, and has failed to prevent divergence of policies and performance. The switch to economic expansion by the new Socialist government in France in May 1981 didn't help, and the rate of realignments has accelerated:

23 September 1979	D-Mark upvalued by 2 per cent, Danish krone devalued by 3 per cent, each against all other EMS currencies.
29 November 1979	Danish krone devalued by 5 per cent.
22 March 1981	Italian lira devalued by 6 per cent.
4 October 1981	D-Mark and Dutch guilder upvalued by 5.5 per cent, French franc and Italian lira devalued by 3 per cent.
21 February 1982	Belgian franc devalued by 8.5 per cent and Danish krone by 3 per cent.
12 June 1982	D-Mark and Dutch guilder upvalued by 4.25 per cent, French franc devalued by 5.75 per cent and Italian lira devalued by 2.75 per cent.
21 March 1983	D-Mark upvalued by 5.5 per cent, French franc and Italian lira devalued by 2.5 per cent, Dutch guilder upvalued by 3.5 per cent, Danish krone by 2.5 per cent and Belgian franc by 1.5 per cent, Irish pound devalued by 3.5 per cent.

Nevertheless, the EMS has had an effect; the Mitterrand government bowed to pressure in March 1983 to make its economic policies more restrictive to avoid a fourth devaluation of the franc.

The EMS's architects intended the EMS to develop further after two years, when EEC countries would pool their reserves; FECOM could become a genuine pan-European central bank, called the European Monetary Fund, and would issue ecus against national currencies. But the EMS's shaky life, plus legal objections from West Germany on the transfer of reserves, has led to stage two of the EMS blueprint being postponed indefinitely. The EMS survives – but as nothing grander than a supersnake.

Exchange controls. Artificial life support system for a CURRENCY. Britain had controls on the outward flow of sterling from 1939 (when controls were slapped on as a wartime emergency) until October 1979. Individuals could buy only a limited amount of foreign exchange for holidays; all overseas direct investment by firms was vetted by the BANK OF ENGLAND, which elbowed companies to raise funds abroad rather than exporting it from Britain; portfolio investment abroad had to be financed from a fund of 'investment dollars', skilfully managed to ensure scarcity. The aim of controls was to 'protect the pound', an argument with some (but not much) justice in the days when sterling was a RESERVE CURRENCY, but clearly inappropriate once sterling soared on a wave of North Sea oil revenues in 1979. Then the Conservative government abolished controls. Other countries use (and have used) controls to help prop up their currencies; France, for instance, imposed controls in 1981 to defend the franc; Italy has long had controls.

Exchange equalization account. British means of intervening in the FOREIGN EXCHANGE markets. It was set up in 1932, after Britain left the GOLD STANDARD in 1931. The EEA holds the country's foreign exchange reserves, which can be sold if the BANK OF ENGLAND wishes to support sterling. It also holds quantities of sterling assets (mainly TREASURY BILLS) which can be sold to foreigners if the Bank does not want the pound to rise. When the EEA stays on the sidelines, the sterling exchange rate is determined in the private market.

Exchange rate. Price at which one currency can be converted into another. Currencies freely traded on the FOREIGN EXCHANGE markets have a spot rate (see SPOT MARKETS) for immediate exchange, and a forward rate (see FORWARD MARKETS) for dealing at some date in the future. Countries manage their exchange rates in five ways:
● Fixed. As under the GOLD STANDARD, or BRETTON WOODS, currencies can have a narrow margin of flexibility, 1 per cent either side of their central parity. Some currencies – for example, the Swedish krona, the Finnish markka and the Norwegian krone – are fixed against a special basket of currencies suited to their trade pattern, others to the SPECIAL DRAWING RIGHTS (SDR). Under fixed rates, governments and CENTRAL BANKS alter rates by announcing DEVALUATION or REVALUATION.
● Floating. Here the currency is freely traded on the foreign exchange markets, and finds its own level. If the central bank attempts to guide this level and to smooth fluctuations by intervention and adjusting INTEREST rates, this is called DIRTY FLOATING; if the bank chooses not to interfere, this is CLEAN FLOATING. Since the SMITHSONIAN AGREEMENT collapsed in 1972, most major currencies have floated, though some Europeans have opted for:

- Restricted floating in the SNAKE and the EUROPEAN MONETARY SYSTEM.
- Crawling peg. Here the rate is officially fixed, but is altered regularly by small amounts to spread a devaluation or revaluation over a longer period. In Latin American countries with HYPERINFLATION, crawling pegs never seem to stop crawling.
- Two-tier rates. A few countries, such as Belgium, set two exchange rates, one for financial transactions and the other for commercial (trade) purposes.

Exchequer. The British government's bank account of revenue and expenditure, run by the Treasury, and kept at the BANK OF ENGLAND. Britain's finance minister is known officially as the Chancellor of the Exchequer.

Ex dividend. Without DIVIDEND. Shares bought ex dividend usually carry no dividend during the payment period, or for some fixed period immediately preceding payment. Many shares have two prices: an ex-dividend price and a higher CUM DIVIDEND price.

Ex-Im bank. Short for the Export-Import bank, America's EXPORT CREDIT agency – the biggest of them all. Set up in 1934, this government agency provides INSURANCE for United States EXPORTS, and lends money to foreigners to buy American goods. In fiscal year 1981 the Ex-Im bank disbursed $5.4 billion of loans, supporting 6 per cent of American exports. The biggest loans were for aircraft purchases.

Expectations. Hopes and fears about the future. Economists have long agreed that expectations play a big role in all kinds of economic decisions, from investing in a new factory to wage negotiations, to buying and selling foreign currency. But expectations are hard to define, harder still to measure; only in the theory of RATIONAL EXPECTATIONS have they been accorded full dress status.

Export credits. Loans (often subsidized) to boost EXPORTS. Government agencies such as the EX-IM BANK (United States), the Export Credit Guarantee Department (Britain) and Hermes (West Germany) lend foreign buyers money to help them buy goods from domestic producers. Producers like the idea, because they are effectively insured against non-payment. And since money is often what buyers lack, customers can be swayed as much by the financial terms of the deal as by the goods themselves. When governments are anxious to boost exports, therefore, they start competing with ever more attractive export credits.

This has produced an export credit competition that at times has threatened to turn very nasty. In the late 1970s and early 1980s, the big industrial countries raced to out-subsidize each other's exports. Credits to LDCs alone expanded from $28 billion in 1978 to $36 billion in 1981. To try to control the credit war, the big countries (the United States, France, Japan, West Germany, Britain) agreed in the arena of the ORGANIZATION FOR ECONOMIC CO-OPERATION AND DEVELOPMENT to standardize the INTEREST rates given to countries, to be divided into three groups: (1) poor, for example, China, India; (2) intermediate, for example, Brazil, Mexico, Taiwan; (3) rich. In December 1982 the permitted minimum interest rates under the consensus were: (1) 12.15 per cent (two to five years), 12.4 per cent (loans over five years); (2) 10.85 per cent (two to five years), 11.35 per cent (over five years); (3) 10 per cent. Yet although the rates were fixed, countries evade the voluntary deal, and can still compete on volumes.

Table 2 shows the pattern of export credits in the 1970s.

Table 2 *Export credits to less developed countries.* Gross disbursements by DAC members* ($ billion).

	Total DAC	France	Japan	US	Germany	Britain	Italy
1970	6.7	1.0	1.1	0.3	1.1	1.0	0.7
1971	8.3	1.1	1.4	1.1	1.6	1.2	0.8
1972	8.1	1.4	1.1	1.6	1.2	1.3	0.7
1973	9.4	2.0	1.3	1.8	1.5	1.2	0.5
1974	11.3	1.7	1.3	2.6	2.4	1.3	0.4
1975	14.9	2.3	1.6	2.9	3.4	1.4	1.8
1976	19.0	3.3	2.1	3.5	3.2	2.3	1.2
1977	22.8	4.1	3.2	3.2	3.0	2.5	2.2
1978	27.7	4.0	4.1	3.1	3.6	3.6	4.0
1979	28.6	4.9	3.4	3.5	3.2	4.9	4.5
1980	34.9	5.4	4.2	5.1	4.1	4.9	4.2
Average annual % change 1970–80	17.9	18.4	14.3	32.8	14.1	17.2	19.6

* Members of Development Assistance Committee.
Source: OECD.

Exports. Sales abroad. VISIBLE (TRADE) exports, known in America as merchandise exports, are manufactures, machines, raw materials and other goods that physically pass through customs; INVISIBLE (TRADE) exports are of services like INSURANCE, BANKING and shipping, INTEREST payments, tourism inside the country, and emigrants' remittances. Exports are normally reckoned as 'FREE ON BOARD' – that is, priced at the moment they arrive on board ship, train, lorry or aircraft — so the cost of transport and insurance are charged as an IMPORT for the recipient country. Imports are priced including COST, INSURANCE, FREIGHT. See BALANCE OF PAYMENTS.

External financing limits (EFL). Maximum available credit for British NATIONALIZED INDUSTRIES. EFLs set the amount that companies such as British Steel, British Rail or the National Coal Board can borrow from public or private sources in the financial year concerned.

Externality. Side effect. Externalities are normally social costs rather than straightforward financial ones. A factory, for example, creates externalities such as pollution, noise, its ugliness and the need for residents to move house, all of which are hard to quantify. Nonetheless, some COST-BENEFIT ANALYSIS attempts to put a price on them. Externalities can be benefits, too. A new road saves users' time, and perhaps their nerves.

F

Factor cost. Way of measuring output according to the costs of factors of production (land, labour, CAPITAL), rather than market prices (which are affected by indirect taxes and SUBSIDIES). See GROSS DOMESTIC PRODUCT.

Factors of production. Land, labour and CAPITAL, the three generic requirements for production. Some textbooks add a fourth – enterprise.

Federal funds market. A market involving several hundred American banks. Federal funds are reserve assets (that is, non-interest-bearing deposits) that commercial banks hold at the FEDERAL RESERVE. The market involves trading in these reserves: those banks with surplus reserves lend to those who do not have enough to meet their reserve requirements. The term is sometimes used generically, to cover interbank lending in Federal funds and other related instruments.

Most transactions in the Fed funds markets are for one day only, though some longer-term deals are made. The interest rate is called the Federal funds rate: as in other markets, it contains a 'spread' (usually about $\frac{1}{4}$ per cent) between the rate paid to lenders and the rate charged to borrowers. The spread is effectively the commission for the brokers who specialise in bringing borrowers and lenders together. The Fed can influence the Fed funds rate (which has an important influence on other rates) by OPEN MARKET OPERATIONS that increase or decrease the volume of member bank reserves.

Federal Open Market Committee. Governing body of American monetary policy. See MONETARY CONTROL, FEDERAL RESERVE SYSTEM.

Federal Reserve System. The United States CENTRAL BANK. Set up in 1913, and popularly known as the Fed, the system divides the United States into twelve Federal Reserve districts each served by a Federal Reserve bank. In addition, the Fed consists of a Federal Reserve Board, a board of seven governors based in Washington; the FEDERAL OPEN MARKET COMMITTEE; the Federal Advisory Council; and member COMMERCIAL BANKS. The Federal Reserve Board, along with the Open Market Committee, fulfils the standard functions of a central bank: it issues coins and notes; it manages the United States's monetary policy (see MONETARY CONTROL); it regulates the banking system and acts as LENDER OF LAST RESORT; it acts as a fiscal agent for the American Treasury, issuing and redeeming treasury bonds; and it can intervene in FOREIGN EXCHANGE markets to influence the international value of the dollar. Federal Reserve banks also manage cheque clearing and transfers of funds for member banks.

Only 'national' banks – those who have been granted a federal charter – have to belong to the Federal Reserve system; state-chartered banks can choose not to be members. Roughly 40 per cent of America's 14,000-plus banks are members, but they hold almost 75 per cent of commercial bank deposits.

The Fed manages the United States MONEY SUPPLY in three ways:

- By setting reserve requirements for member banks. Banks must deposit a percentage of their liabilities as reserves, either at Reserve banks or in their own vaults as cash. In 1982, the basic reserve requirement was set at 3 per cent. The money held in reserve earns no interest – the main deterrent to state-chartered banks joining the Fed.
- By fixing the DISCOUNT RATE. The INTEREST RATE at which the Fed lends to banks, the discount rate influences interest rates – but only marginally, as only a small chunk of banks' funds are borrowed from the Fed. However, shifts in the discount rate are widely taken to reflect the Fed's approach to its third, and most powerful, weapon:
- OPEN MARKET OPERATIONS. The Federal Open Market Committee (FOMC), consisting of the board of governors, the president of the Federal Reserve Bank of New York and four other reserve bank presidents (shared in rotation), meets roughly eight times a year to fix open market policy – and hence, normally, American monetary policy. The FOMC decides how much reserves to supply to member banks – creating those reserves when the Fed buys government securities, reducing them when it sells securities. The New York Fed is responsible for carrying out the FOMC's decisions.

The Fed does have other monetary powers up its sleeve – including REGULATION Q, to fix ceilings and interest rates for time and savings deposits – but these are rarely used. Like the BUNDESBANK, the Fed is independent from the administration. Board members are appointed for fourteen years, so they can outlast any president. However, the Fed is constitutionally responsible to Congress; under the Full Employment and Balanced Growth Act, 1978 (known as the Humphrey-Hawkins Act, after its congressional sponsors), the Fed chairman must report his objectives to the congressional banking committees. Its chairman is appointed by the president. Independence is a two-edged sword – while trying to influence Fed policy discreetly, the administration can at the same time publicly blame its economic problems on the Fed's monetary policy.

Federal Trade Commission. America's competition watchdog, set up in 1914. See ANTI-TRUST.

Financial futures. Big growth area in the 1970s and early 1980s. Like FUTURES in COMMODITY and FOREIGN EXCHANGE markets, they consist of contracts to buy or sell something at a future date, but with the price fixed at the time of the deal. In this case, what is being traded are financial SECURITIES. Like other FORWARD MARKETS, financial futures offer opportunities for HEDGING and SPECULATION, and need both hedgers and speculators to function successfully.

To take a simple example, the manager of a company's pension fund may know that in three months' time he will have $1 million to invest, but may suspect that before then bond prices will have risen and yields fallen. As he does not have the cash now, he cannot lock into today's prices and yields by buying bonds directly. But he may be able to buy a futures contract at something very close to today's yield. He buys the contract 'on margin', which means he just pays a small percentage now (say 5 per cent – the fee varies between markets) and the rest in three months time when his cash arrives.

Financial futures were invented in Chicago in the early 1970s when marketmen realised that money could be viewed as a commodity just like pork bellies. The timing was no accident. When EXCHANGE RATES were fixed under BRETTON WOODS, and INTEREST rates were fairly stable, there was no need for financial futures. Floating rates changed all that, introducing a need for hedging in currencies and interest. In 1972 the International Monetary Market (IMM, part of the Chicago Mercantile Exchange) introduced foreign currency futures, making it the world's first centralized market for transferring financial risk. In 1975 Chicago's second big commodities market, the Chicago Board of Trade, developed the idea by launching an interest rate contract. The IMM followed suit, and both have since generated other contracts. Between 1972 and 1981 annual volume on the IMM grew from 144,000 currency futures contracts to more than 6.1 million. Growth in interest rate futures was even faster: between 1976 and 1981 volume jumped from 110,000 to more than 6 million contracts a year.

Other markets have tried to follow Chicago – in Canada, Australia, and the New York Futures Exchange, for example – but none have matched its success. It took ten years for financial futures to come to London, when the LONDON INTERNATIONAL FINANCIAL FUTURES EXCHANGE opened its doors in September, 1982. That, too, is struggling to get up steam.

Financial Times (FT) index. Barometer of London's STOCK EXCHANGE, the index is compiled and published by the daily newspaper, the *Financial Times*. The main FT measure is the 'industrial ordinary', which gauges movements in the shares of thirty representative industrial companies. The index has a base of 1 July, 1935 as 100. The *Financial Times*, together with the Institute of Actuaries and the Faculty of Actuaries, calculates other indices for each main sector (e.g., oil companies, gold mines) based on market capitalization rather than crude price movements. Collectively, these sectoral indices are known as the FT actuaries indices. See also DOW JONES INDEX.

Fine tuning. Once likened by Frank Paish of the London School of Economics to driving a car with the front and side windows blackened and just a rear view mirror to see where the car is going, and with brake and accelerator pedals that take effect some time after they are applied. Fine tuning was a favourite government tool in the KEYNESIAN 1950s and 1960s, and involved frequent adjustments to FISCAL POLICY in order to adjust the level of aggregate demand (see STOP–GO). Snag: information about what is going on in the economy, and the effect of fiscal policy changes, is imperfect. Statistics on output, consumer spending and UNEMPLOYMENT, for instance, take several weeks or months to compile. Add on delays in taking decisions, and the supposedly 'fine' tool looks very blunt. Nevertheless, pressure on governments to react to economic indicators means that tuning still goes on.

First in, first out (FIFO). Opposite of LAST IN, FIRST OUT (LIFO). Both ACCOUNTING conventions, FIFO and LIFO are alternative ways of valuing stocks. As the term indicates, FIFO assumes items are used, or sold from stock, in the order in which they arrived there; LIFO assumes the newest items leave first. FIFO means stocks are valued at historic, or original, cost; LIFO values stocks at current prices. As a result, FIFO tends to produce a higher level of profits than LIFO does, because it includes the gains from stock appreciation. See ACCOUNTING, CURRENT COST ACCOUNTING, HISTORIC COST ACCOUNTING.

Fiscal drag. INFLATION's way of helping governments to increase TAXATION without saying so. If tax allowances, progressive tax rates and thresholds stay constant while pre-tax incomes rise in nominal terms, then tax payments increase, too; allowances are worth less, and people jump into higher tax brackets. Good for government revenue, but bad for demand, output and activity, as a higher tax burden 'drags' down post-tax incomes and hence demand. If the government's aim is to dampen demand, however, then 'drag' can be a built-in stabilizer. In the 1970s, most governments agreed to adjust allowances and thresholds in line with inflation, to reduce fiscal drag (see INDEXATION). But this is normally done just once a year, so the government still has the benefit of 12 months of drag each time. See ROOKER–WISE AMENDMENT.

Fiscal policy. Government use of taxing and spending powers to influence aggregate DEMAND, and much else besides. Normally said in the same breath as monetary policy (see MONETARY CONTROL), governments' attempts to influence the rate of growth of the MONEY SUPPLY.

Fiscal policy is the more straightforward of the two. In managing public expenditure and raising the revenue to pay for it, governments have to decide on:

Forms of taxation. TAXATION can influence spending and working behaviour, and the distribution of INCOME in a society. So governments choose a balance between direct and indirect taxation (for example, income tax versus value added tax); progressive or regressive taxation; taxing companies or individuals; the balance between earned and unearned income. Fiscal policy aims to plug loopholes, and must constantly adapt to new tax dodges – like DEEP DISCOUNT BONDS. One eye has to be kept on other countries' policy, too, as more favourable taxation policy elsewhere may lure away not just pop stars and poets but also MULTINATIONAL companies.

The volume of spending. Governments choose not just the amount of their spending, but also its division between current (pencils, salaries, textbooks) and capital items (sewers, roads, hospitals). See PUBLIC EXPENDITURE for how total spending has grown as a proportion of GROSS DOMESTIC PRODUCT. Bids to cut spending since 1979 have, almost without exception, managed to cut capital spending more quickly and easily than current – it is easier to scrap planned projects than to sack dustmen. Snag: capital spending, as INVESTMENT, may have a bigger MULTIPLIER effect on total spending; also, sewers eventually collapse.

The size of the budget deficit or surplus. The BUDGET balance is the fiscal kingmaker. An overall government deficit (see PUBLIC SECTOR BORROWING REQUIREMENT) adds to aggregate demand; a surplus subtracts from it. So KEYNESIANS and other advocates of FINE TUNING favour the management of this deficit or surplus to regulate economic activity. Problem 1: information is poor, so regulation is accident prone. Problem 2: the deficit, if it is financed by printing money, adds to the money supply and so, say MONETARISTS, fuels inflation. When it is borrowed, it competes with the private sector for savings (see FLOW OF FUNDS), so CROWDING OUT can occur, raising interest rates.

In a recession, budget deficits widen automatically; unemployment rises, so ex-workers pay less tax and draw more SOCIAL SECURITY benefits. This is a built-in stabilizer for demand; that is, as demand falls, extra government borrowing plugs some of the gap. To try to strip this automatic effect out and isolate the impact of the government's deliberate fiscal policy, economists calculate a cyclically adjusted budget balance. The choice of starting-point is important. Figure 10 shows five countries' budget balances both unadjusted and cyclically adjusted, using 1979 as the base – relatively FULL EMPLOYMENT. The chart shows that in 1979–82 only France's budget looked actively expansionary, after cyclical adjustment. America's wobbled around neutral, and West Germany and Japan were both in deficit, though steadily cutting it back. Britain, by contrast, was extremely

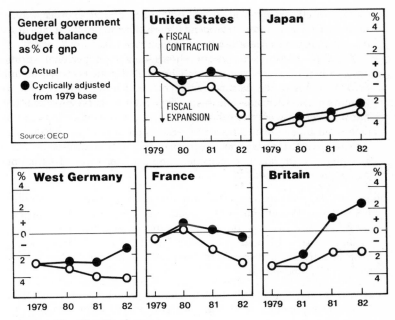

Figure 10 *The fiscal stance*

restrictive – with a cyclically adjusted surplus equivalent to more than 2 per cent of GDP.

Fixed charge. When particular assets of a person or a company are singled out as collateral for DEBT. So if the debtor goes bankrupt, only those assets go to the creditor, the rest being left intact. Compare with FLOATING CHARGE.

Floating charge. When a borrower offers his total ASSETS as security for a loan, the lender has a floating charge on them, that is, not one tied to a particular asset.

Flow of funds. The financial face of the economy – who is borrowing how much from whom – and a useful cross-check on how the economy is running. Users of this analytical technique start by dividing the economy into four sectors: government, households, companies (including public corporations) and foreigners. Each is either a borrower (in which case they run a financial deficit) or a lender (enjoying a financial surplus). Households typically run a surplus which they lend, via BANKS and SAVINGS instruments, to domestic borrowers (that is, governments and domestic companies). If households' savings are not large enough to satisfy those borrowers, then

Flow of funds

73

foreigners effectively bridge the difference. This is another way of saying that when a country spends more than it produces, it runs a trade deficit and so needs to attract foreign CAPITAL.

The flow of funds technique shows how high personal savings need to be to finance company and household deficits. So it can also provide a clue to the demand for CREDIT, and how easily savings are going to satisfy demand (and hence how high INTEREST rates will go). But it never answers the question 'why?'. Abundant savings can be motivated by gloom and worry in a recession in which companies are loth to invest. Or they can mean that ample money is being made available for the keen, expansionist-minded borrower. To find out which, look at the 'real' economy.

Food and Agriculture Organization. UN agency, based in Rome, that helps Third World countries' agriculture. Set up in 1945, the FAO sends teams of advisers, often on secondment from national ministries or universities, to help poor countries develop farming, eradicate crop and livestock disease and improve studies and statistics about the world's food supply.

Forecasting. Economists' informed guesses about the future. Using ECONOMETRIC models of the way variables have been related in the past – for example, prices, profits and wages – economists feed in guesses (called exogenous assumptions) about some of the major outside influences on the economy like world trade and oil prices. They then run these through their computer model of the past, to produce forecasts of growth in output, incomes, prices and so on. Often forecasts differ because of their exogenous assumptions, rather than because of the intrinsic qualities of the model. For any given model, the room for random error is usually considerable – for example, 1–2 percentage points in the forecast for GDP growth. So treat forecasts as a guide, not a certainty.

Foreign exchange. Hard CASH in a foreign CURRENCY. Foreign exchange markets deal in currencies. A country earns foreign exchange by exporting goods or services. With the single exception of the United States, all countries have to pay for imports out of foreign exchange; America can use its own dollar, giving it powers of SEIGNORAGE. When a country lacks foreign exchange and does not want to let its own currency depreciate, it is forced to rely on trade and EXCHANGE CONTROLS. Traders with eastern Europe (and other non-convertible currency areas) get round the problem of foreign exchange shortages by using BARTER.

Foreign investment. Purchase of assets (direct investment) or securities (portfolio investment) abroad by a company or individual. Foreign investment by, for instance, ICI in America shows up in Britain's BALANCE OF PAYMENTS as an outflow in the capital account. Income from the investment is entered in the INVISIBLE (TRADE) section of the current account. Similarly, in the American balance of payments, the investment will be a capital inflow; the transferred profits or DIVIDENDS will be a current account outflow.

During the 1960s, the strongest flow of direct foreign investment was from the United States to Europe, by American MULTINATIONAL companies. They set up manufacturing operations in Europe, helped by a strong dollar, also to avoid the EEC tariff wall and Atlantic freight costs. The flow spawned a book *Le Défi Américain* (the American challenge) by the French political gadfly, Jean-Jacques Servan-Schreiber, who warned of a *de facto* American invasion of Europe, an economic and cultural take-over. By the late 1970s, recession, high labour costs in Europe and a weak dollar turned the tide – there was a rush of European foreign direct investment into the United States. If the yen strengthens in the next two years, the next challenger in Europe and America could be the Japanese.

Forward markets. Where currencies can be traded for delivery at some specified date in the future. Forward prices are expressed as a premium (higher) or a discount (lower) on the spot rate (see SPOT MARKETS). It would be simple if a premium meant that the market expected the currency to appreciate, a discount, that it was expected to depreciate. However, this equation is also affected by interest rates. Suppose you can earn 10 per cent interest from holding your money in sterling for a year, but only 5 per cent if you put it in dollars. To eliminate the risk of losing money through currency fluctuations, you sell your sterling forward – that is, you undertake to swap it into dollars in 12 months' time at an agreed rate. That rate is bound to be lower than the spot rate – otherwise you could, without risk, earn an extra 5 per cent by holding sterling rather than dollars.

Since every market man will smell out such opportunities, they will go on selling sterling forward until the 5 per cent interest rate differential is reflected in sterling's 5 per cent discount against the dollar (the process known as ARBITRAGE).

For commodities and financial securities, forward markets also exist but are known as FUTURES – except in the silver market, where 'forward' is sometimes used.

Franchise. A licence, often exclusive, to sell a company's goods and use its trade name. Coca Cola is sold throughout the world by local franchisers, most of them millionaires. Many fast food restaurant chains, for example, McDonalds, Wendy and Pizza Time Theatre, sell franchises for restaurants to be run under the company name, according to strict rules about design, quality and so on, and sometimes taking supplies from the parent company. Some companies misuse franchises in order to enforce high prices, demanding that licensees buy only direct from the manufacturer, and adhere to recommended prices. Competition law in the United States and Europe attempts to control this.

Free on board (FOB). The way of valuing EXPORTS by eliminating transport and insurance costs which are deemed to fall to the importing country. See COST, INSURANCE, FREIGHT.

Free trade. Free trade implies the removal of government imposed barriers to trade, whether TARIFFS, QUOTAS or administrative obstacles (for example, safety rules designed to favour domestic manufacturers). Advocates of free trade think that an open trading system encourages a fast growth in world trade which generates fast growth in output, and, by increasing COMPETITION, fast improvements in efficiency. Free trade has been a rare commodity; retaliatory increases in tariffs cramped trade in the 1930s. With this in mind, in 1945, the western powers set up the GENERAL AGREEMENT ON TARIFFS AND TRADE (GATT), undertaking to follow rules of fair play and gradually reduce tariffs and other barriers. See Figure 11 for the relation between trade and GDP growth in the OECD.

Thanks to successive 'rounds' of GATT negotiations, tariffs on manufactured goods have fallen far and fast, with the average tariff for industrial goods in 1982 at 5 per cent for the EEC, $4\frac{1}{2}$ per cent for the United States and 4 per cent for Japan. World trade grew by, on average, 5.9 per cent a year in the 1950s, 8.5 per cent a year in the 1960s and 6.4 per cent a year in the recession-hit 1970s, slowing to 2.3 per cent in 1980 and then falling in 1981. By 1982, recession was inducing a swing back towards PROTECTIONISM in America and Europe; not actually restoring tariffs but raising administrative bar-

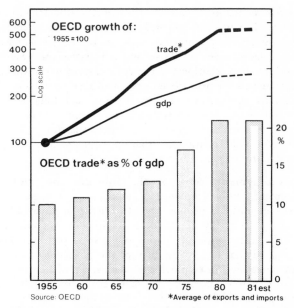

Figure 11 *OECD output and trade*

riers to trade, and demanding 'voluntary restraint agreements' on exports from Japan and other Far Eastern suppliers.

Note, also, that protectionism ebbs and flows with movements in EXCHANGE RATES if these do not reflect trade competitiveness. Two periods when the dollar became overvalued – 1970–71 and 1981–82 – have coincided with the fiercest bouts of American protectionism since 1945, because other countries' exports, especially Japan's, became super-competitive.

There is only one genuine economic justification for trade barriers: to nurture a new, 'infant industry', and to allow time for a country to build up the infrastructure necessary to make the industry internationally competitive. This takes time, and heavy fixed costs, so short-term protection can be justifiable. But a country must decide as soon as possible when to dismantle the barrier, and force its industry to compete. Otherwise the 'infant' quickly becomes senile, and unable to live without protection.

Frictional unemployment. That part of the jobless total caused by people simply changing jobs. Contrast with the tougher nut to crack, STRUCTURAL UNEMPLOYMENT.

Friedman, Milton (born 1912–). American economist and polemicist who did most to put MONETARISM on the map and to revive the

QUANTITY THEORY OF MONEY. He won the NOBEL PRIZE for economics in 1976. Apart from theoretical works on the importance of free markets, his major empirical work has been *A Monetary History of the United States 1867 to 1960*, written with Anna Schwartz, which charted a close relationship between movements in the MONEY SUPPLY and the general price level. Friedman's empirical proof is powerful but far from conclusive: his study is of such long periods that cause and effect are hard to separate, and annual blips in the series – irrelevant for Friedman's needs, but crucial for policy-makers – are ignored. This guarantees that pro-Friedmanites will always be matched by large numbers of antis.

Full employment. Jobs for all. This does not mean zero unemployment; fully employed economies always have some people between jobs, or people who, by virtue of their skills (or lack of them) or disability are hard to employ. Full employment is everybody's aim: a government proposal (white paper) in Britain in 1944 stipulated that it was the duty of the government to secure 'a high and stable level of employment'. An earlier white paper, in 1942, had defined full employment as there being more job vacancies than unemployed people.

Broadly, all industrial countries had full employmment most of the time between 1950 and 1970. Since then, only Switzerland and Austria can fairly claim the accolade. Compare with NATURAL RATE OF UNEMPLOYMENT.

Full employment budget balance. Technique of calculating the deflationary or expansionary impact of FISCAL POLICY. By deducting unemployment related expenditure, and adding extra tax revenues that the unemployed would pay if in work, the underlying fiscal stance can be calculated.

The United States regularly publishes figures of the 'employment adjusted' budget balance. Other countries do not, partly because the concept is itself controversial. Some economists argue that fiscal deficits do little more than raise interest rates (see CROWDING OUT), which therefore aggravates recession and unemployment. On this view, expanding the deficit when unemployment rises will only make things worse. See FISCAL POLICY for a chart applying a form of full employment budget balance to five countries.

Funding. Colloquialism for all kinds of DEBT management. In its narrower, technical sense, funding means shifting costly short-term debt into cheaper long-term debt. Companies and governments take advantage of lower or falling long-term rates to borrow long term, or sell long-term SECURITIES to pay off short-term debts.

Futures. Forward markets in COMMODITIES and in financial SECURITIES. See also HEDGING, FINANCIAL FUTURES, LONDON INTERNATIONAL FINANCIAL FUTURES EXCHANGE.

G

Game theory. Not the belief that selling video games or grouse could earn billions, but a technique for describing decision-making. Competition between two firms is analysed as a game; each defines its own optimal marketing strategy, but, aware of the effect of the others' actions on the market, tries to anticipate what the other will do. This anticipated reaction means that neither achieves its optimal result, nor behaves in an economically ideal manner (see OLIGOPOLY and MONOPOLISTIC COMPETITION). The worst case of game theory is the ZERO-SUM GAME, where players see that total winnings are fixed; some must lose if others win. See also PRISONERS' DILEMMA.

Gearing. Polite way of evaluating a company's indebtedness. The most common formula is the DEBT RATIO; another is the debt/equity ratio. The higher the number, the deeper a company is in the mire, and the more vulnerable it may be to BANKRUPTCY.

General Agreement on Tariffs and Trade (GATT). The nearest thing the world has to a set of laws on international trade. GATT was signed by twenty-two countries in 1947, in a bid to set a FREE TRADE ball rolling and avoid the PROTECTIONISM prevalent in the 1930s. Now more than 100 countries have signed. GATT is based on two principles — reciprocity in liberalizing trade, and non-discrimination, and has acted in two main ways:
● Eliminating QUOTAS. There was substantial progress on this in the 1950s and 1960s, although countries have been left escape clauses for 'temporary' quotas — BALANCE OF PAYMENTS difficulties, or injury to domestic producers from imports.
● Reducing TARIFFS in a series of negotiating 'rounds'. By the seventh round (the Tokyo round), completed in 1979, tariffs applied to industrial products were down to 6.6 per cent for the EEC, 6.4 per cent for the United States, and 5.5 per cent for Japan and were set to be reduced to 4.7, 4.4 and 2.8 per cent respectively by 1 January 1987.

GATT has two weaknesses that have thwarted its efforts in other areas: it has precious few weapons, and it depends on countries being aware of mutual self-interest. In particular, GATT has had to resort to toothless 'codes' for trade issues like government PROCUREMENT, subsidies and anti-DUMPING action. Agriculture and services have been virtually untouched. Tariffs are relatively easy to police: hidden NON-TARIFF BARRIERS are more tricky.

Figure 12 shows the pattern of world trade growth since 1930.

General arrangement to borrow. CREDIT line for the INTERNATIONAL MONETARY FUND set up in 1962 by the GROUP OF TEN (G10). Until January 1983 the credit line could be used only for loans to G10

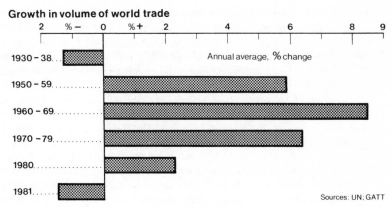

Figure 12 *The rise and fall of world trade*

members (Britain, for instance, borrowed from it in 1976). But the
G10 then threw the line open to all IMF members as an emergency
fund, and lured Saudi Arabia in to contribute to it.

Gilt-edged stock. A safe bet, at least as far as payment of INTEREST and
eventual redemption are concerned. In Britain, all government SECURI-
TIES except TREASURY BILLS are known as gilts. However, their price
varies inversely with interest rates (see BOND MARKET), so little old
ladies should be careful. Note that some gilts are now INDEXED and
some carry variable interest rates.

Gini coefficient. A measure of equality derived from the LORENZ CURVE.
As incomes become more equal, the curve moves closer to a 45° line;
the Gini coefficient measures this proximity by the following
formula:

$$G = \frac{\text{area between Lorenz curve and } 45° \text{ line}}{\text{area above the } 45° \text{ line}}$$

The smaller the value of G, the more equal are incomes – or whatever
else is being measured.

Glass–Steagall Act. Popular name for America's Banking Act of 1933
that forbade deposit-taking banks (that is, RETAIL BANKS) to deal in
SECURITIES. This forced, for instance, the Morgan bank to set up a
separate securities subsidiary, Morgan Stanley. The Glass–Steagall
Act was part of a series of Acts designed to mop up the mess from the
crash on Wall Street in 1929 and the banking crisis that followed.
Others in the series set up the SECURITIES AND EXCHANGE COMMISSION,
strengthened the FEDERAL RESERVE SYSTEM and injected new LIQUIDITY

into the banking system by allowing the Federal Reserve to buy government securities and hence increase the MONEY SUPPLY.

Gold standard. Benchmark for EXCHANGE RATES before 1914, that returned briefly to prominence in the 1920s and 1930s. CURRENCIES were CONVERTIBLE into gold, at a fixed price, and international debts were transacted in gold; gold itself was then usable as a currency.

In 1914 the First World War disrupted world trade and payments, and all first world warriors left the gold standard. Along with others, Britain returned to the standard in 1925. But, in a vain bid to prove national virility, the pound was set at its pre-war parity against gold. Britain was forced to abandon gold and devalue in 1931, floating the pound from 1931 to 1939. The gold standard broke down generally in 1930–33, under pressure of slump and the huge cutbacks in international lending. The United States suspended the dollar's convertibility to gold in March 1933, returning to it, with restricted convertibility, in January 1934.

After the Second World War, a limited form of gold standard survived, but only for the dollar. Even that was abandoned in 1971. See also INTERNATIONAL MONETARY SYSTEM, EXCHANGE RATE, BRETTON WOODS, SMITHSONIAN AGREEMENT.

Goodhart's law. Coined by Charles Goodhart, a senior official at the BANK OF ENGLAND. It states that any measure of the MONEY SUPPLY will start behaving differently the moment it becomes an official target for monetary growth.

Green money. Bewilderingly complicated system used by Europe's COMMON AGRICULTURAL POLICY to convert common prices expressed in EUROPEAN CURRENCY UNITS into national CURRENCIES. Originally, actual EXCHANGE RATES were used – possible because, in the 1950s and 1960s, the INTERNATIONAL MONETARY SYSTEM used fixed exchange rates. But a French DEVALUATION in 1969, and then the shift to floating rates in 1971–3, led to the use of 'green money', employed to protect farmers from wobbling exchange rates that would involve wobbling farm prices. Green rates are special agricultural exchange rates that ensure that movements in currencies are not reflected in national farm prices, unless governments want them to be.

Example: if the real pound increases in value against the ECU, then Britain's government has two choices for its 'green' pound:

• It can revalue the green pound in line with sterling. The effect of this will be to reduce British farm prices, hurting farmers but benefiting consumers.

• It can keep the green pound where it is, so holding British farm prices steady. To do this, special border taxes and subsidies known as 'monetary compensatory amounts' (MCAs) are enforced to bridge the gap between real rates and green rates for exporters. In this example, Britain would impose a positive MCA – which acts as a tax on imports and a subsidy on exports. This option prevents consumers from benefiting from the pound's strength (which would normally cut import prices), and protects farmers. This was Britain's choice in 1980–82. If, conversely, the real pound weakens against the ECU, then a negative MCA can be imposed.

Table 3 shows the effects of MCAs. MCAs have two unwelcome consequences. First, they encourage smuggling in order to evade taxes and collect subsidies. Second, they tend to stay in place, if the movement in actual exchange rates is long lasting. So the European Commission tries to force governments to eliminate long-lasting MCAs, by revaluing or devaluing the green currency.

Table 3 *Effect of MCAs compared with a nil rating*

	Negative MCAs	Positive MCAs
Food exports	taxed	subsidized
Food imports	subsidized	taxed
Food prices	lower	higher
Consumers	gain	lose
Farmers	lose	gain
Smugglers	reimport	reexport
To eliminate MCA	devalue*	revalue*

* green currency.

Gross domestic product. The best measure of economic activity in a country. Normally abbreviated to GDP, it is arrived at by adding the total value of a country's annual output of goods and services. GDP equals private consumption + investment + government expenditure + the change in stockbuilding + (exports minus imports). It is normally valued at market prices; by subtracting indirect taxes and adding subsidies, however, GDP can be calculated at FACTOR COST. This measure more accurately reveals the incomes paid to FACTORS OF PRODUCTION. To avoid double counting of goods and services produced for intermediate use, only final production for consumption and investment is aggregated. To eliminate the effect of inflation, GDP growth is normally expressed in CONSTANT PRICES.

GDP can be measured in three ways:

• By adding incomes of residents, both individuals and firms, derived directly from the production of goods and services.

• By adding the output contributed by different sectors.
• By adding expenditure on the goods and services produced by residents, before allowing for depreciation or capital consumption.

As one man's output is another man's income which in turn becomes expenditure, these three measures ought to be identical. They rarely are, because of statistical imperfections. Also, for example, tax dodgers and the BLACK ECONOMY escape the output and income measures but should, if the earnings are spent, turn up in the expenditure measure.

Although GDP is the best available measure of economic activity, it is not perfect. As well as the BLACK ECONOMY, activities that are not paid for and so cannot be priced, such as housework or voluntary work, are excluded. See also GROSS NATIONAL PRODUCT.

Gross national product. GROSS DOMESTIC PRODUCT plus residents' income from economic activity abroad, and property held abroad, minus the corresponding income of non-residents in the country.

Group of Ten. The ten leading capitalist countries – the United States, Britain, West Germany, France, Belgium, Holland, Italy, Sweden, Canada and Japan and an honorary eleventh member, Switzerland – that agreed to provide CREDIT of $6 billion to the INTERNATIONAL MONETARY FUND in 1962, known as the GENERAL ARRANGEMENT TO

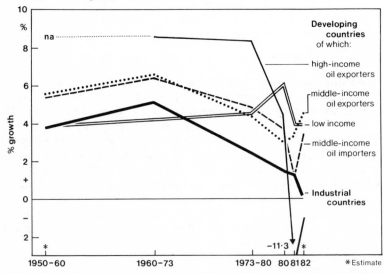

Average annual gdp growth

Figure 13   *Who grew fastest*

BORROW. The G10 is a convenient forum for discussing international monetary arrangements; it hatched up the SMITHSONIAN AGREEMENT and CURRENCY changes in 1971. The G10 also meets through its CENTRAL BANK, the BANK FOR INTERNATIONAL SETTLEMENTS.

Growth. Bounteous source of jobs and prosperity. Growth means an increase in real GROSS DOMESTIC PRODUCT, which implies higher output and incomes. Economists have never pinned down the precise causes of growth; but TECHNICAL PROGRESS has a lot to do with it. As Figure 13 shows, from 1950 until 1973 growth came like manna from heaven; since 1973, the industrialized countries have found growth harder to get. The result: UNEMPLOYMENT, slower rising INCOMES, and disgruntled voters.

H

Hawley–Smoot tariff. Passed into law by the United States Congress in 1930, against the near-unanimous advice of American economists. TARIFFS were raised on virtually all imports, and agricultural exports were subsidized. The tariff marked a new and more intense phase of TRADE WAR, producing a new and more intense phase of the Great Depression.

Hedge. Cautious behaviour, of two kinds:
- In COMMODITY and financial markets, investors who want to eliminate the risk of price movements do so by hedging. Example: a company holding 100 tonnes of copper for use in three months' time wants to avoid the risks of price fluctuations. It therefore sells its 100 tonnes in the FORWARD MARKET. If, during the three months, the spot price (see SPOT MARKETS) of copper falls, the company's 100 tonnes will be worth less than it paid for them. But the finance director will escape a rocket from the board, because his forward contract will offset the spot loss. Conversely, if the price rises during the three months, the company will show a tidy profit on its holdings – but one that is offset by the loss it will make having to honour its forward contract. Note that markets will provide opportunities for hedging only if there are enough SPECULATORS ready to take an 'uncovered' risk – that is, not to match every spot purchase with a forward sale. Speculators, oft maligned as they are, serve to give others a quiet life.
- More broadly, 'hedging' involves trying to live with inflation. In the 1970s the best hedge for most people in Britain and the United States (helped by tax breaks) was property. An Englishman's home is his hedge.

Historic cost accounting. Traditional method of ACCOUNTING, whereby ASSETS are valued according to their original cost. The onset of rapid INFLATION sharply increased the cost of replacing those assets; a company's historic cost accounts could therefore make it look profitable, even if it is in fact not making enough money to replace its assets. Also, inflation can make STOCKS look more valuable than they really are. As a result, CURRENT COST ACCOUNTING has now largely taken over in countries with rapid inflation (see also LAST IN, FIRST OUT and FIRST IN, LAST OUT).

Hiving off. Getting rid of unwanted subsidiaries, or departments, either by selling them wholly, or perhaps contracting out particular functions to outsiders. Wandsworth Borough Council in London, for instance, hived off its refuse collection department to private contractors in 1982.

Hog cycle. See COBWEB THEOREM.

Hot money. Burns CENTRAL BANKERS' fingers. Hot money is CASH that is held in one CURRENCY, but is liable to switch to another at a moment's notice. Fast selling by hot-money owners often pushes a currency down. Hot money may be SPECULATORS' cash, or oil sheikhs' bank balances. These deposits chase the highest INTEREST rates and/or the best prospects for currency appreciation. Britain suffered especially from hot money surges in the 1960s and 1970s in and out of sterling.

Human capital. People. Computer buffs are wont to define three sorts of 'wares': hardware, software and 'wetware'. Wetware is brainpower and skills that make up an eminently marketable commodity known as human capital. Investment in human capital involves education and training.

Hyperinflation. Big, big trouble. It is a matter of taste when a country tips from rapid inflation – 100 per cent plus? – into hyperinflation. The term tends to imply that inflation must not only be high but accelerating as well. Germany's hyperinflation after the First World War got up to 23,000 per cent before the system broke down completely.

I

Import controls. PROTECTIONISTS' delusion. Controls aim to reduce IMPORTS by imposing TARIFFS, QUOTAS, import surcharges (taxes akin to tariffs) and NON-TARIFF BARRIERS in a bid to boost domestic output and employment without running into BALANCE OF PAYMENTS problems. Controls by country A against imports from countries B, C, and D are self-defeating because:

- They provoke retaliationary action, thus shrinking demand for country A's exports.
- By cutting all B, C and D's exports they reduce these countries' ability to buy country A's exports.
- They divert B, C and D's exports to other countries thus increasing competition for A's exports.
- Country A's exports may be diverted to satisfy domestic demand, so any improvement to the balance of payments may be small.
- By limiting or excluding competition, country A ensures that its consumers have to pay higher prices than necessary for their goods and services. This cuts their real incomes, probably cancelling the alleged income gains achieved by increased output and employment.

See also FREE TRADE and GENERAL AGREEMENT ON TARIFFS AND TRADE.

Imports. Purchases of foreign goods and services. Imports of goods – for example, manufactures, raw materials – are known as VISIBLES in Britain, merchandise trade in America; purchases of foreign insurance, foreign shipping or banking and national tourists spending money abroad are all examples of INVISIBLES. Imports are normally valued at COST, INSURANCE, FREIGHT (CIF), that is, including transport and insurance costs.

Income. The flow of money (or goods in the case of income in kind) to FACTORS OF PRODUCTION; wages for labour, profit and INTEREST for CAPITAL, RENT for land. Incomes are not exclusive – in an economy, incomes move in a circular flow: labour earns wages which it spends on goods and services produced by firms; firms pay interest for capital, rent for land, and wages for labour, all of which are again spent in some form on goods and services. Yet although incomes flow in this way, it does not all pass through all hands: one central problem of macroeconomics is how the income flow is determined, and how it is allocated between factors.

NATIONAL INCOME is a snapshot of this circular flow, and is the aggregate of all factor incomes – rent, wages, interest and profits during any one period. More conventionally, it is determined statistically as the value of the economy's output – see GROSS DOMESTIC PRODUCT – or expenditure.

The degree of equality in a society is measured by its income distribution – how total personal income is divided between rich and poor. This is best depicted by a LORENZ CURVE, which plots the shares of different groups of the population in total income (see also GINI COEFFICIENT). Governments use TAXATION to try to close this gap, but the biggest shifts in distribution in the industrialized world have been outside direct government control – for example, the transformation from mass unemployment in the 1930s to FULL EMPLOYMENT in the 1950s brought with it a large redistribution of income. See DISPOSABLE INCOME, EARNED INCOME, UNEARNED INCOME, LIFE-CYCLE HYPOTHESIS, PERMANENT INCOME HYPOTHESIS, RELATIVE INCOME HYPOTHESIS for how income is used and taxed.

Incomes policy. Seductive means of controlling INFLATION (see PRICE CONTROLS). Governments keen to put a lid on wages slap on controls in one of four ways:

● A statutory freeze or wage rise limit. Infringements can be punished by fines (for example, in Britain 1966–68, France 1982).

● Voluntary controls, where the government sits down with unions and employers to agree guidelines for wage rises (for example, in Holland 1977–80, Britain 1975–78). The success of this depends on the commitment of the workers and bosses to the deal, and the degree of say-so held by the big TRADE UNION federations over what happens at factory level.

● Variant of voluntary controls, where the government sets a norm, often through its deals with its own employees, and asks the PRIVATE SECTOR to follow (for example, in Britain 1971–72, the United States 1972–73).

● Where a wage norm is enforced by penal taxes on companies that exceed the norm, so acting as a disincentive to inflationary deals.

Any of these approaches is usually accompanied by controls on prices and DIVIDENDS, often also with complicated guidelines for allowable increases.

Incomes policy can be extremely effective at dampening inflation in the short run; in theory, it can be used at a time of GROWTH to restrain the inflationary effects of fast expansion. However, incomes policies have rarely been operated successfully for any length of time because (1) they multiply the rigidities in the labour market, suppressing wages in firms with fast-growing PRODUCTIVITY, increasing them in less dynamic firms and thus breaking links between pay and productivity; (2) they store up trouble for when the controls are removed, in the form of leapfrogging wage demands; and (3) by pitching the government into every level of wage bargaining, they encourage political confrontation over wages, a guaranteed election loser. Incomes policies have been operated successfully only in small countries, like Holland, Sweden and Austria, where a high degree of social consensus exists (even in Holland, a powerful lobby is building up against incomes policy from both unions and employers), or in cases where other economic policy assures success, for example, West Germany. There, tight FISCAL POLICY and MONETARY CONTROL have given little opportunity for wages to explode; also a highly centralized trade union movement makes bargaining at a national level relatively easy. See Figure 14 for how Britain's succession of incomes policies have made little dent on inflation.

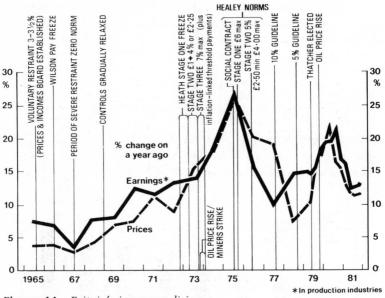

Figure 14 *Britain's incomes policies*

Income tax. Universally disliked source of government revenue. In Britain, a tax or levy on personal income was first introduced in 1799 as a 'temporary' tax to finance a war against Napoleon. It was abolished in 1816, reintroduced in 1842 – and has remained ever since.

In Britain, income tax is levied according to a complicated formula: first, each person has a personal allowance (say, £1,500) free of tax, and can deduct this, and other tax-free items, such as mortgage interest and life insurance premiums, from his income. Then the remainder, known as taxable income, is taxed in slices; the first, say between 0 and £10,000 is taxed at the 'basic rate', normally around 30 per cent; then the next £5,000 is taxed at a higher rate, say 40 per cent, the next £5,000 at 45 per cent, and so on. So higher incomes pay out a larger chunk of income in taxes – this is known as pro-

gressive taxation. In April 1983, Britain's tax thresholds were as in Table 4.

Table 4 *Bands of Taxable Income*

£	Per cent
0–14,600	30
14,601–17,200	40
17,201–21,800	45
21,801–28,900	50
28,901–36,000	55
over 36,000	60

Governments aim to strike a balance between direct and indirect TAXATION. During the inflationary 1970s, however, FISCAL DRAG has helped to raise the share of total tax receipts provided by income tax in many countries. Figure 15 shows by how much.

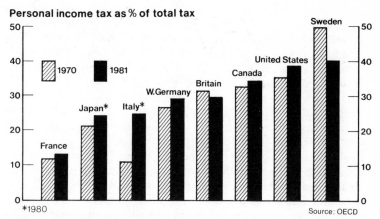

Figure 15 *The income taxman's take*

Indexation. Inflationary way to keep pace with INFLATION. Wages, UNEMPLOYMENT benefits, or other sources of income are automatically raised according to the movements in the retail price index. The changes may be made annually, quarterly – or even monthly in countries like Israel and Brazil, where inflation rates run to three figures. Worthy idea, favoured by some MONETARISTS who argue that indexation will minimize the cost of DISINFLATION. They maintain that indexation is not a driving force of inflation (which is caused only and always by excessive monetary growth). However, most governments that have adopted indexation have done so as an alternative to disinflation; and some have found it a positive hindrance.

Examples are European countries like Belgium, Italy and Holland, where indexation has had three results:

● The indexed rise becomes a minimum, not the maximum intended. As a result, there is little link between pay and productivity. Wage bargainers then add to the indexed rises, so the overall increase is well above inflation, stoking up the cost of living index.

● The cost of social security spending rises steeply – awkward for governments beset by big fiscal deficits and costly foreign borrowing.

● Other economic policies – notably devaluation – become ineffective. If wage indexation had not been suppressed in Belgium in 1982, the 8 per cent devaluation of the Belgian franc in February would have fed straight back into industry's costs, and hence inflation, through indexed wage rises.

Index numbers. The purpose of all index numbers is to distil many different ingredients into a single index, and then to measure changes in that index by changes in its parts. To do that involves giving weights to the components: in the case of a consumer price index, a doubling in the price of pepper seems intuitively less significant than a doubled petrol price. Each item is therefore weighted according to its importance in what is being measured: in industrial countries, roughly 25 per cent of consumer spending goes on food, so it has a correspondingly large weight in their consumer price indices. Although consumer prices are the best known brand of price index, many others exist: wholesale prices (both raw materials and factory gate), share prices, commodity prices, prices of exports and imports, etc. The same goes for indices of production: GNP, industrial production, manufacturing output, and so on, all of which can in turn be expressed as index numbers.

The obvious virtues of index numbers still beg the question of how best to construct them. In particular, should the weight given to each component be determined by its current or its historical importance? Example: an index of Britain's industrial production, based on 1975 weights but measuring changes in the 1980s, would give misleadingly little value to oil and gas production because North Sea oil was pumped on a significant scale only in the late 1970s.

Paasche index. An accurate measure of changing industrial production would require up-to-date weighting, and this is what the Paasche index does. It takes current year weights and applies these to both past and current production or prices, or whatever it happens to be measuring. For the record, a Paasche price index takes the form:

$$\frac{\sum_{t=1}^{n} P_2, t \cdot Q_2, t}{\sum_{t=1}^{n} P_1, t \cdot Q_2, t}$$

where P is price, Q is quantity and t is time.

Laspeyres index. By contrast, a Laspeyres index is based on historical weights:

$$\frac{\sum_{t=1}^{n} P_2, t \cdot Q_1, t}{\sum_{t=1}^{n} P_1, t \cdot Q_1, t}$$

Both approaches have their drawbacks, especially when weights change abruptly. Although the Paasche index is more capable of picking up that sort of change, it may be impossible to construct if information on the newly important component in the index was not previously being collected.

Indicative planning. Tightrope walking between providing economic FORECASTING and information to industry, and trying to talk up growth. The heyday of indicative planning in Europe was the 1960s, as whole departments were devoted to drawing up national plans for GROWTH and development, sector by sector. In CENTRALLY PLANNED ECONOMIES, the planners actually have some control over their subject; in indicative planning there is little control (except on infrastructure construction). The plan is intended as a guide, a co-ordinator, and an encouragement.

In Britain, George Brown's Department of Economic Affairs set up by the Labour government in 1964 tried to talk up growth in the belief that if '4 per cent' was said loudly enough, businessmen would come to believe growth was coming, would invest and lo, growth would come. It didn't. In France, where state interference (*dirigisme*) has long been the rule, '*planification*' has been more successful, and has remained a central part of economic policy (though its effect is probably only marginal). Some other European countries – for example, Belgium and Holland – still have national planning offices, but their role is now little more than an economic forecasting unit.

Industrial and Commercial Finance Corporation (ICFC). British attempt to provide capital for small- and medium-sized firms finding it hard to get cash from the markets or the banks (see MACMILLAN GAP). The ICFC was formed in 1945 and raises loan capital using its top credit rating for on-lending to industry. The ICFC has, however, proved inflexible about providing VENTURE CAPITAL for new industries.

Inelastic. Where the supply or demand of something is relatively insensitive to changes in another variable, for example, price. See ELASTICITY.

Inflation. Wasting disease of modern economies. Inflation is normally a shorthand for consumer price inflation expressed as an annual rate, but can apply to other prices, for example wholesale prices, wages, etc. Rises in consumer prices steadily erode the purchasing power of a given CURRENCY unit. Inflation would matter little if it was smooth, uniform, and all INCOMES were adjusted perfectly in line. But it does not work like that (see INDEXATION).

Economists differ in their analysis of the causes of inflation, and therefore in their prescribed cures. MONETARISM holds that inflation can be reduced only by slowing down the growth of the MONEY SUPPLY: in the words of Milton FRIEDMAN, 'inflation is always and everywhere a monetary phenomenon'. KEYNESIANS tend to believe that inflationary pressures can exist independently of monetary conditions; to run a modern economy at low inflation and low unemployment, they say, governments need an INCOMES POLICY.

Inflation accounting. Accounting method designed to abstract from the effects of inflation on stocks, costs and profits. See CURRENT COST ACCOUNTING.

Input–output analysis. Method developed by Wassily Leontief (see NOBEL PRIZE) to analyse the productive capacity of an economy. The user lists inputs – basic commodities – and, from empirical data, calculates the amount of any input needed to produce given outputs. Once these coefficients are found, input–output analysis can trace the PRODUCTIVITY of an economy and measure the changes in inputs needed to produce a given set of outputs.

Institutional investors. The big brothers of the financial markets, these are INSURANCE companies, pension funds, unit trusts and other investment trusts. They have huge funds to invest either to maintain their own reserves and employ customers' premiums (insurance companies), or to manage other people's money (pension funds, unit trusts). Their investment policy is typically cautious. Institutional investors in Britain own 64 per cent of all traded company SECURITIES.

Insurance. Coverage of a RISK (fire, theft, damage, death, shipwreck) in return for a fee, known as a premium. Insurance companies employ actuaries to evaluate frequent risks (for example, how often teenagers crash their motor cars) by collecting and computing statistics; this can be highly accurate, especially in life assurance. For one-off risks (for example, insuring Betty Grable's legs, or the Titanic), insurers must follow their own hunches in setting the premium. Insurance BROKERS shop around to find the best insurer; UNDERWRITERS literally write the insurance policy. See LLOYD'S and REINSURANCE.

Integration. Marriage, for companies or economies. Merging companies can lead to VERTICAL INTEGRATION if the companies are at different stages of a production chain (for example, steel mills and car plants); or horizontal integration if at the same stage (for example, two steel mills). Economies achieve integration by trading more with one another and co-operating in policies. One of the principal aims of the EUROPEAN ECONOMIC COMMUNITY is European integration.

Interbank market. Where banks borrow and lend to each other, normally for very short periods. The market is invaluable for ensuring that banks match their assets and liabilities after a day's trading. Alongside national varieties of interbank markets, a huge international version has grown up to serve the EUROMARKETS. The bulk of the money deposited and lent in the Euromarkets comes from the banks – prompting sceptics to wonder whether a single bank failure would knock down all the dominoes.

Interest. The cost of money, with interest rates varying according to the demand for and supply of money. Developed financial systems offer a wide range of interest rates, depending on the kind of instrument and for how long money is being lent or borrowed. The ones that attract most attention are the DISCOUNT RATE, and those paid on TREASURY BILLS and in the BOND MARKET. As far as BANKS are concerned, they set a rate for their best customers – known as the prime rate in the United States, base rate in Britain.

Interest rates are influenced by INFLATION, both tending to rise and fall together. There are exceptions, though: in the mid 1970s, interest rates in the main industrial countries did not rise as much as inflation did, and in the early 1980s did not fall as much. Stripping out inflation gives a 'real' interest rate – which is easy enough to compute for short periods, but much harder when it comes to bonds. An investor in a 10-year bond at a fixed interest rate will only know what real rate he earned when he finally redeems his money.

Internal rate of return. Measure used in project evaluation. See RATE OF RETURN.

International Bank for Reconstruction and Development. See WORLD BANK.

International Monetary Fund (IMF). Supervisor and safety net for the INTERNATIONAL MONETARY SYSTEM. The Fund was set up at BRETTON WOODS, along with its sister institution just across the road in Washington DC, the World Bank, to supervise the fixed EXCHANGE RATE system. These surveillance powers – member governments had to ask permission from the IMF for changes in their exchange parity of more than 10 per cent – largely died with fixed rates in 1971–73. Now the IMF is more closely involved with members' economic as well as exchange rate policies, making loans while trying to enforce ADJUSTMENT for payments problems. In 1967 it devised the SPECIAL DRAWING RIGHT which aimed to relieve the dollar of its RESERVE CURRENCY functions and help steady FOREIGN EXCHANGES.

Each of the more than 140 members (recent new boys include Hungary) pay subscriptions, or quotas, to the IMF – partly determined by the size of their economies. So the United States provides 20.8 per cent of quotas, West Germany 5.3 per cent, Japan 4.1 per cent and Britain 7.2 per cent. Quotas are paid 75 per cent in national CURRENCIES – so the IMF's coffers are stuffed with useless pesos and gourdes – and 25 per cent in foreign currencies (formerly gold, now dollars and SDRs). This means that only about half of the quota money can actually be lent.

Members can withdraw cash from the kitty: the 25 per cent 'gold tranche' may be withdrawn at will; another 25 per cent of quota may be drawn on certain (fairly easy) conditions; for subsequent tranches the conditions attached to loans get stiffer, so that countries have to agree their economic policies with the IMF. There are also special loans such as the compensatory financing facility for countries with falling EXPORT earnings from COMMODITIES. In all, a country can draw up to four and a half times its quota.

The IMF is run by a board of executive directors, six of whom are appointed by the world's five largest economies plus Saudi Arabia (one of the fund's biggest creditors). Countries group into constituencies to elect the other fifteen. Decisions are made by the 'interim committee' of the finance ministers which make up the board, and in an annual meeting of all members where more bilateral and private business is done than real IMF work. The fund has a managing director (currently Jacques de Larosière) and makes its views known in speeches and an annual report, which is a veritable goldmine of information. The IMF had better be well informed: DEBT crises in 1982 gave it plenty to find out about.

International monetary system. Shorthand for the way that countries settle their debts with each other. Apart from observing the obligations to pay what is due, this comes down to the question of what value different currencies have against each other – that is, to EXCHANGE RATES. During the twentieth century countries have juggled with different methods:

● From 1900 until 1914, the GOLD STANDARD was used for CURRENCY CONVERTIBILITY and settlement of DEBTS. This was largely abandoned during the First World War, but returned in a modified form in the 1920s. In 1930–32, however, slump destroyed the gold standard.

● From 1932 to 1939 a mixed system of floating rates (for example, sterling) and a restricted gold standard (for example, the dollar) was used.

● From 1945 until 1971 the BRETTON WOODS agreement ruled. Under it, countries were enjoined to reduce EXCHANGE CONTROLS and obstacles to international trade, and to allow their currencies to be freely convertible into one another. However, it was not until 1958 that full currency convertibility was achieved – D-marks being exchangeable for French francs or sterling just as easily as for the dollar. Exchange rates were fixed against each other, being allowed to move within a band of 1 per cent on either side of their announced parity. According to the rules of the INTERNATIONAL MONETARY FUND, these parities could be changed if currencies suffered from 'fundamental disequilibrium', as evidenced by their balance of payments and foreign reserves. Only the dollar was convertible into gold, at a fixed rate of $35 an ounce, and then only on transactions between central banks.

● In August 1971 the United States suspended convertibility of the dollar into gold. After six months of confusion the GROUP OF TEN signed the SMITHSONIAN AGREEMENT in December 1971. The yen and the D-mark were upvalued against the dollar, and new fixed rates were allowed a wider margin of movement – $2\frac{1}{4}$ per cent on either side of parity.

● In 1973 Smithsonian collapsed too, and most countries began a DIRTY FLOAT, still in operation in 1983.

Although the international monetary system affects all countries, in practice it is run by the rich few. Bretton Woods, for instance, was really a deal between the USA and Britain. Nowadays the GROUP OF TEN and particularly the United States, calls the tune.

Intervention. Term normally used to describe efforts by CENTRAL BANKS to influence EXCHANGE RATES. When exchange rates were fixed, a central bank intervened if its currency came under pressure – buying it (and therefore using the country's foreign exchange reserves) or selling it (and therefore adding to the country's MONEY SUPPLY). If such intervention failed to ease the pressure, and an exchange rate was in 'fundamental disequilibrium', the government concerned eventually devalued or revalued the currency to a new fixed rate.

With floating rates, intervention has become more problematic. Economists, bankers and governments debate endlessly whether intervention can alter market behaviour, particularly to prevent currencies from OVERSHOOTING. Most think that intervention can help to smoothe day-to-day fluctuations (as it does in the EUROPEAN MONETARY SYSTEM); and beyond that, domestic changes – to interest rates and fiscal policy – are needed. See ADJUSTMENT, CLEAN FLOATING, DIRTY FLOATING.

Inventory. American word for what are called STOCKS in Britain.

Investment. Engine of GROWTH and PROFIT. Popularly, an investment is the purchase of any ASSET with a view to making money, often shares (see EQUITIES). But that kind of investment involves only a transfer of ownership; no new spending has taken place. Economists define investment to be spending on factories or houses or machinery – known as 'fixed investment'; the accumulation of STOCKS is sometimes treated as investment as well.

Since investment is the most volatile component of GROSS DOMESTIC PRODUCT, its behaviour is a constant focus of economists' attention. And a constant source of controversy: some economists put most emphasis on ENTREPRENEURS' ANIMAL SPIRITS and on INTEREST rates. Others say that companies invest primarily when they run short of capacity, so that the pressure of DEMAND is the most important influence. The debate has not been settled to anybody's satisfaction, though perhaps there is a growing consensus that part of investment is done for cost-cutting reasons and to keep up with the latest tech-

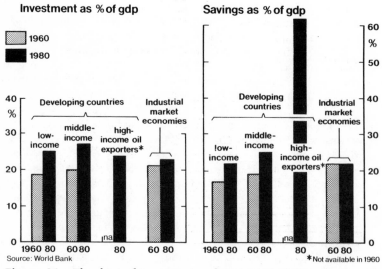

Figure 16 *The share of investment and savings in GDP*

nology, almost irrespective of the level of demand or of interest rates. This does little to explain the variety of investment and saving rates among different countries, as shown in Figure 16.

Invisible hand. Adam SMITH's visible shorthand for the way the capitalist system works − or might work, ideally. If all individuals act from self-interest, spurred on by the profit motive, then society as a whole prospers, with no apparent regulator at work. It is, wrote Smith, as if an 'invisible hand' guided the actions of individuals to combine for the common wealth. Alas, visible hands are needed too, as some individuals are clever enough to pull the wool over others' eyes and make a dishonest buck; examples of visible controllers

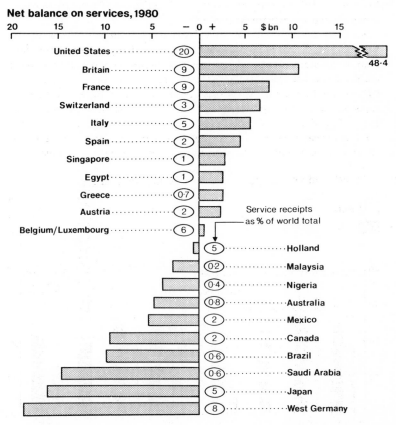

Source: Committee on invisible exports

Figure 17 *The invisibles men*

include policemen, governments and ANTI-TRUST agencies. Too much regulation, though, can give the invisible hand the shakes.

Invisible trade. EXPORTS and IMPORTS of things you cannot drop on your foot, that is, services, such as shipping, INSURANCE, BANKING, and INTEREST payments, DIVIDENDS, and foreign travel. These are entered on the current account of the BALANCE OF PAYMENTS, and make up roughly a quarter of world trade. The industrial countries have a surplus on invisible trade; the DEVELOPING COUNTRIES and the oil-producing countries have big deficits. Some rich countries are big exceptions: West Germany had a deficit of $12 billion on invisible trade in 1981, Japan $14 billion.

Figure 17 shows the invisible trade balances of various countries.

Issuing house. CITY (OF LONDON) MERCHANT BANKS that specialize in arranging an issue of shares (see EQUITIES) or bonds (see BOND MARKET) on the STOCK EXCHANGE. Fifty-six banks belong to the Issuing Houses Association – an altogether less exclusive club than the ACCEPTING HOUSES committee. Swanky merchant banks can of course be on both.

J

Jaw-boning. Talking your way out of trouble, particularly applied to governments running an INCOMES POLICY, or trying to do so without becoming too formal. They talk down INFLATION, trying to persuade companies not to raise their prices too much, or TRADE UNIONS their wage demands.

J-curve. Graphic description of the trend of a country's trade balance after a DEVALUATION. Devaluation immediately reduces the value of EXPORTS and increases the value of IMPORTS, so that the current account (see BALANCE OF PAYMENTS) actually gets worse before it gets better. After a lag, the volume of exports should increase because of their lower price, and the volume of imports should be squeezed. The improved volume balance should then outweigh the unfavourable price effects, and the current account will turn into surplus (see Figure 18). Note that an inverted J-curve can follow from an appreciation of the currency.

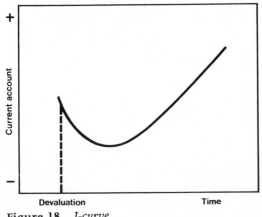

Figure 18 *J-curve*

J-curves may be flattened or even eliminated if traders do not react to EXCHANGE RATE changes by changing their price. If exporters choose to take wider profit margins after a devaluation, for example, then the value of export earnings will not fall. Ditto if importers choose to maintain market share by accepting squeezed profit margins. But the current account can still improve, because the bigger profits may lure more firms on to the export trail, while some importers will quit.

Jobber. British STOCK EXCHANGE barrow-boy; a dealer in stock exchange SECURITIES. Only jobbers can deal in shares, and jobbers can act only for STOCKBROKERS, not directly for clients. Requirements for jobbers: quick wits, a strong pair of legs and a pocket calculator.

Job-sharing. The splitting of one full-time job into two or more part-time jobs. In vogue in the 1980–82 RECESSION as a panacea for mass UNEMPLOYMENT, it founders on the reluctance of full-timers to give up part of their wages. Also SOCIAL SECURITY costs are often increased by splitting jobs. Nevertheless some firms, such as Britain's GEC, claim that PRODUCTIVITY is boosted by job-splitting as there is less motive for absenteeism.

Junior creditors. Unlucky second-line CREDITORS. When a debtor defaults, senior creditors get priority in the distribution of assets, leaving junior creditors to wait for the scraps.

K

Kennedy round. See GENERAL AGREEMENT ON TARIFFS AND TRADE.

Keynes, John Maynard (1883–1946). English economist, he studied under MARSHALL at Cambridge but went on to reject large chunks of NEO-CLASSICAL ECONOMICS. His best-known work was the *General Theory of Employment, Interest and Money*, published in 1936 in the depths of the Great Depression. A complicated, sometimes obtuse book, its central message was clear: economies could be in EQUI-LIBRIUM at less than FULL EMPLOYMENT, so it was for governments, through their taxing and spending policies, to ensure enough effec-tive DEMAND to produce full employment.

Keynes therefore switched the emphasis of policy away from MICRO-ECONOMICS and on to MACROECONOMICS, where it remained for almost forty years. His influence was enormous; governments everywhere came to accept responsibility for full employment. His critics were not silent, however; as INFLATION rose in the late 1960s and early 1970s, their claim that Keynesian policies were inevitably inflationary began to receive new attention. It was President Richard Nixon who, acknowledging in 1971 that 'We are all Keynesians now', simply proved the truth of one of Keynes's most famous dicta: 'Practical men, who believe themselves to be quite exempt from any intellec-tual influences, are usually the slaves of some defunct economist. Madmen in authority, who hear voices in the air, are distilling their frenzy from some academic scribbler of a few years back.'

From 1973 on, governments ceased to be Keynesian in any literal sense. They allowed UNEMPLOYMENT to rise without trying to expand BUDGET deficits enough to prevent it. Keynesians – the breed remains robust, despite the practical demise of their beliefs – argue that rising unemployment proves the need for Keynesian policies. Non-Keynesians reply that the mess is caused principally by inflation, itself the product of Keynesian policies. The debate, be assured, will continue.

Apart from his macroeconomic theorizing, Keynes was an active *homme d'affaires*. He was long an adviser to the British Treasury, a director of the BANK OF ENGLAND, editor of the *Economic Journal*, bursar of King's College, Cambridge, director of several CITY (OF LONDON) financial institutions, architect of the BRETTON WOODS system, and occasional member of the Bloomsbury Group.

Keynesians. Adherents of Keynesianism; followers of KEYNES.

Kondratieff cycle. Named after a Russian economist, Nikolai Kondra-tieff (1892–died, date unknown), who identified cycles of economic activity spanning 50–60 years. His book *The Long Waves in Economic Life* was published in 1925. It implied that CAPITALISM had a secular stability, while Russia's Marxist leaders claimed it was self-destructively unstable. Kondratieff therefore fell from favour, and died in one of Stalin's prisons.

His work has attracted new attention recently as economists seek to explain the causes of the post-1973 recession. Unfortunately, Kondratieff does not prove very enlightening. His statistics established cycles from the late 1780s to 1844–51, from 1844–51 to 1890–96, and an upswing from 1890–96 to 1914–20 (which was followed, his adherents point out, by about twenty-five years of downswing, then the twenty-five golden post-war years, and now by RECESSION). But Kondratieff's analysis was, at best, sketchy. The enigma remains.

L

Labour intensive. A relative term, used to describe a way of making a good or service which depends a lot on labour and only a little on CAPITAL. Example: a jersey can be knitted by hand or by machine. Both methods use the same amount of wool. The first is labour intensive, the second is capital intensive. For a poor country with abundant (and cheap) labour and scarce (and relatively expensive) capital (for example, India), it is sensible to use labour-intensive production methods. For a country like Sweden – scarce labour, abundant capital – capital-intensive production makes sense. (See also COMPARATIVE ADVANTAGE.)

Labour theory of value. The notion that the value of any good or service depends on how much labour it incorporates. Suggested by Adam SMITH and developed by David RICARDO, it assumed a central place in the philosophy of Karl MARX. These CLASSICAL economists later spawned a school of NEO-CLASSICAL dissenters – the main cause of dissent being the latter's disagreement with the labour theory of value. They argued that price was independent of how much labour had gone into producing something, being determined solely by supply and demand.

Laffer curve. Named after a young academic at the University of Southern California, Arthur Laffer, who received instant acclaim in the 1970s for a theory devoid of empirical content. His curve relates average TAXATION rates to total tax revenues. Legend has it that Laffer first drew his curve on a napkin in a Washington bar in November 1974. Since then it has been drawn and redrawn a thousand times.

In the hands of advocates of supply-side tax cuts, the curve 'proves' that most governments could raise more revenue by cutting tax rates. Drawn by those of a different persuasion, it 'proves' that raising tax rates will bring more revenue.

Which curve is right? Some academics have started to estimate where the curve really is. Honest answer: nobody knows.

Laissez-faire. The belief that, by and large, economic activity should be left free of regulation or interference by government. This, say *laissez-faire* supporters, will maximize production and consumers' satisfaction. For how that is supposed to happen, see INVISIBLE HAND.

Laspeyres index. See INDEX NUMBERS.

Last in, first out (LIFO). LIFO is a way of valuing company STOCKS and of firing employees. The personnel manager's LIFO – the last person hired will be the first to go – is a way of rewarding long service. The finance director's LIFO – everything in the warehouse, from a gallon of oil to a finished widget, will be priced by how much the latest arrival cost – is a way of preventing INFLATION from bankrupting his company (see CURRENT COST ACCOUNTING). By contrast, HISTORIC COST ACCOUNTING is based on FIRST IN, FIRST OUT (FIFO): it ignores any extra cost that may be involved in replacing a firm's ASSETS, whether INVENTORIES or plant and machinery. As such, it produces artificially high profits, which are then taxed (see TAXATION) and distributed as DIVIDENDS. The left-overs are not enough to maintain the company's real value.

Leading indicators. Also known as cyclical indicators, these are groups of statistics used to indicate the future path of economic activity and the BUSINESS CYCLE. Experience suggests that movements in certain variables tend, fairly consistently, to precede movements in production. They are combined as an INDEX NUMBER, each variable being given a particular weight according to what has been found to give the best statistical 'fit'. There is not necessarily any causal connection between the variables in the index and production, merely a statistical relationship that has proved reliable and therefore useful for forecasting purposes. Note that an index may be asymmetrical as between peaks and troughs in the business cycle: it may turn well before production resumes its cyclical upswing but only slightly before the downswing begins.

In Britain, four sets of cyclical indicators are compiled:

• A 'longer leading index' indicating trends about a year in advance, composed of the rate of INTEREST on three-month prime bank bills; the financial balance of industrial and commercial companies; housing starts; the Financial Times–Actuaries 500 share index; and the quarterly survey of business confidence conducted by the Confederation of British Industry.

• A 'shorter leading index', indicating trends about six months ahead, composed of new car registrations; CBI quarterly surveys on the expected change in new orders and in STOCKS; credit granted; and gross trading profits of companies excluding stock appreciation and oil and gas extraction.

• A 'roughly coincident' index, showing current movements in production, composed of GROSS DOMESTIC PRODUCT; retail sales volume; output in manufacturing industry; and CBI quarterly surveys of capital utilization and actual changes in stocks.

• A 'lagging index', indicating the path of production about a year after it has happened, composed of UNEMPLOYMENT; unfilled vacancies; investment in manufacturing plant and machinery; orders in engineering; and the level of manufacturers' stocks and work in progress.

In the United States, three main cyclical indicators are used,

● The 'leading index', which uses 12 indicators to mark out future trends about nine to ten months ahead of peaks and about two to three months ahead of troughs, is composed of the average working week in manufacturing; average weekly first claims for state unemployment insurance; new orders for consumer goods and materials; speed of delivery of goods; net formation of businesses; contracts and orders for plants and equipment; new building permits for private houses; net change in inventories (stocks) on hand and on order; change in some materials prices; change in credit outstanding to businesses and consumers; prices of 500 stocks and shares; the MONEY SUPPLY measure M2.

● The 'roughly coincident' indicators, that move broadly in line with the general business cycle, composed of employees on non-agricultural payrolls; personal income minus TRANSFER PAYMENTS; industrial production; and manufacturing and trade sales.

● The 'lagging indicators', that move on average about four to five months behind peaks and about 10 months behind troughs, composed of the average duration of unemployment; the ratio of inventories (stocks) to sales in manufacturing and trade; the labour cost per unit of output in manufacturing; the average prime interest rate charged by banks to borrowers; commercial and industrial loans outstanding; and the ratio of consumer hire purchase credit to personal income.

Lender of last resort. One of the classic functions of a CENTRAL BANK. If a bank's depositors ever decided to withdraw all their money simultaneously, no bank would be able to produce the cash in time, because it lends out most of its DEPOSITS and cannot quickly liquidate its loans. Should a run develop, however, the central bank stands ready to provide as much cash as necessary. Except *in extremis*, that knowledge is enough to stop depositors worrying that their cash is not there in the till.

In return for providing this safety net, the central bank imposes certain prudential controls on banks to try to make sure they never need to use it.

Letter of credit. Common lubricant of trade. If company A is buying widgets from company B, A's bank (usually its merchant bank) can issue a letter of credit as proof that B will be paid. B can then take the letter into the market (usually the commercial paper market) and swap it for cash. Also known as bill of exchange, or COMMERCIAL BILL.

Liability. Opposite of an ASSET on a company BALANCE SHEET. Liabilities represent sums owed or ultimately belonging to other people. Examples are SHAREHOLDERS' FUNDS, and DEBTS of all kinds. Short-term debts, bank loans and overdrafts are often known as current liabilities.

Life-cycle hypothesis. Attempts to explain the way that people split their INCOMES between SAVING and spending (see also PERMANENT INCOME HYPOTHESIS and RELATIVE INCOME HYPOTHESIS). The life-cycle school places great store by DEMOGRAPHIC factors: the fact that people with low incomes tend to spend a high proportion of their incomes is attributed to their age. The young have small incomes, but big spending commitments and ambitions. As people get older, their incomes tend to rise – and they also tend to save more. When they retire, their incomes fall back: they join the young set again, spending a large proportion of their income. Averaged out over a lifetime, people have a stable PROPENSITY to consume and to save – which is consistent with the evidence for economies as a whole, where the propensities do not change as incomes rise.

Liquidity. The speed with which financial ASSETS could, if so desired, be spent. CASH is wholly liquid, whereas non-transferable twenty-year bonds (see BOND MARKET) are as close to being wholly illiquid as makes no difference.

Liquidity preference. The way that individuals and corporations choose to hold their ASSETS in varying degrees of LIQUIDITY. Cash is totally liquid; a ten-year loan in a non-negotiable instrument is effectively illiquid; most other assets come somewhere in between, depending on how quickly they can be turned into cash. Liquidity preference therefore indicates the demand for money, which plays a central role in the theoretical and practical debate over MONETARY CONTROL.

Liquidity ratio. Most commonly used as a CENTRAL BANK method of prudential control over COMMERCIAL BANKS. The central bank stipulates that banks must keep a certain ratio of their assets in liquid form – cash, plus short-term, marketable instruments (such as TREASURY BILLS) – to meet day-to-day demands for cash. For details of how this fits into the broader framework of economic management, see MONETARY CONTROL.

Liquidity trap. Identified by KEYNES, its very existence is denied by non-Keynesians, especially MONETARISTS. Keynes acknowledged that, as a result of recession or deliberate monetary expansion by the CENTRAL BANK, INTEREST rates would fall, and that this might encourage individuals and companies to borrow and spend more. But he maintained that it was quite possible for the supply of CREDIT to exceed demand even when interest rates fell to zero. If that were to happen, then recession would not be self-correcting via interest rates; the economy would be 'trapped' in a surfeit of unlent and unspent liquidity.

Monetarists and other non-Keynesians see no conceptual or empirical reason why this trap should be sprung. They believe INVESTMENT and consumer spending are both sensitive to interest rate changes, and can find no historical instance of liquidity remaining unborrowed – especially if it is 'given away' at zero interest rates.

Lloyd's. Ever since Edward Lloyd opened his coffee house in London's Lime Street in 1688, Lloyd's has been the world's leading INSURANCE market. Lloyd's is organized in idiosyncratic style: competing syndicates are responsible for writing policies and accepting business, and they in turn derive their financial backing from external 'names'. These names (some 16,000 in 1982) are wealthy individuals who accept unlimited liability – down to their last bottle of Bollinger – in support of their syndicates. Their cash is rarely needed; but in return for sharing the risk, they receive a share of their syndicate's profit.

Lloyd's used to enjoy an unblemished reputation, and it remains true that no legitimate insurance claim has ever gone unpaid. However, a series of scandals hit Lloyd's in the early 1980s – the result of individual syndicate managers allegedly channelling near-riskless business into reinsurance companies in which they held an undeclared stake. Lloyd's had always run its own affairs; these scandals showed up the weaknesses in its self-policing ways, and the market is likely to become more closely under the wing of its titular authority, the Department of Trade.

Lombard rate. The rate of INTEREST which West Germany's CENTRAL BANK, the BUNDESBANK, charges BANKS when it lends them money for up to three months against the collateral of certain high-quality SECURITIES. These include TREASURY BILLS, bills of exchange (see COMMERCIAL BILLS) and fixed interest bonds (see BOND MARKET) issued by particular institutions (for example, the federal government). Lombard loans are made to help banks over temporary shortages of LIQUIDITY.

Lomé Convention. Successor to the YAOUNDÉ CONVENTION, it is a trade and aid agreement between the EEC and various DEVELOPING COUNTRIES. It was signed in Lomé (capital of Togo) in 1975, and renewed in 1980. The 63 developing countries that now belong to Lomé are in Africa, the Caribbean and the Pacific (ACP), and are mainly ex-colonies of EEC countries. But note that they exclude Asia – and therefore Britain's largest ex-colonies like India, Pakistan and Bangladesh. The other EEC countries were not prepared to grant trade concessions to such large countries.

Those concessions include duty-free access to the EEC market for all ACP manufactures and most tropical agricultural products (which therefore do not compete with EEC farmers). Lomé also set up a scheme called Stabex, designed to compensate primary producers for part of any decline in their export earnings from the EEC caused by falling COMMODITY prices.

London interbank offer rate (LIBOR). Applies to the INTEREST rates in the EURODOLLAR market. It is most widely used in setting the terms for a loan where the interest rate will vary. The borrower agrees to pay a margin (known as the 'spread') above LIBOR – usually between half and two percentage points. The loan agreement will stipulate which LIBOR rate is to be used – for example, three-month or (more usually) six-month.

London international financial futures exchange (LIFFE). Pronounced 'life', and set up in September 1982. It does roughly what its name suggests: just as people buy and sell CURRENCIES and COMMODITIES in FORWARD MARKETS, so they can with various financial instruments. LIFFE offers anything from three-month TREASURY BILLS to long-dated GILT-EDGED STOCK. It faces stiff competition: FINANCIAL FUTURES were first traded in Chicago in 1972; Canada and Australia have followed suit, and the New York Stock Exchange opened a futures market in 1980. Chicago is still streets ahead of the rest.

Long run. The phrase that spawned one of Keynes's best-known aphorisms. Discussing the classical view that economies have a long-run tendency to settle at FULL EMPLOYMENT EQUILIBRIUM, he observed that 'in the long run we are all dead'. Perhaps a little more precision is possible. Politicians, cultivating an image of responsible economic management and hoping for many years in office, invariably proclaim that theirs are long-term policies. On their desks they keep a four-point memo from their leader:

- The long run is what happens after the next-but-one election.
- The medium run is what happens after the next election.
- The short run is anything between tomorrow's newspapers and the next chance the voters have to say whether they like our 'long-term' policies.
- We don't want to die in the short run.

Lorenz curve. Named after an Italian economist, it describes the degree of inequality in the distribution of numbers. Usually applies to INCOMES, with the cumulative percentage of income recipients along the horizontal axis and the cumulative percentage of income received on the vertical axis. The Lorenz curve would be at 45° if everybody had identical incomes. The further the curve is away from the 45° line, the more unequally are incomes distributed. (See also GINI COEF-FICIENT.)

M

Macmillan gap. Identified by the Macmillan Committee on the financing of British industry, which reported (Cmnd 3897) in 1931. The 'gap' was the difficulty that small- and medium-size companies had in raising CAPITAL; to help fill it, the INDUSTRIAL & COMMERCIAL FINANCE CORPORATION (ICFC) and the Finance Corporation for Industry (FCI) were set up in 1945. Criticism of the City's failure to raise money for small companies has since rumbled on, producing another institution, Equity Capital for Industry, in 1976. However, the Wilson Committee's report on the City (Cmnd 7937, 1980) concluded that Macmillan-type gaps no longer existed.

Macroeconomics. The big picture, in contrast to MICROECONOMICS which deals with the behaviour of individual markets, households and firms. Macro issues usually involve government FISCAL POLICY and MONETARY CONTROL, and focus on aggregates like the rate of economic GROWTH, the level of EMPLOYMENT, the BALANCE OF PAYMENTS, INFLATION and so on. However, as many economists have pointed out, such aggregates grow from micro roots: a proper understanding of UNEMPLOYMENT and inflation requires studying labour markets as well as monetary and fiscal policies.

Malthus, Thomas (1766–1834). English economist and the original doomster. His laboriously titled book, *Essay on the Principle of Population as it Affects the Future Improvement of Society*, was published in 1789, the year of the French Revolution; its message had nothing to do with liberty, equality and fraternity, but has become almost as well known. Malthus argued that population growth would always exceed the growth in food supply; real wages would be forced down to subsistence level and population growth would be checked by periodic wars and famines.

Malthus underestimated the scope for technological progress in

agriculture. More important, he failed to anticipate how it would be rising real incomes, not falling ones, that would slow down population growth. Latter-day Malthusians fear that his grim predictions, unfulfilled in Britain and other industrial countries, will come true in places like Bangladesh. See DEMOGRAPHY.

Marginal analysis. The core of NEO-CLASSICAL ECONOMICS, though subsequently adopted and adapted by KEYNES and his followers. There are numerous 'marginals' − revenue, cost, product, price, propensity to consume, save, invest, and so on − and the essence of all of them is the same. They are the cost (or whatever) of the extra unit − as opposed to the AVERAGE cost, which simply divides, for example, total costs by the total number of units produced.

Alfred MARSHALL, father of neo-classical economics, used this simple idea to develop all kinds of theory about economic behaviour. Example: a profit-maximizing firm will produce up to the point where marginal revenue (MR) equals marginal cost (MC). Reason: if MR is less than MC, a firm will be losing money from the production of that extra widget; if MR exceeds MC, the extra output is still adding to total profits, so the firm will be encouraged to produce more. See COMPETITION, Figures 4, 5 and 6, for the way that this rule explains differences in prices and production along the spectrum from PERFECT COMPETITION to MONOPOLY.

Market forces. Convenient shorthand, often abused. In some mouths it is a term of uncritical praise; others treat it as a slur, akin to the law of the jungle. But 'market forces' does not mean that open (still less perfect) COMPETITION prevails, that all market participants are well informed, and that the deals struck in the market could be legally enforced. It simply means that some buyers and sellers have been able to meet, bargain and agree; the price has been set where their supply and demand curves meet. The conditions under which markets operate are clearly important, because their ability to tell producers about consumer preferences, and CONSUMERS about available choice, cannot be taken for granted.

Market prices. Prices actually paid. See also GROSS DOMESTIC PRODUCT.

Market socialism. To some, a happy blend of freedom and fraternity; to others, as nonsensical as dry water. The idea, in abstract, is simple: to replace centralized economic planning with markets where consumers signal their preferences, that are then answered by producers organized on socialist lines. 'Socialist', in that context, means different things to different people: workers' control, workers' self-management, labour hiring capital (instead of capital hiring labour).

Jugoslavia claims to have adopted market socialism in the mid-

1950s; some other East European countries, notably Hungary, have reduced their reliance on central planning and placed more faith in flexible prices and wages. None of the experiments can be counted a triumph; but the search for a third way – not communist, not CAPITALIST – seems bound to continue. See CENTRALLY PLANNED ECONOMIES.

Marshall, Alfred (1842–1924). English economist and professor at Cambridge from 1885 to 1908. His best-known work, *The Principles of Economics*, combined many of the standard beliefs of CLASSICAL ECONOMICS with new ways of looking at the way markets determine prices and quantities. Marshall kept some of the classical emphasis on COSTS as a determinant of prices, but expanded this to highlight the importance of demand factors as well. He introduced the idea that DEMAND curves slope downwards from left to right, a staple of economics texts ever since. He incorporated MARGINAL ANALYSIS into his treatment of markets, and invented the notion of the ELASTICITY of demand.

Marshall Plan. Named after America's secretary of state, General George Marshall, who proposed giving aid to Western Europe after the Second World War. A total equal to 1 per cent of American GNP (about $47 billion in 1981 dollars) was given between 1948 and 1952, the great bulk of it by the United States and some by Canada. (See also the ORGANIZATION FOR ECONOMIC CO-OPERATION AND DEVELOPMENT.)

Marx, Karl (1818–83). German economist, sociologist and superstar. Claimed as the inspiration of all kinds of things he probably never thought of, his two best-known works were the *Communist Manifesto* (1848, jointly with Friedrich Engels) and *Das Kapital* (published in four volumes between 1867 and 1910).

Contrary to popular belief, Marx was not wholly against CAPITALISM. It was rescuing millions from 'the idiocy of rural life', and had an impressive dynamic. It was doomed, none the less. It would founder, Marx thought, through a shortage of DEMAND; would CONCENTRATE economic power and wealth in ever fewer hands; and would produce a larger and ever-more-miserable proletariat. It would be replaced by the 'dictatorship of the proletariat', leading eventually to a 'withering away' of the state. For progress reports, watch this space.

Marxists. Adherents of Marxism; followers of MARX.

Mass production. Wide-eyed 1920s phrase for what has now become the norm of industrial life. See ECONOMIES OF SCALE.

Matrix. A collection of numbers, arranged in a rectangle. The size of the rectangle is usually described with algebraic symbols – for example, $a \times b$, which indicates that it has a rows and b columns. An input–output (see INPUT–OUTPUT ANALYSIS) table is one example of a matrix. Contrast this with a vector, which is a string of numbers set down either in a row or in a column.

Mean. One of three measures that can be collectively (and loosely) called 'averages'; the other two are the MEDIAN and the MODE. The mean is the simplest of the three – the total divided by the number of units. Thus if a company's annual wage bill is $1 million, and it has forty employees, the mean wage is $25,000 a year.

Median. One of three measures that can be collectively (and loosely) called 'averages'; the other two are the MEAN and the MODE. Taking a series of numbers, the median is the middle one with 50 per cent of the rest lying above it and 50 per cent below. Example: in the numbers 1 to 9, the median is 5; it is also 5 in a range of 1, 2, 3, 4, 5, 8, 9, 10, 11. If there are an even number of figures, the median is the average of the middle two – for example, in 1 to 10, the median is $5\frac{1}{2}$.

Merchandise trade. American version of VISIBLE TRADE.

Mercantilism. Seventeenth-century conventional wisdom, bidding to make a come-back in the late twentieth century. The central goal was the accumulation of national treasure, to be achieved by exporting as much as possible and importing as little as possible. It took Adam SMITH to show that exports were a sacrifice, desirable only in as much as they allowed a country to import. Although the crudest forms of mercantilism have been banished, contemporary PROTECTION-ISM is motivated by the same beliefs.

Merchant banks. British term for BANKS whose tasks include helping companies raise money, advice on portfolio management, and so on. See ACCEPTING HOUSES.

Microeconomics. The study of ECONOMICS at the level of the individual household or firm, in contrast to MACROECONOMICS. Price theory has a central role in microeconomics: how prices emerge and change, and how people respond to them. This brings in issues such as COM-PETITION and availability of information, both important elements in micro behaviour. The formal distinction between micro- and macro-economics, though embodied in most textbooks, is often less than helpful. Since the early 1970s economists have renewed attempts to fuse the two, recognizing that certain key macroeconomic questions like INFLATION and UNEMPLOYMENT have their roots in the way prices are fixed and labour markets operate.

Mill, John Stuart. English economist and philosopher (1806–73), he is best known among economists for his *Principles of Political Economy* (1848). Modern-day political liberals and CLASSICAL ECONOMISTS still regard the book – essentially a textbook of classical economic thought that updated Adam SMITH's *Wealth of Nations*, rather than introducing startlingly new concepts – as an exemplary statement of their faith. Mill's upbringing was decidedly unusual, though – he learned Greek at three, Latin at eight, and algebra, geometry and differential calculus by the time he was twelve.

Minimum lending rate. Born October 1973, laid to rest August 1981, MLR was the rate at which the BANK OF ENGLAND would lend money to the DISCOUNT HOUSES. As such it had a key effect on all other INTEREST rates. MLR replaced the old bank rate, and was initially intended to vary according to market interest rates. In practice, the Bank of England continued to use it to direct market rates, formally admitting this in May 1978. MLR's suspension in 1981 was part of the broader change in Britain's MONETARY CONTROL.

Mode. One of three measures that can be collectively (and loosely) called averages; the other two are the MEAN and the MEDIAN. In a range of numbers, the mode is the one that occurs most frequently. In a golf foursome, for example, if two players are aged 45 and the other two are 55 and 67, the modal age is 45, even though the mean is 53.

Monetarism. Like all isms, the term is loosely used. This one is applied to the school of economic thought that places growth in the MONEY SUPPLY at the centre of its thinking. Specifically, monetarists believe in the QUANTITY THEORY OF MONEY. And they say that monetary expansion or contraction has only transitory effects on 'real' variables like output and employment; ultimately it feeds through solely into the price level. See MONETARY CONTROL for a broader discussion.

Monetary base. The narrowest measure of MONEY SUPPLY: just CURRENCY in circulation, the CENTRAL BANK's surplus cash in its vaults, and any COMMERCIAL BANK's reserves deposited at the central bank.

Monetary control. Commonly confused with monetary restraint, its meaning is more mundane: how can central bankers get the MONEY SUPPLY to do what they want – whether that be to grow at 5 per cent a year or 50 per cent? Answers come in several forms; yet even the seemingly simple are, in practice, hard to implement. Choose from any of the following, in the paraphrased words of their advocates:
Control the monetary base. This involves the CENTRAL BANK acting on something over which it has direct control, because the MONETARY BASE is its liabilities – that is, notes and coins, plus whatever balances

it holds on behalf of COMMERCIAL BANKS. Known by its other name – high-powered money – the significance of the monetary base becomes clearer: banks have to hold high-powered money to transact their day-to-day business and to insure against an uncertain pattern of withdrawals, so restraining this 'power' directly affects their business. Because it can control its own liabilities, a central bank can affect the banks' lending capacity by expanding or contracting the monetary base. The banks will react precisely because high-powered money is so essential to their operations. If their reserves are squeezed, they will bid for cash and short-term deposits in the INTER-BANK MARKET, paying a higher rate of INTEREST than if they were able to borrow from the central bank. They will then translate this extra cost into higher lending rates, which will choke off lending and so constrain monetary growth.

Several central banks set their monetary targets in terms of the monetary base, the BUNDESBANK being the most notable example. Others continue to target some measure of the money supply, but operate on the monetary base as an indirect way of controlling the money supply. This is what the FEDERAL RESERVE did in October 1979, when it stopped trying to use interest rates as its operating instrument for monetary control. Of course, control of the monetary base is not the same thing as controlling the money supply, on any definition of the latter. But the relationship between the monetary base and the money supply is fairly predictable; a central bank that sets and hits a target for monetary base expansion will know pretty well how much monetary growth there will be.

Control interest rates. This involves the central bank affecting market INTEREST rates through changing the interest rate which it controls itself – its DISCOUNT RATE, which is what it charges banks (and other selected institutions) for swapping their COMMERCIAL BILLS for cash. This will then affect all other interest rates, which in turn will affect (1) bank lending and deposits and (2) the prospects for selling government paper so as to finance the PUBLIC SECTOR BORROWING REQUIRE-MENT without expanding the money supply.

Apply direct controls to bank lending. These can take several forms. In an informal way, the central bank may try to arm-twist commercial banks into limiting their lending for certain kinds of business (for example, property speculation) and expanding it for others that are deemed virtuous (for example, exporting, manufacturing). More formally, the central bank may require banks to make special deposits with it, on top of their usual reserve requirements. The special deposits approach was long favoured by the BANK OF ENGLAND: in effect, it neutralized part of the banks' deposits and therefore restricted their ability to lend.

Another method employed by the Bank of England became known as the CORSET. It tried to limit the growth of banks' interest-bearing liabilities by requiring banks to make special supplementary deposits with the Bank of England if liabilities exceeded growth rates laid down in advance. Even its supporters accept that the corset encouraged DISINTERMEDIATION – that is, lending that had hitherto been done through banks simply moved into other channels not subject to corset controls.

Monetary control can be rather like squeezing a balloon: squeeze hard in one place, and bulges appear round the edges. See GOODHART'S LAW.

Money. Replaced BARTER and cowrie shells, and has been giving trouble ever since. Textbooks intone that money has three qualities: (1) as a unit of account (good for adding up apples and pears in some common value); (2) as a medium of exchange (less awkward than cowrie shells); and (3) as a store of value (doesn't rot, like wheat would). By comparison with hypothetical agrarian alternatives, money indeed appears admirable. But it has proved a lousy store of value, and this DEPRECIATION has affected its ability to carry out its other tasks. For an account of money as it really is, see INFLATION, MONETARY CONTROL and MONEY SUPPLY.

Money illusion. Misplaced belief that the value of MONEY is not changing. In the good old days of the 1950s and 1960s, when prices in the OECD countries rose at an average 2.8 per cent a year, many people suffered from money illusion. Rapid INFLATION stripped away this veil; when opinion pollsters asked what the current rate of inflation was, more replies came in over the actual rate than under it. (Even when British inflation went above 25 per cent in 1975, however, a resolute 5 per cent or so of the opinion polls' sample continued to say that prices were rising in the range of 0–5 per cent.)

Money illusion is more than a quirk. It was KEYNES who coined the phrase, arguing that workers would be more willing to accept a cut in real wages (see REAL VALUES) if it came from higher prices eroding their nominal pay than from an outright reduction in pay packets. MONETARISTS have long argued that KEYNESIAN pump-priming could work only as long as money illusion persisted. Once people came to learn that pump-priming led to inflation, Keynesian policies would have less and less effect on the 'real' economy (output and employment), and a more immediate effect on inflation. Eventually, say monetarists, inflationary consequences are wholly anticipated: the mere announcement of a stimulative package lowers the EXCHANGE RATE, pushes up INTEREST rates, causes businessmen to start planning price rises, and prompts bigger wage demands from TRADE UNIONS. (See RATIONAL EXPECTATIONS.)

Money market. Generically, any market where money and other LIQUID assets (for example, Treasury bills, bills of exchange) can be lent and borrowed for periods ranging from a few hours to a few months. Compare with CAPITAL MARKETS, where long-term capital is raised. In London the 'money market' usually refers to the market dominated by the DISCOUNT HOUSES and a few money BROKERS, where cash is lent on call (See CALL MONEY).

Money market funds. One of America's growth industries in the 1970s. As INTEREST rates rose, established financial institutions like SAVINGS AND LOAN ASSOCIATIONS were prevented by law from offering their depositors more than a prescribed maximum interest rate (see REGULATION Q). Moneymen being nothing if not adaptable, new institutions were set up to get round these limits. The most successful were money market funds, run by newcomers as well as household names like Merrill Lynch. They took DEPOSITS, invested the proceeds in short-term, high-quality paper (like TREASURY BILLS), and offered their depositors higher interest rates and even a limited banking service. Depositors can write up to three cheques a month on their money market accounts.

The funds have been a huge success. Having been virtually non-existent in 1970, by 1978 they had deposits of $10 billion; by 1980, their total had risen to $75 billion, and by 1981 to $185 billion. Their future, however, may not be so rosy. Interest rate ceilings are gradually being abolished, and the money market funds will have to compete directly with BANKS, savings and loan associations and others once held back by outmoded laws.

Money supply, measures of. Money is as hard to measure and define as it is to control (see MONETARY CONTROL). Money is graded according to its LIQUIDITY – notes and coins being completely liquid, whereas some kinds of bank deposits become spendable only after notice to withdraw them has expired.

In Britain,

● M1 is notes and coins in circulation, plus sterling sight deposits (that is, those withdrawable without notice) held by the private sector.

● Sterling M3 (£M3) is M1 plus sterling time deposits (those requiring notice of withdrawal) of the British private sector, plus all sterling deposits of the British public sector, plus the foreign currency deposits of all British residents.

● PSL2, short for private sector liquidity, is notes and coins in circulation; all sterling deposits (that is, including time deposits and CERTI-FICATES OF DEPOSIT); other money market instruments (for example, TREASURY BILLS, bank bills and local authority debt held by the non-bank private sector); BUILDING SOCIETIES' share and deposit accounts, and some national savings securities.

The United States uses three measures:

• M1, defined as currency in circulation, travellers' cheques, demand deposits of the private sector at commercial banks, automatically withdrawable deposit accounts at banks and thrift institutions, credit union share draft accounts, and demand deposits at mutual savings banks.

• M2 is M1 plus savings and small-denomination time deposits, over-night deposits at commercial banks, overnight Eurodollars held by American residents (other than at Caribbean branches of Fed member banks, and balances of accounts with MONEY MARKET FUNDS.

• M3 is M2 plus large denomination time deposits, companies' term REPURCHASE AGREEMENTS at commercial banks and SAVINGS AND LOAN ASSOCIATIONS, and money markets funds held by institutions.

West Germany is simpler. Though it uses measures of M1, M2 and M3 similar to the American measures, it only targets one:

• Central bank money stock, defined as currency in circulation and banks' required reserves on domestic deposits. This is a version of what is generically known as the MONETARY BASE.

Monopolies and Mergers Commission. British government agency set up in 1948 to study possible monopolistic abuses, and to vet mergers likely to result in MONOPOLIES or an undesirable reduction in competition. See ANTI-TRUST.

Monopolistic competition. Halfway house between PERFECT COM-PETITION and MONOPOLY, independently constructed during the 1930s by two economists – American E. H. Chamberlin and British Joan Robinson. They argued that few firms enjoyed a pure monopoly; that OLIGOPOLY was more common; but that even where there are many competitors, they enjoyed some discretion in setting their prices because their products were differentiated from those of their com-petitors. As a result, they did not make monopoly profits, though their prices were higher and output lower than they would be under perfect competition. Figures 4, 5 and 6 (under COMPETITION) show the differences.

Monopoly. Production solely in the hands of a single firm. The word implicitly asserts that the firm will exploit its monopoly – producing less, at a higher price, than would happen under PERFECT COM-PETITION. This assertion is supported by the investigations of ANTI-TRUST bodies, and by Figure 6 (under COMPETITION).

In practice, monopolies are rarely absolute. A few are enshrined in law – for example, Britain's Post Office Act 1953 used to give the Post Office sole rights to carry letters, though this was repealed in 1981. Patent and copyright laws also grant temporary monopolies. In general, though, the scope for absolute monopoly is limited by near-competitors (see MONOPOLISTIC COMPETITION), international trade, and anti-trust laws. Some of these limitations apply to a favourite branch of the monopoly family – TRADE UNIONS. (See also OLIGOPOLY.)

Monopsony. A market dominated by a single buyer, as opposed to MONOPOLY's single seller. Again, with harmful consequences: the monopsonist will change all the prices under its monopsonistic control (for example, wages, raw material prices) whenever it wants to vary its purchases by even a single unit. Under perfect competition, by contrast, no individual buyer is large enough to affect the market price of anything.

In practice, monopsony is even rarer than monopoly; perhaps the best example is the Central Selling Organization (CSO), the diamond-buying arm of De Beers. Since the 1930s, it has bought up about 80 per cent of the value of world diamond production, and then (acting as a monopoly) regulated the amount of diamonds it sold. Its grip has recently been weakened a little by recalcitrant producers, notably Zaire and Australia, who have sold some of their diamonds outside the CSO.

Most favoured nation (MFN). A convention most frequently employed in trading arrangements. If country A grants country B MFN treatment, it means that B's exports will face TARIFFS that are no higher (and also no lower) than those applied to any other country with which A has an MFN agreement. MFN clauses are usually reciprocal. That does not mean that B's tariffs will be identical to A's, merely that neither will give an advantage to any third country in the tariffs they impose on each other's products.

Multinationals. Firms with operations in more than one country; also known as transnationals. A United Nations report has estimated that multinationals are responsible for 20 per cent of industrial production in the non-communist world; and their internal trade – that is, between branches of the same company – may, according to other estimates, account for perhaps 10 per cent of all world trade.

Multinationals were favourite whipping boys in the 1960s, held responsible for destabilizing governments, cheating on their taxes (see TAXATION) through TRANSFER PRICING and generally stripping the world of all that was most dear. Their image has since improved, partly because host governments have become more confident and skilful in their dealings with multinationals, and partly because conventional multinational operations are increasingly rare. Few companies now set up wholly owned subsidiaries in foreign countries and expect to carry on their business as they see fit. Instead they go in for TURNKEY CONTRACTS and BUYBACK DEALS; they are happy to split the ownership with local shareholders; and they may be more interested in selling and adapting patented technology than producing the widgets themselves.

Multiplier. Shorthand for the way in which a change in spending produces an even larger change in income. Example: suppose spending in an economy is increased by £100 million, by, for example, higher INVESTMENT. The first-round effect is to boost the incomes of those who produced the buildings or machinery that make up the extra investment. Those people will in turn spend part of their extra incomes, which puts more money into the pockets of others, who spend it . . . and so on.

In theory, this process could continue indefinitely, in which case the multiplier would have an infinite value. In practice, not all of the extra income is spent: some of it leaks abroad in the form of IMPORTS, and some of it is saved rather than spent. The remainder is defined as the marginal PROPENSITY to consume – that is, that proportion of an extra pound of income that is spent. The value of the multiplier can be derived from the simple formula of $1/(1 - \text{MPC})$. If 50 pence of each extra pound is spent at home, then the multiplier has a value of 2.

The practical value of this knowledge is considerable when governments come to decide their FISCAL POLICY. If they want to boost NATIONAL INCOME by £100 million, and they know that the multiplier is 2, they need inject only £50 million in the form of higher PUBLIC EXPENDITURE or TAXATION cuts in order to achieve their ultimate target. This, at least, is what KEYNESIANS argue: non-Keynesians, while accepting that spending does have a multiplier effect, argue that the notion (1) gives a misleading impression of precision and (2) implies that the extra spending will produce more real GROWTH whereas it could all dissipate in INFLATION instead.

N

National debt. The total outstanding DEBT of a country's government (usually defined to include local as well as central government). Economists have long pondered whether the national debt is a 'burden', and if so whose burden it is. Consensus opinion: debt due to foreign creditors is burdensome, because it has to be serviced and repaid out of a country's FOREIGN EXCHANGE earnings (themselves a sacrifice, because EXPORTS are produced but not consumed). But debt owed to domestic creditors is not a burden for the country as a whole, with two qualifications:

● If one generation incurs the debt, leaving the next to redeem it, there is some inter-generational transfer.

● If the debt is not held evenly, those who have lent money to the government will benefit at the expense of taxpayers generally, because it is the latter's TAXATION that services the debt.

Even this last point needs qualifying when INFLATION benefits debtors at the expense of creditors. Since most national debt is issued at fixed INTEREST rates, this kind of erosion of its real value has been common in the 1960s and 1970s. Though national debt has everywhere risen steeply in nominal terms, in real terms it has fallen in some countries: see Table 5.

Table 5 *National debt of six major economies 1960–1980*

	1960		1970		1980	
	($ billion) nominal	as % GNP	($ billion) nominal	as % GNP	($ billion) nominal	as % GNP
United States	82.5	16.3	370.9	39.4	931.8	34.5
Japan	3.7	8.7	17.3	8.3	424.4	40.2
West Germany	5.4	7.5	12.9	7.7	127.8	15.6
France	17.2	28.4	17.8	12.6	66.2	10.1
Britain	79.2	109.1	80.2	63.6	262.8	48.8
Canada	18.3	46.1	24.5	30.0	70.8	28.5

Source: national accounts.

National Economic Development Council. Known as Neddy, it is Britain's tripartite forum (government, employers, unions) for considering economic issues. Established in 1962, its early years were concerned with studies on speeding up the rate of economic GROWTH. This drew the council into examining the implications for individual industries, and various 'little Neddies' were set up. Even when relations between the three parties have been at their chilliest, Neddy has continued to function. Some say that shows its value; others its harmless irrelevance.

National income. Generic term for all that is produced, earned and spent in a country. See GROSS DOMESTIC PRODUCT.

National Insurance. The British name for a PAYROLL TAX. Both employers and employees pay contributions, expressed as a percentage of earnings but with an upper limit. These contributions are used to pay SOCIAL SECURITY benefits – UNEMPLOYMENT and sickness pay, pensions, etc. The self-employed also pay national insurance contributions, but at a different rate and with different entitlements to benefits.

In Britain, the rates (as of April 1983) are: employers 9.00 per cent: employees 11.95 per cent, with an upper earnings limit of £235 per week.

Nationalized industries. Part of the mix in mixed economies. Countries differ widely in the size and shape of their PUBLIC SECTOR: government-provided services like education or health are controversial enough, but nothing compared to the heat generated over how many industries should be owned and run by the state. And the caricatures seldom fit neatly: in the 1970s, none of the BANKS in 'socialist' Sweden were state-owned, whereas 'capitalist' France had two of its three largest banks in the public sector.

Figure 19 shows how nationalization differs between countries.

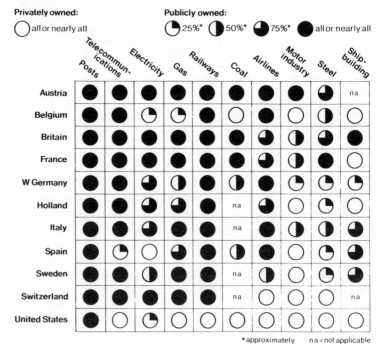

Figure 19 *Who owns what, and where*

Natural rate of unemployment. Phrase that raises hackles and confusion, yet means little more than the equilibrium rate. Like any EQUILIBRIUM, it depends on the characteristics of its market and the behaviour of those supplying labour and those demanding it. If, for example, people become more choosy about the jobs they will take, being prepared for longer spells of unemployment until they find what they want, the equilibrium will tend to rise.

The notion of a natural unemployment rate is central to the debate about the PHILLIPS CURVE – is there a trade-off between INFLATION and unemployment? MONETARISTS (and others who would not call themselves that) answer no: any attempt to steer unemployment below its natural rate will produce not just higher, but accelerating, inflation. For this reason, the natural rate is sometimes known by the acronym NAIRU – the non-accelerating-inflation rate of unemployment. Not very elegant, but it makes the point that a market is not in equilibrium if the price it is setting (in this case the price of labour) is continuously accelerating.

Neo-classical economics. Like painters, philosophers and cooks, economists split into different schools. 'Neo-classical' applies to all those who built on the foundations of classical economists like Adam SMITH and David RICARDO, with a strong belief in free markets and their ability to steer economies towards FULL EMPLOYMENT EQUILIBRIUM. However, neo-classicals developed a full-scale theory of prices and markets that did not depend on the LABOUR THEORY OF VALUE. The greatest neo-classical economist was Alfred MARSHALL, the father of MARGINAL ANALYSIS.

Net national product. GROSS NATIONAL PRODUCT minus DEPRECIATION. This measure of activity is rarely used.

Net present value. Measure used in project evaluation. See RATES OF RETURN.

Net worth. The value of a company after total liabilities have been subtracted from total ASSETS. Liabilities include deferred as well as current obligations, whether they be taxes or outstanding bills; assets – plant and equipment, cash, and so on – should be valued at current MARKET PRICES.

New Deal. Name given to the policies of President Franklin Roosevelt, enacted from 1933 on to counter the DEPRESSION. The Roosevelt administration adopted largely KEYNESIAN MACROECONOMIC policies: the federal BUDGET, which balanced in 1930 with spending of $3.6 billion, had a deficit of $5 billion in 1936 (and spending of more than $9 billion). The national debt roughly doubled, from $16 billion to $32 billion.

MICROECONOMIC policies were also more interventionist. TRADE UNIONS were encouraged; agricultural prices were raised and farmers were for the first time paid to restrict their acreage (see AGRICULTURAL POLICY); and the National Industrial Recovery Act of 1933 established the FEDERAL TRADE COMMISSION to enforce ANTI-TRUST laws.

The results of the New Deal will remain controversial as long as economists have breath in their bodies. Keynesians point to the 8 million rise in employment between 1933 and 1937 (though there were still 7 million unemployed in 1937), and the doubling of industrial production between 1932 and 1937. Non-Keynesians say that recovery was already beginning in 1932, before the New Deal started. Private investment in 1937 was still 8 per cent below its 1929 level because, critics say, ENTREPRENEURS were suspicious of the New Deal and profits were artificially held down. And the recovery ran out of steam in 1937, despite the continuing growth of the budget deficit – in the sceptics' view, the fate of all Keynesian recoveries.

New issues. Generic term for all forms of new long-term CAPITAL raised by borrowers. New issues are the bread and butter of many financial institutions – for example, MERCHANT BANKS, investment banks, and underwriters. They offer the shares of bonds (see BOND MARKET) to the public, usually on the basis of prospectuses for which they are paid handsome fees; and they agree to underwrite the issue – that is, guarantee that they will provide the borrower with his cash if the issue flops – in return for an underwriting commission of about $\frac{1}{2}$ per cent.

Contrast with 'RIGHTS ISSUES', which are offered by companies to their existing shareholders: 'for every five shares you hold, you can now buy one more at a price slightly below the market price prevailing when we announced the rights issue'.

Newly industrializing country (NIC). Those countries that are no longer poor but are not yet rich. Definitions vary, but the ORGANIZATION FOR ECONOMIC CO-OPERATION AND DEVELOPMENT (whose members are starting to feel the NICs' hot breath coming up behind) puts the following countries in the NIC class: Brazil, Greece, Hong Kong, South Korea, Mexico, Portugal, Singapore, Spain, Taiwan and Yugoslavia. Note that three of these (Greece, Portugal and Spain) already belong to the OECD: others may join before the end of the century.

Nobel prize. An annual economics prize has been awarded since 1969 – financed not by the Nobel foundation but by Sweden's CENTRAL BANK. In every other respect, the winner is regarded as a Nobel laureate. Take a bow,

1969	Ragnar Frisch	Norway
	Jan Tinbergen	Netherlands
1970	Paul Samuelson	United States
1971	Simon Kuznets	United States
1972	Kenneth Arrow	United States
	Sir John Hicks	Britain
1973	Wassily Leontief	United States
1974	Gunnar Myrdal	Sweden
	Friedrich von Hayek	Austria
1975	Leonid Kantorovich	USSR
	Tjalling Koopmans	United States
1976	Milton Friedman	United States
1977	James Meade	Britain
	Bertil Ohlin	Sweden
1978	Herbert Simon	United States
1979	Sir Arthur Lewis	United States
	Theodore Schultz	United States
1980	Lawrence Klein	United States
1981	James Tobin	United States
1982	George Stigler	United States

Nominal values. The value of anything – wages, GDP, EXPORTS, antiques, potatoes – expressed in the money of the day. Since INFLATION means that money loses its value, nominal figures are very misleading when used to compare values in different periods. They are therefore deflated by some appropriate INDEX NUMBER to produce values in CONSTANT PRICES. Compare with REAL VALUES.

Non-tariff barriers. Aside from QUOTAS and TARIFFS, international trade can be hindered or distorted by legal and administrative obstacles. Examples: invoicing requirements (all invoices must be completed in fourteen different languages) and safety standards (which change frequently and without warning).

Perhaps the most blatant recent instance comes from perfidious France. In 1982, the French government announced that all imports of video tape recorders would have to pass through Poitiers, a tiny customs post in central France with only a handful of customs officers. Being methodical chaps, they were able to okay only 2,000 recorders a week; before that about 15,000 a week had been coming into France, mainly from Japan. Poitiers was the place where the French defeated advancing Arab armies in 792. In 1983, the Japanese hi-fi firm Hitachi put advertisements in French newspapers proclaiming that 'We are not Saracens'.

O

Offshore banking. Collective term for banking that is free from domestic regulations, the most prominent form being the EUROMARKETS. The biggest 'offshore' centres are London, Nassau, Hong Kong, Singapore and Luxembourg.

Oligopoly. Where a few producers dominate an industry. Sometimes they collude in a CARTEL, producing results similar to a MONOPOLY; sometimes they are anti-competitive only by default, because they fear that direct COMPETITION would damage all of them. Their actions therefore try to take account of the reaction of other oligopolists: since that is uncertain, the behaviour of an oligopoly is hard to predict. If a price war breaks out, oligopolists will produce and price much as a perfectly competitive industry would; at other times they act very like a monopoly. See GAME THEORY.

Open market operations. CENTRAL BANKS buying and selling SECURITIES in the open market, as a way of controlling interest rates or monetary growth. They deal mainly in government paper – bonds (see BOND MARKET) and TREASURY BILLS – though they also enter the market for COMMERCIAL BILLS if they wish to channel corporate demands for LIQUIDITY away from the banking system. (See MONETARY CONTROL.)

Operational research. Fancy name given to a way of looking at an age-old economic and business problem – how best to use scarce resources to achieve particular goals. OR relies heavily on building mathematical models of, for example, cash flow or INVENTORY management, and then watching computers spew out solutions that supposedly satisfy the finance director, marketing director and production director. Wonderful, when it works.

Opportunity cost. Limited resources always have alternative uses – building a bridge, for example, involves using labour and cement that could build a road instead. These alternatives are known as the opportunity costs, and they provide a useful way of measuring the value of different activities. An afternoon's leisure can be priced according to how much a person should be earning if he had chosen to work instead. Opportunity costs can be zero: from the point of view of national production, any kind of job, however menial, is worth doing if the alternative is to be unemployed. (From the individual's viewpoint, things may be rather different. If unemployment pay is higher than the wage he is offered, the opportunity cost of working may be too great for him to take the job.) See COST–BENEFIT ANALYSIS.

Optimizing. Doing well in the circumstances. All economic decisions are subject to constraints – for example, a household's spending is constrained by its INCOME, SAVINGS and creditworthiness. Economic theory assumes that a household will try to optimize its spending by what it considers the best possible combination of the three sources of cash. On a broader scale, countries are constrained by scarce resources – labour, capital, and so on – and try to improve on their use. When they succeed, economic GROWTH is the result.

Option dealing. Not recommended for little old ladies or the faint-hearted. SPECULATORS expecting a share price (see EQUITIES) to rise take out a CALL OPTION to buy the share at some agreed price at some agreed date in the future. If they are right and the share price rises above their agreed level, they can immediately resell the share when the time comes to exercise their option. If they believe the price will fall, they take a put option to sell at some point in the future.

'Double options' allow a person to buy or sell – which sounds like a licence to print money. That they are not. Any option is expensive, because it can be bought only at a premium or discount to the spot price (see SPOT MARKETS). As such, the spot price needs to change quite sharply in order to make option dealing profitable. If you buy a double option only to find, on the appointed day, that the spot price hasn't budged, you will have lost – perhaps 10 per cent or more.

Organization for Economic Co-operation and Development (OECD). The capitalist world's club, the OECD has twenty-four member countries and a secretariat based in Paris. Its origins go back to the MARSHALL PLAN, when the Organization for European Economic Co-operation (OEEC) was set up to organize Europe's recovery. In 1961, the OEEC became the OECD, the principal forum for countries to discuss economic issues of mutual interest.

Sceptics believe that the OECD is little more than a talking shop and a massive collector of statistics. Others point to more concrete achievements, such as the gentleman's agreement on EXPORT CREDITS, the co-ordination of rich-country views in north–south negotiations, and fruitful work on particular industries like shipbuilding and steel, where capacity in OECD countries clearly needed to be cut. The OECD's publications are also valuable, the annual economic surveys on each member country and the biannual *Economic Outlook* being particularly useful.

The OECD secretariat is conventionally regarded as KEYNESIAN in its views. In its early years its staff was disproportionately British, becoming known as the 'Treasury in exile'. Old hands swear that the OECD once published a paper which referred to West Germany as 'an overseas country'.

The OECD's twenty-four members are Australia, Austria, Belgium,

Canada, Denmark, Finland, France, West Germany, Greece, Iceland, Ireland, Italy, Japan, Luxembourg, the Netherlands, New Zealand, Norway, Portugal, Spain, Sweden, Switzerland, Turkey, the United Kingdom and the United States. In addition, Yugoslavia, communism's maverick, has a special status halfway between member and observer. The secretary-general of the OECD is by tradition a European (currently a Dutchman, Emil van Lennep).

Organization of Petroleum Exporting Countries (OPEC). OPEC became a household term in 1974, after oil prices were quadrupled within the space of a few weeks. It was established in 1960 to try to co-ordinate production among the main oil exporters. Its success as a CARTEL is hotly disputed; some economists argue that market pressures were leading to a sharp rise in oil prices anyway, and OPEC merely capitalized on them. Certainly OPEC has had difficulty maintaining the unity it achieved in 1974.

The key role belongs to Saudi Arabia; it needs to produce about 5 million barrels of oil a day for its own FOREIGN EXCHANGE requirements, but is capable of producing about 11 million b/d. This margin gives it enormous power to decide how much OPEC as a group will produce, and therefore the prices at which oil will sell. Saudi Arabia has generally used this power to moderate the ambitions of the 'OPEC hawks', such as Algeria and Venezuela.

Not all oil exporters belong to OPEC (Britain and Mexico being two obvious exceptions), and the world's largest oil producer, the Soviet Union, is not a member either. These outsiders are one reason why OPEC's importance is diminishing. In 1974, 53 per cent of all the world's oil came from OPEC members; by 1981, their share was down to 40 per cent. Current OPEC members, with 1981 production figures in brackets, are: Saudi Arabia (9.8 million barrels a day), Iran (1.3), Iraq (0.9), Kuwait (1.1), UAE (1.5), Qatar (0.4), Venezuela (2.1), Nigeria (1.4), Libya (1.1), Indonesia (1.6), Algeria (0.8), Gabon (0.1), Ecuador (0.2).

Overnight money. The shortest of short-term loans, commonly involving BANKS that need to square their books at the end of each day. Those who are short of DEPOSITS will borrow from those with 'too much', literally overnight until trading starts the next morning. Rates vary enormously depending on market conditions: if the monetary authorities have started to drain LIQUIDITY from the markets in the afternoon, overnight rates can rise to (an annual rate of) 50 per cent or more.

Overshooting. Term used to describe the tendency of floating EXCHANGE RATES to move further than is necessary to offset differential changes in the costs of traded goods. 'Necessary' is itself hard to define, because much depends on your starting point for comparison. But suppose an exchange rate of £1 = $2 in year 1 accurately reflected the costs of producing similar goods and services in Britain and the United States. In year 2, those costs rose by 10 per cent in Britain, only 5 per cent in America. The dollar ought to appreciate against the pound, so that in dollar terms the two countries' exports would still cost the same. That would happen if the new rate was £1 = $1.91. If, however, the pound went to $1.80 and then stayed there, it would have overshot the mark.

Since generalized floating started in 1973, overshooting has become common. The yen and the D-mark were undervalued against the dollar and most other currencies in 1976–78, and again in 1980–82. This gave Japanese and German exporters a competitive advantage in world markets, increasing pressures for PROTECTIONISM in countries with overvalued exchange rates.

P

Paasche index. See INDEX NUMBERS.

Pareto optimum. Named after an Italian economist, Vilfredo Pareto (1843–1923), the phrase describes circumstances in which nobody can be made better off without making somebody else worse off. If an economy's resources are allocated inefficiently, a Pareto improvement ought to be possible – that is, making one person (or more) better off without harming anybody else. In practice, such uncontroversial opportunities are rare: change usually involves losers as well as winners, and the Pareto criterion has nothing to offer on how the balance should be judged. See GAME THEORY.

Paris Club. The name given to the arrangements through which countries RESCHEDULE their official (but not commercial) DEBT. The Club is actually based on the Avenue Kléber in Paris, and the French Treasury provides a small secretariat for its meetings. Other institutions, like the WORLD BANK, attend in an informal role.

With the growth of rescheduling operations in recent years, the Paris Club has come under pressure from COMMERCIAL BANKS to include private debt in its negotiations. The pressure has been firmly resisted: governments argue that the Club would become too unwieldy (there are rarely more than 20–25 official creditors; but 1,400 commercial banks had lent money to Mexico, for example). They also say that official rescheduling can take account of geopolitical and historical factors, whereas commercial bankers are interested only in getting their money back. Official and private creditors do share one prejudice, however: they dislike rescheduling INTEREST payments.

Partial equilibrium. An unkind joke has a farmer, an engineer and an economist on a desert island, with piles of tinned food as their only means of survival. Sharpen a stone to act as a tin opener, suggests the farmer. Light a fire and use the heat to weaken the seams on the tins, opines the engineer. They turn to the economist, asking for his view. Brimming with confidence, he begins: 'Assume a tin opener . . .'.

Partial equilibrium is a bit like that. Economists assume that all prices and quantities in an economy are constant, save for one particular industry or market. They then put that chosen bit under their microscope to see how it reaches equilibrium. But economists also recognize that changes in any industry have ripple effects throughout the economy – for example, by bidding up wages. To incorporate all these is more complicated, and involves studying the conditions under which general EQUILIBRIUM is achieved.

Pay-as-you-earn (PAYE). The automatic deduction of INCOME TAX from the weekly or monthly pay packet of employees. It was introduced in Britain in 1944, partly on the recommendation of John Maynard KEYNES, replacing the system where employees paid their own income tax over to the taxman every six months. The United States has had PAYE since 1943, and other industrial countries have since switched to it.

Note that PAYE does not apply to the self-employed. For these, elaborate schemes are devised to bring in the tax. In Belgium, for example, the self-employed can 'voluntarily' pay tax every three months, that is, in advance of their annual declaration. Failing to pay in advance is penalized by a final tax bill often 20 per cent higher than the advance payers'. In Britain the self-employed are responsible for declaring their income after the tax year has ended and then, later still, paying tax when the taxman demands it; this system has been nicknamed PAYP (pay-as-you-please).

Payroll tax. Levied on both employers and employees, usually as a percentage of each worker's salary. The revenues are generally used to finance SOCIAL SECURITY payments like UNEMPLOYMENT and sickness benefits. Payroll taxes are important revenue raisers in most industrial countries, accounting for 26.5 per cent of all taxes in the United States in 1980, 21.0 per cent in Britain, 45.3 per cent in France, and 34.3 per cent in West Germany. Critics brand them a 'tax on jobs'; at a time of rising unemployment, their size and purpose are increasingly questioned.

Percentile. Part of the 'ile' family that signposts positions on a scale of numbers (see also QUARTILE). The percentile is the most common member of the clan, with 99 appearances on the scale. The 'top percentile' on, for example, the distribution of income, is the richest 1 per cent; the size of their incomes is expressed as the income of the 99th per cent – Mr Bulging-Wallet's £100,000 a year – 'and above'.

Perfect competition. The textbook paradigm of a market for a perfectly homogeneous product, where there are so many buyers and sellers that none can individually affect the price, there are no BARRIERS to entry or exit, and where full information about market conditions is available to all. In such circumstances, output will be maximized, prices minimized, and competition will eliminate all save 'normal' profits – that is, those that are just large enough to keep firms in business. To compare this world with that of MONOPOLY and MONOPOLISTIC COMPETITION, see Figures 4, 5 and 6 (under COMPETITION).

Perks. Short for perquisites – income in kind, provided with the thinly disguised purpose of avoiding tax. Perks – company cars, subsidized lunches, private health insurance and so on – tend to flourish in countries with high marginal tax rates and/or a history of INCOMES POLICY. They are therefore more common in Britain than the United States (where company cars are very much the exception).

Since the mid-1970s, many governments have been taking a tougher line with perks. The Briton caricatured by John Betjeman:

I am a young executive. No cuffs than mine are cleaner;

I have a Slimline brief-case and I use the firm's Cortina.

is now having to pay for the privilege. His tax allowance has been reduced according to the size of the car and how much he uses it for private motoring as opposed to his work. The financial advantages of a company car have largely disappeared. In the United States, President Carter made it harder for companies to write off entertainment against tax, calling it a crackdown on the 'two-Martini lunch'. Most slimline American executives had turned to Perrier long before.

Permanent income hypothesis. One explanation for a crucial issue in economics – the way in which people split their INCOME between spending and SAVING. Developed by Milton FRIEDMAN in 1957, the hypothesis suggests that people have an idea of what their 'permanent', long-run income is, and will spend a constant proportion of this. Month by month, though, their actual income will differ from their notional norm. It might be higher, because of, for example, unusual overtime, windfall gains from gambling, the chance of some unexpected moonlighting, and so on. For most people, however, actual income is lower than permanent income – because most can look forward to rising incomes as they get older and are promoted.

Since consumption and savings are determined by permanent income, not actual income, the hypothesis helps to explain why people have different PROPENSITIES to save at different income levels. It also has important policy implications for tax-cutting politicians: to the extent that people believe that tax cuts are only an aberration, they will tend to save the extra cash, not spend it.

Phillips curve. Named after a New Zealand economist, A. W. H. Phillips (1914–75), who lectured at the London School of Economics from 1950 to 1967. His curve appeared in an article published in 1958; looking at the rate of change in NOMINAL wage rates and the UNEMPLOYMENT rate in Britain between 1861 and 1957, Phillips saw that the figures formed a definite smooth curve. To many, the conclusion was plain: INFLATION could be controlled simply by varying the amount of unemployment. Specifically, it seemed possible to combine unemployment of only 2.5 per cent with wages rising by only 2 per cent a year, which could be offset by PRODUCTIVITY growth to provide stability.

That sublime innocence was soon shattered. STAGFLATION, the antithesis of the Phillips curve, has in Britain produced combinations of 25 per cent inflation and rising unemployment. Figure 20 shows

Figure 20   *Britain's Phillips curve*

how the 'curve' has disappeared in the 1970s. MONETARISTS were not surprised by the demise of the Phillips curve, claiming that it mistakenly implied a permanent trade-off between inflation and unemployment. To monetarists, such a trade-off would be temporary at best; any attempt to regulate unemployment below its NATURAL RATE would not merely raise the inflation rate, but would accelerate it.

Pigou effect. Falling inflation and interest rates producing a rise in spending: see WEALTH EFFECT.

Poll tax. Generic term for a tax levied on everybody, irrespective of their INCOMES or spending. Historically common (because administratively simple), poll taxes are now virtually unknown.

Pollution. Generally used to describe damage to the environment – smoky air, dirty rivers, and so on. Economists have long recognized pollution as an example of how private and social costs and benefits can diverge (see COST–BENEFIT ANALYSIS, EXTERNALITY). Pressure groups have come to regard it in more lurid terms – for example, the indifference of big business to nature, the threat that continued economic growth poses to mankind's future, etc.

Population. Self-evident definition. However, this is a useful opportunity to show (Table 6) how the world's population has changed over time.

Table 6   *World population*

	Millions	Average annual % growth
1650	500	–
1750	790	0.46
1800	980	0.43
1850	1,260	0.50
1900	1,650	0.54
1950	2,490	0.83
1980	4,430	1.94
2000	6,490	1.93
2050	11,200	1.10

Source: World Bank; UN.

The estimates for 2000 and 2050 come from the United Nations; the only certain thing about them is that they are wrong. Initially, DEMOGRAPHERS tended to underestimate future population growth – in recent years, their forecasts have been too high.

Portfolio balance. Highlighted by monetary economists from KEYNES onward. All wealth holders, from the poorest pensioner to the largest pension fund, make important decisions about the form in which they will hold their ASSETS. They shift this balance depending on the level and structure of INTEREST rates, the rate of INFLATION (actual and expected) and the competing attractions of LIQUIDITY versus security. In running its monetary policy (see MONETARY CONTROL), a CENTRAL BANK needs to have a close understanding of what influences portfolio choices. If it does, it can, for example, operate effectively on interest rates and sell the right mixture of TREASURY BILLS and GILT-EDGED SECURITIES at minimum cost.

Positive economics. All economic issues are controversial: to try and lower the temperature, economists like to distinguish between positive and normative economics. 'Positive' means the world as it is, devoid of subjective judgements and morality: 'if a government imposes RENT CONTROLS, my professional prediction is that it will reduce the availability of rented accommodation'. Whether that result is desirable or not is a normative issue, on which economists are no better qualified to speak than anybody else.

Poverty trap. The combination of paying INCOME TAX and losing welfare benefits can mean that poor people's incomes fall (or rise only slightly) when their pay is increased or when they take a job instead of being unemployed. An actual example, from Britain in 1982, is given in Figure 21.

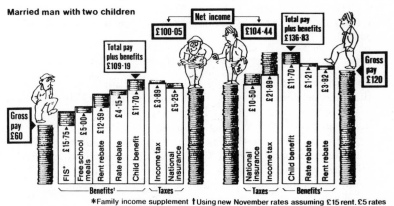

Figure 21 *The poverty trap*

Price controls. Governments' attempts to tame MARKET FORCES and INFLATION by rigging prices. Normally this is in conjunction with an INCOMES POLICY. Usual results: distorted demand and supply, under-investment, a price explosion when controls are eventually taken off. Worst sufferers from price controls are farmers in the Third World, where many governments set low prices to keep unruly town dwellers happy. Inevitably, farmers produce less, get poorer, and are forced to go to the towns in search of work. In CENTRALLY PLANNED ECONOMIES, price controls often go hand-in-hand with a major tourist attraction: the food queue. See also RATIONING.

Price discrimination. Where a firm charges different prices in different markets for the same product, depending on each market's ELASTICITY of demand. This is usually made possible by differing degrees of COMPETITION – the closer a firm gets to monopolizing a particular market, the more it has discretion over the prices it charges. But other factors may also be involved – for example, what consumers regard as a commonplace in one market may be highly prized in another.

The profit maximizing producer will, as ever, set his price and output at the point where marginal revenue (see MARGINAL ANALYSIS) equals marginal cost. Where elasticities differ, he will charge most in the market where demand is the most inelastic (see also MONOPOLY).

Price–earnings ratio. A useful measure of share prices (see EQUITIES), it is the ratio of the market price of an ordinary share to the earnings per share. The higher the P/E ratio, the more the stock market (see STOCK EXCHANGE) is buying a company's shares in the expectation that it will make larger profits in future. P/E ratios therefore vary widely: at the end of 1982, the New York stock market offered a range from 1 to 681, while London had P/E ratios from as low as 2 to as high as 79.

Price index. See RETAIL PRICE INDEX, INDEX NUMBERS.

Price supports. Most commonly used in agriculture, they have much the same purpose as wage and PRICE CONTROLS (see INCOMES POLICY): to prevent markets from reaching an EQUILIBRIUM at which supply equals demand. With one big difference: wages and prices are controlled to try and keep them below their market equilibrium, whereas agricultural support tries to hold prices above equilibrium. Predictable result: supply exceeds demand, piling up butter and wheat mountains, filling wine and olive oil lakes (see COMMON AGRICULTURAL POLICY).

So long as CONSUMERS are willing to finance these mountains and lakes through unnecessarily expensive food, price supports will be maintained by politicians anxious to please farmers. Note, though, that a free agricultural market would cause problems of its own – first, because prices would tend to vacillate very wildly (see COBWEB THEOREM), and second, because farmers' incomes would fall steadily behind those of other groups, because the demand for food is income inelastic (see ELASTICITY and ENGEL'S LAW).

Price takers and makers. Derives from the models of PERFECT COMPETITION and MONOPOLY, plus the hybrid of MONOPOLISTIC COMPETITION. Under perfect competition, all producers are price takers: they have to accept the market price and can do nothing to influence it. At the other extreme, a monopolist obviously makes his own price. In between, some firms are price leaders in their industry. They decide the price of their product, believing that their smaller competitors will follow suit because they fear that they would lose a price war. A CARTEL turns this kind of leadership into collusion.

Prisoners' dilemma. Part of GAME THEORY, it helps to explain how, in economics, individual and collective interests can diverge (compare with INVISIBLE HAND). Imagine several prisoners, jointly accused of an offence and being held in separate cells. They face three options:
- If one becomes a state witness, he could be freed while his comrades are harshly sentenced.
- Provided they all keep quiet, all will receive only a light sentence for lack of firm evidence.
- If all confess, individual sentences will be lighter than if only one had squealed, but sterner than if all had kept quiet.

Individually, each has an incentive to confess, hoping to get off altogether. But if all act in this rational way, then their punishment would be tougher than if all had kept quiet.

Private sector. Accurate but unhelpful definition: any economic activity that is not in the PUBLIC SECTOR. Most capitalist economies have more than half of their output produced by companies and individuals working not for the state but for private profit. Most communist countries are becoming less intolerant of private enterprise, especially among farmers and small traders. (For details of the private–public split in various countries, see NATIONALIZED INDUSTRIES.)

Probability. When a layman says that rain is 'probable', he means to be more confident than if he had said rain was possible. Economists use the word entirely neutrally: the probability of rain may be 1 in 100 or 9 in 10. These ratios are often strung together in a probability distribution which – in a graph or a table – shows where the outcome is most likely to be and what it depends on.

Procurement. Generic term for how governments buy goods and services from the PRIVATE SECTOR – anything from power stations to paper clips. Since those purchases involve a sizeable chunk of all spending (see PUBLIC EXPENDITURE), they are often used to favour domestic industries. This kind of PROTECTIONISM is frowned on by both GATT and the EEC; but their codes of conduct are hard to enforce and rarely invoked – partly because all governments are guilty of favouritism, so cries of 'foul' would fall unconvincingly from their lips.

Product cycle. Like people, products follow a life-cycle. They are typically invented and developed in industrial countries, and initially produced there. Once the technology matures, however, MASS PRODUCTION – as cheaply as possible – is the order of the day. The goods may then be produced in those developing countries with the human skills and the infrastructure to do the job effectively (see NEWLY INDUSTRIALIZING COUNTRIES). By that stage, the product is being steadily refined by new technological developments and may be overtaken completely by a different kind of product. Obsolescence, for a product, is roughly equivalent to human senility.

Productivity. The key to affluence, yet horribly elusive. It is a term that can be applied to any FACTOR OF PRODUCTION – land, labour or capital – to measure the output of each unit. Statisticians labour long hours to produce half-decent figures, and then economists spend their careers pondering exactly what (if anything) the figures mean.

The least bad statistics are for labour productivity – variously defined as output per worker, output per worker-shift, and output per worker-hour. Ironing out these wrinkles is nothing compared

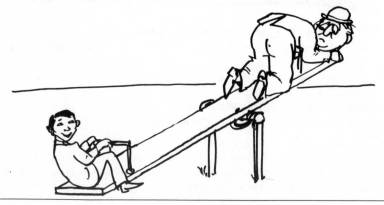

Table 7 *Output per man-hour in manufacturing* (*constant 1973 dollars*).

	1978	1981	Annual average % change
United States	9.42	10.44	1.3
Japan	4.73	7.43	5.8
West Germany	6.23	8.55	4.0
France	5.26	7.31	4.2
Britain	3.28	3.91	2.2

Source: NIESR.

with the problems involved in making comparisons between different industries and countries. The least distorted figures come from manufacturing, because it is easier to measure the output from a car factory than from an insurance company. Some recent figures are given in Table 7.

Although these absolute levels are interesting, they are rarely computed on anything like a comparable basis for different countries. More common is the kind of comparison of productivity growth shown in Table 8.

Table 8 *Comparison of productivity growth* (*annual average percentage changes*)

	Real GDP per employed person				
	1950–59	1960–69	1970–79	1980	1981
United States	2.6	2.4	0.8	−0.6	0.9
Japan	5.6	9.2	4.5	3.1	2.1
West Germany	5.2	4.5	3.5	0.9	0.6
France	4.4	5.0	3.6	0.9	1.0
Britain	2.1	2.6	2.1	0.2	2.7
Canada	3.1	2.6	1.4	−2.6	0.4

	Output per man-hour in manufacturing				
	1950–59	1960–69	1970–79	1980	1981
United States	2.1	2.9	2.5	−0.3	2.8
Japan	8.7	11.1	8.0	6.8	3.0
W. Germany	6.1	6.0	5.0	1.1	2.6
France	4.5	5.9	5.2	0.6	2.3
Britain	1.8	4.3	2.9	0.5	5.8
Canada	3.8	4.5	3.1	−1.9	0.6

Source: OECD; US Department of Labour.

Profit and loss account. Company's statement of its revenues and costs during a given period, showing its overall profit or loss, and what has been done with the profits – that is, how much is paid out as DIVIDENDS and how much is being retained in the business. Contrast with BALANCE SHEET, which shows just ASSETS and liabilities and always, by definition, balances.

Profit margin. The percentage mark-up over the cost of each good sold.

Profit maximization. The presumed goal of businessmen. Profits are maximized at the point where marginal revenue equals marginal cost (defined under MARGINAL ANALYSIS). This is so whether the company is a MONOPOLY, an OLIGOPOLY or operating under PERFECT COMPETITION; but the market structure will determine how large its profits are (see Figures 4, 5 and 6 under COMPETITION).

Many economists doubt that firms really aim to maximize profits; they think other goals are more likely – for example, maximizing sales, or expanding assets. Some of these alternatives have been incorporated into the theory of SATISFICING behaviour.

Propensities. Economics abounds with propensities to do various things – consume, save, invest, import, and so on. In each case, the critical distinction is between the average propensity and the marginal one: the average propensity to consume (APC) is simply c/y, consumption divided by income (with a typical value of about 0.9 in Britain, rather more in the United States, significantly less in Japan). The marginal propensity to consume (MPC) is how much each *extra* pound of income is consumed; formally $MPC = \Delta c/\Delta y$. The value of the MPC is harder to predict than APC (note, though, that if MPC is less than APC, then APC will fall over time as income rises). Note, too, that propensities determine the value of the MULTIPLIER.

Property taxes. American version of Britain's RATES.

Protectionism. Generic term for obstacles to international trade. See MERCANTILISM, TARIFFS, QUOTAS, IMPORT CONTROLS, NON-TARIFF BARRIERS, FREE TRADE and the GENERAL AGREEMENT ON TARIFFS AND TRADE.

Public expenditure. For bookkeeping purposes, it is usually divided into three: central government, local government and state industries. For economic purposes, two other sets of distinctions are more important:
- Current spending (pensions, pay and so on) versus capital spending

(roads, sewers, bridges and so on). Governments usually find it easier to cut their capital programmes, because that does not involve them in politically unpopular decisions on welfare payments or public sector pay and employment. Capital spending has therefore become less important in all the major countries except West Germany (see Table 9).

Table 9   *Public expenditure by type, percentage shares*

	United States		Japan		W. Germany	
	1950	1980	1950	1980	1950	1980
Current expenditure						
Goods and services	54.2	52.2	56.4	30.8	45.7	42.6
Transfer payments	27.7	32.5	19.2	37.5	44.3	39.5
Debt interest	7.4	9.4	—	9.6	1.4	4.1
Capital expenditure	10.7	5.9	24.4	22.1	8.6	13.8
	France		Britain		Canada	
	1950	1980	1950	1980	1950	1980
Current expenditure						
Goods and services	38.9	32.8	46.8	48.2	46.4	53.0
Transfer payments	38.6	56.1	29.0	32.5	26.9	31.6
Debt interest	3.3	3.5	11.1	11.3	12.1	8.0
Capital expenditure	19.2	7.6	13.1	8.0	14.6	7.4

Source: OECD; UN; national accounts.

● Spending on goods and services versus TRANSFER PAYMENTS. The latter include pensions, unemployment pay, industrial subsidies, and so on – anything where the government acts purely as a channel between taxpayers and beneficiaries. By contrast, the government also buys goods and services from the private sector – for example, when it spends money on roads, railway engines, teachers' pay. This expenditure on goods and services counts as part of GROSS NATIONAL PRODUCT; transfer payments do not, because statisticians want to avoid double counting and therefore register only *final* expenditure. Pensions, for example, are computed as part of personal income and expenditure.

Double counting is a common trap for politicians wanting to prove that the state is gobbling up more and more of the national cake. Figure 22 shows what has really been happening.

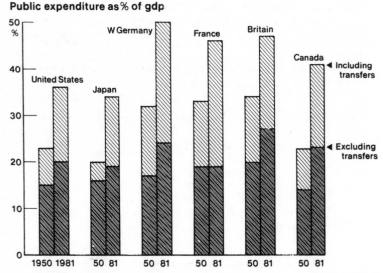

Figure 22 *The rise and rise of the public sector*   Sources: OECD; UN

Public goods. Several services, by their very nature, will not be properly provided by private markets. Lighthouses are a favourite textbook example: no ship owner will bear all the cost of a lighthouse if all his competitors are going to get the benefits for nothing, yet all will be harmed if no lighthouse is built. Solution: some public body builds and runs the lighthouse, and pays for it by taxing shipowners.

Other relatively uncontroversial examples of public goods include the judiciary, the police and the armed services. Thereafter, opinions start to differ. Some politicians and economists believe that private markets are capable of providing many things that are treated largely as public goods – for example, health care (backed by private insurance schemes) and education (with means-tested vouchers to ensure that all parents can afford the fees). Others reply that such facilities only became widely available when they were publicly provided; and that the indirect benefits of a healthy, educated population are shared by all, so the cost should be shared as well.

Public sector. Catch-all phrase for all the activities performed by the state and its agencies. They include central government, local government and the nationalized industries. (For details of where these frontiers are drawn in various countries, see NATIONALIZED INDUSTRIES.) Contrast with PRIVATE SECTOR.

Public sector borrowing requirement (PSBR). Shortfall between spending by the PUBLIC SECTOR and revenues, financed by borrowing. Take care: the term 'budget deficit' is often loosely applied to just the central government's budget shortfall. The PSBR takes in spending by the whole of the public sector, that is, including local authorities and nationalized industries, and it is the best measure of the impact of a government's FISCAL POLICY on aggregate DEMAND. Nevertheless, in a RECESSION the PSBR tends automatically to increase because of higher unemployment and therefore higher social security costs. See also DEFICIT FINANCING, FINE TUNING.

Purchase tax. British SALES TAX superseded by VALUE ADDED TAX in 1973.

Purchasing power parity. Basis for comparing living standards between countries; more accurate than simply translating figures for GDP per caput from the domestic CURRENCY into some common currency (like the dollar) by using EXCHANGE RATES. The flaws in exchange rates are considerable:

● They are influenced only by goods and services that are traded internationally (and therefore exclude things like housing and many welfare services).

● More important, exchange rates also depend on capital flows, and can fluctuate wildly from year to year. In dollar terms, country A's GNP might be higher than country B's in year 1, and lower in year 2 – but only because its exchange rate depreciated, not because it had grown 'poorer' in any meaningful sense.

Purchasing power parities (PPPs) try to eliminate these distortions by looking at how much goods and services can be bought by a certain amount of currency. For both rich and poor countries, the results are very different from those obtained by simple exchange rate comparisons: see Table 10.

Table 10   *Comparisons of 1980 GDP per caput*

	(1) $ at current exchange rates	(2) $ at PPP exchange rates	(2) as % of (1)
United States	11,365	11,365	100
Japan	8,905	8,465	95
W. Germany	13,305	9,430	71
France	12,135	9,040	69
Britain	9,335	7,630	82
Philippines	730	1,565	214
Brazil	2,020	3,050	151
Zambia	660	850	129

Sources: OECD; IMF; World Bank.

Q

Quantity theory of money. The foundation stone of MONETARISM, it maintains that prices are determined by how much money is in circulation. It was formalized into an equation by an American economist, Irving Fisher (1867–1947):

$$MV = PT$$

where M is the money supply, V is its VELOCITY OF CIRCULATION, P is the price level, and T is the volume of transactions in goods and services. If V is constant – that is, if money changes hands at a constant rate – and the volume of transactions is constant (over the short term at least) then there is a direct link between the volume of money M and the price level P.

The same principle is embodied in a modified form of this equation, expressed as

$$M = kPT$$

where k is the reciprocal of V and is defined as the proportion of spending which is held in the form of cash.

Those who dispute the theory do so on two main grounds: (1) that V is not constant, and that it does not even vary in some predictable way; and (2) that even if there is a link between M and P, it need not be a causal link, still less one that leads from money to prices.

These controversies have raged since the 1930s, when KEYNESIANS began to challenge the orthodoxy represented by the quantity theory. The theoretical debate has been supplemented by a mass of empirical research into the value of V and into the time lags between changes in M and changes in P. Monetarists are satisfied that the data bear out their view; Keynesians believe that they are vindicated. The argument, safe to say, will continue.

Quartile. Part of the 'ile' family that signposts positions on a scale of numbers (see also PERCENTILE). Divide the scale into four and the lower quartile is the value below which 25% of the numbers lie; the upper quartile starts on the 75% mark. Example:

Number of taxpayers	Income range (£)	Total income (£m)
100	0–7,000	0.5
150	7,001–12,000	1.5
50	12,001–15,000	0.7
50	15,001–17,500	0.8
50	17,501 and above	1.0
400		4.5

This table shows that the lower quartile of income is £7,000, the upper one £15,001. Another conclusion is that the bottom quartile received one-ninth (0.5 ÷ 4.5) of all income, while the top quartile received two-ninths. This gives a rough guide to the degree of income inequality (see also GINI COEFFICIENT and LORENZ CURVE).

Quasi-rent. A refinement of the notion of RENT − any surplus that accrues to a producer over and above his costs of production. The concept of quasi-rents was developed by MARSHALL to define the short-term surplus derived from inputs whose supply cannot quickly be increased. Any good or service that depends on, for example, a rare skill will earn quasi-rents until more people develop those skills and prices are then forced down by competition.

Quotas. A direct, quantitative form of trade PROTECTIONISM: 'country A will import 5,000 pairs of shoes from country B this year, but no more', irrespective of price, quality or latent consumer demand. Unlike TARIFFS, which raise the price of imports by taxing them, quotas do not yield any direct revenue to the government. But they may also be relied on to raise the price of the imported good above what it would have been had its supply been unrestricted. If indirect taxes are expressed as a percentage of price, therefore, the government's coffers will be affected.

Quotas are also used in another context − by producers who allocate production quotas to members of CARTELS. Again, the purpose is to restrict trade, so that (well organized) producers gain at the expense of (usually incoherent) consumers.

R

Radcliffe Committee. Set up in 1957, under the chairmanship of a judge, Lord Radcliffe, to report on the working of the British monetary system. Its report, published in 1959, was the high-water mark in KEYNESIAN influence over economic policy. It maintained that monetary policy, as exercised through changes in bank rate, had little effect on the supply of money – which in turn had little effect on INFLATION and other variables. The report concluded that more use should be made of credit controls and the direction of financial institutions. It was not until 1971, with the publication of *Competition and Credit Control*, that British monetary policy started to depart from the lines advocated by the Radcliffe Report.

Random walk. A theory (most commonly applied to share prices; see EQUITIES) which asserts that there is no systematic relationship between prices on successive days. Prices respond only to new and unexpected information, since all market participants are equally well informed about the factors that influence those prices. In the absence of a surprise, therefore, prices on day 2 will be the same as prices on day 1, and will in turn determine prices on day 3. Since surprises – wars, government policy, boardroom disputes – are common, prices jump around; but, says the theory, they do so in a random way, so that even assiduous investors will never master the Midas touch.

Rate of return. Simple in outline, in detail a statistical minefield. Most commonly used to measure annual profits as a percentage of CAPITAL employed. However, rates of return also apply to the rewards from investing in HUMAN CAPITAL (that is, education), while COST–BENEFIT ANALYSIS calculates rates of return by including a variety of hard-to-quantify social benefits like clean air and safer roads.

Even in common business usage, rates of return are difficult to pin down, largely because of the way that INFLATION distorts both profits (especially from company STOCKS) and capital. (See CURRENT COST ACCOUNTING). Even when these issues are sorted out, rates of return are not an unambiguous criterion for judging the relative merits of different investments, because they do not distinguish between profits earned quickly and those earned slowly.

Economists therefore emphasize alternative ways to evaluate the future profitability of a project. They are interested in finding out the value of future profits if an investor could bank them today. This can be approached in one of two ways, known together as DISCOUNTED CASH FLOW (DCF) techniques.

The net present value. Each year's prospective costs and revenues are recalculated in terms of today's money. Simple example: £110 a year from now is worth £100 today if the INTEREST rate is 10 per cent. All these future £110s or whatever are expressed in today's money by using some chosen interest rate, and then added up. If total revenues are greater than costs, it looks like a profitable project.

The internal rate of return (IRR). This is a variation on the NPV, but seeks to calculate the interest rate rather than to choose it as an assumption. Prospective profits are added up, and the IRR is whatever interest rate makes this stream of future income equal, in today's money, to the cost of the project. Investors can then decide whether that is an adequate return.

Rates. The British term for what are known as property taxes in the United States. Levied by the local council (and by state and local governments, in America), they tax (see TAXATION) all property, commercial, industrial and residential. The bill that British ratepayers actually pay depends on two things:

● Rateable value. This is assessed according to the local authority's estimate of a property's rental value, and depends on things like area, number of rooms, and so on. The rateable value is changed only infrequently, since local authorities do not have the resources to make proper assessments.

● The rate itself, expressed as *x* number of pence per pound of rateable value. This can be changed very simply, and is; over the five years 1976–81, average rates in England and Wales rose by 97 per cent.

Exemptions are possible: agricultural land is derated in Britain, and some 3.4 million households received rate rebates in 1980–81 (the exact amount depending on income, family size and so on). Even with such exemptions, rates are an important source of finance for local authorities, providing 32 per cent of their income in 1981; in the United States, property taxes provided 18 per cent of all state and local government revenue.

In Britain, the bulk of the rest of local authority income comes as a rate support grant from central government. This grant provides a partial lever on local authority finance, since central government fixes the rate support grant in advance; if local authorities want to spend more, they have to incur the unpopularity of raising rates.

Because they are unrelated to income, rates are frequently criticized for being arbitrary and inequitable. The Layfield Report (1976) in Britain recommended that rental values should be replaced by capital values as the basis for determining rates. It also proposed giving local authorities the right to levy local INCOME TAXES. Politicians agree – in theory, and always while they are in opposition; in government their zeal for reform quickly fades. And rates are not without supporters; depending solely on ASSETS, not income, rates are the only form of WEALTH TAX applied in Britain.

Rational expectations. A wide-ranging approach to explaining economic behaviour in terms of the importance that individuals and
companies attach to expectations about the future. Those expectations, the theory suggests, are based on full knowledge of all available market information: they will be upset, and therefore behaviour
will be changed, only by shocks and the availability of different
information. This is what the RANDOM WALK theory also asserts,
though it is usually confined to STOCK EXCHANGE prices.

Rational expectations theorists push the approach much further, in
the process reaching conclusions profoundly opposed to all types of
KEYNESIAN demand management. For example, they conclude that the
level of UNEMPLOYMENT is as it is because the unemployed have made
a perfectly rational choice between work for a particular wage and
idleness for a particular unemployment benefit. The rational expectations model also maintains that people will react immediately to any
monetary or fiscal stimulus by adjusting for the higher INFLATION
they know will eventually result. Equally they will be reluctant to
believe that monetary restraint will be applied for long enough to
cure inflation, because they know that has never been true in the
past.

Rationing. The price mechanism is the simplest way of rationing –
available supplies going to the highest bidders. Where governments
or other regulators try to fix prices below their market EQUILIBRIUM,
other forms of rationing are necessary. For consumer goods, queues
or coupons are the most common rationing device. Industry usually
ends up being offered some kind of licensing system – for example,
for land development, import QUOTAS, or subsidized credit. In every
case, he who controls the queue or hands out the licence has great

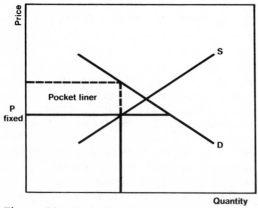

Figure 23   *Rationing*

power – which he generally uses to line his own pocket: see Figure 23.

Real balance effect. Falling inflation and interest rates producing a rise in spending: see WEALTH EFFECT.

Real values. In contrast with NOMINAL VALUES, real values abstract from the effects of INFLATION. If a firm's sales rise from £100 million to £110 million and its prices go up by 10 per cent, the real value of its sales has not changed at all. The same applies to a country's GDP, a worker's wage, a pensioner's pension. The denominator will vary depending on which numerator you are looking at. For real wages, the consumer (or retail) price index is the right deflator; for EXPORTS, the unit value of exports; for GDP, the GDP deflator, because that is the broadest-based measure of output prices in an economy.

Real values are easy to compute historically; they are much harder to calculate in advance if some of the information has to be guesstimated. Real INTEREST rates are the classic example: somebody lending money for five years at 8 per cent will know if he has got a good investment only after five years are up and the rate of inflation is known.

Recession. Colloquially used to describe a period of slow or no economic GROWTH. Has two more precise meanings:

● Any period where GDP growth is below the assumed underlying growth in the economy's productive potential. Since that potential is, in the short term, assumed to be closely related to the availability of labour, rising UNEMPLOYMENT is a fairly good indicator of recession (though note that since changes in unemployment lag changes in output, an economy can be recovering from recession – growing faster than its trend rate of growth – before unemployment starts to turn down).

● In the United States, 'recession' is officially defined as two consecutive quarters of falling GNP.

If recession continues, at some imprecise point it becomes a DEPRESSION.

Reciprocal. In mathematics, a number raised to the power of minus one. The reciprocal of A is $1/A$; the reciprocal of 10 is $1/10$. In international negotiations, any concession or penalty from country A to country B that is matched by country B.

Recycling. Buzz word in the 1970s, with both ecological and financial devotees. Ecologists worried about using up 'the world's stock of finite resources' and therefore urged people and companies to reuse glass bottles, newsprint, scrap metal and so on. The cost of this kind of recycling was often higher than not doing it at all – that is, more resources were used than saved, a powerful disincentive to everybody — save those worried about higher things and indifferent to economics.

The financial version of recycling really meant nothing more than the age-old process of matching lenders and borrowers. It took on particular significance after oil prices were quadrupled in 1973–74, pushing OPEC's current-account surplus (see BALANCE OF PAYMENTS) to $66 billion in 1974 and $32 billion in 1975. These surpluses were the mirror image of deficits run by oil importers, which had to be financed. The surplus cash was therefore 'recycled', largely through the EUROMARKETS, to the deficit countries. At the time it sounded so neat and neutral. By 1980, however, those recycled surpluses came to be seen for what they had been all along — growing debts shouldered by countries that were not well placed to service them. Examples include Zaire, Turkey, Argentina, Brazil, Mexico, Poland. . . .

Redemption yield. Bonds (see BOND MARKET) commonly trade below the price at which the issuer has promised to redeem them at maturity. They therefore offer (1) INTEREST and (2) prospective capital gains, both of which affect the 'return to the investors'. Redemption yields incorporate both elements; they are usually calculated 'gross' — that is, without taking account of possible liability for capital gains tax.

Example: a bond with face value of $100, purchased at $99.50 (a discount of $0.50), and four years to maturity. Coupon rate of interest is $12\frac{1}{2}$ per cent a year. Over the four years, the purchaser would receive $50 in interest; at redemption he would also get the face value of $100. Thus for an initial investment of $99.50, $50.50 would be realized.

$$\text{redemption yield} = \frac{\text{coupon rate} + \left(\dfrac{\text{discount}}{\text{years to maturity}}\right)}{(\text{face value} + \text{purchase price})/2}$$

$$= \frac{12.5 + \left(\dfrac{0.50}{4}\right)}{(100 + 99.50)/2}$$

$$= \frac{12.625}{99.75}$$

$$= 0.1266 \text{ or } 12.66 \text{ per cent a year}$$

Redundancy. Euphemism for losing one's job. Many redundancies are involuntary, brought on by companies closing factories or slimming down their workforce. Since RECESSION started spreading in the

1970s, however, voluntary redundancy has also become more common: firms offer cash to those who volunteer, the size of the payment usually depending on salary and length of service. This practice is almost unknown in the United States.

Reflation. Loosely used, increasingly controversial, term. Usually means a KEYNESIAN stimulus to demand, by TAXATION cuts and/or more PUBLIC EXPENDITURE, which pushes up the BUDGET deficit. This meaning is usually accompanied by implied changes in monetary policy – for example, by lowering INTEREST rates, accepting faster growth in the MONEY SUPPLY.

To non-Keynesians, this type of fiscal and monetary reflation is no more than a harbinger of faster INFLATION. They accept that demand can be reflated (that is, increased in real rather than nominal terms), but to be non-inflationary the reflation must be spontaneous. That means it must happen through falling inflation and interest rates, both of which increase the real value of a flow of monetary demand. See WEALTH EFFECT.

Regional policy. Taking work to the workers rather than expecting them to come to the work. Popular among European governments in the 1950s and 1960s, and still a favourite topic for academics; in the United States, with its greater tradition of job mobility, less common. The weapons of regional policy are grants or cheap loans to companies setting up or expanding in designated areas; wage subsidies (for example, the Regional Employment Premium that operated in Britain from 1967 to 1977); and the dispersion of government offices from the capital to the provinces. The aim of it all: to counter a depressed region's natural disadvantages by offering financial advantages.

Central government is not the only body promoting a regional policy. No self-respecting region or state is complete without some kind of investment promotion board, which extols the beauties of downtown Burbank and the diligence of its workforce. This is the *de facto* form that regional policy takes in the United States, where states compete for investment by offering ever larger carrots. One example: Volkswagen opened a car and truck assembly plant in Pennsylvania in 1978. It was lured there by:

● A $40 million, thirty-year loan at an average interest rate of less than 4 per cent a year.
● A $6 million, fifteen-year loan at 8.5 per cent.
● A five-year property tax abatement, worth about $200,000.
● The plant was designated as a 'foreign trade sub-zone', so the duty that Volkswagen had to pay on a finished car was only 3 per cent.

Regressive taxes. See TAXATION.

Regulation Q. American rule, imposed by the FEDERAL RESERVE, which set ceilings on the INTEREST rates that could be charged to borrowers and paid to depositors. The regulation applied particularly harshly to SAVINGS AND LOAN ASSOCIATIONS, but also affected the COMMERCIAL BANKS. As a result, those banks started moving their dollars to Europe, to lend from there – helping to spawn the EUROMARKETS.

As market interest rates rose sharply in the 1970s, Regulation Q became increasingly eccentric. By discriminating against certain types of deposit takers, it encouraged the development of others – notably MONEY MARKET FUNDS. In 1980, the American Congress belatedly agreed to phase out Regulation Q over a five-year period.

Regulator. The power given to Britain's chancellor of the exchequer to take limited fiscal action without going through the whole rigmarole of a BUDGET. In 1961, parliament agreed that, between budgets, the chancellor could change indirect taxes (see TAXATION) by up to 10 per cent of their level. In 1964, this freedom was amended slightly, to cover only five kinds of indirect taxes – purchase tax, tobacco duty, alcohol duty, oil taxes and betting taxes. After VALUE ADDED TAX replaced purchase tax, it too was covered by the regulator. With VAT at 15 per cent, for example, the chancellor has power to vary it between 13.5 and 16.5 per cent.

Reinsurance. Insurers' way to share out risks. Reinsurance occurs when the primary insurer (or underwriter) pays other insurers to take on part of the risk. See LLOYD'S OF LONDON, INSURANCE.

Relative income hypothesis. One of several attempts to explain how people split their income between CONSUMPTION and SAVINGS. Proposed by the American economist James Duesenberry, who argued that in the long run, people's average PROPENSITY to consume (APC) is determined by their relative income – that is, their position on the income scale. Double everybody's income, he said, and the APC will remain the same.

For the short term, Duesenberry had a different explanation. People dislike reducing their consumption just as much as they like increasing it. Consumption therefore is ratcheted up, each higher level being impossible to reverse. This means, said Duesenberry, that in recessions a person's APC tends to rise if his income falls. Snag: empirical evidence refutes the Duesenberry ratchet, because consumer spending does fall in recessions. Hence the search for alternative explanations: see PERMANENT INCOME HYPOTHESIS and LIFE-CYCLE HYPOTHESIS.

Rent. Economists' term of art, used to describe what is paid to somebody (or to another factor of production) beyond what is needed to keep him in his present occupation. Example: when OPEC quadrupled oil prices in 1973–74, numerous oil producers had their rent vastly increased. They would have been happy to pump oil at $3 a barrel; at $12 a barrel, their rent was $9. Also known as ECONOMIC RENT.

Rent controls. Introduced by well-intentioned politicians (to stop existing tenants being exploited by unscrupulous landlords), they usually end up preventing prospective tenants from getting housing at all. The reason is best explained by a simple demand–supply diagram, Figure 24.

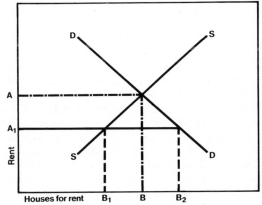

Figure 24   *Rent controls*

If rents are fixed at A_1, below the market clearing rate of A, supply will shrink from B to B_1, while demand will rise from B to B_2. Unsatisfied demand will therefore be B_1 to B_2. Unfortunately for those aspirants, their views are never organized as well as the B_1 body of existing tenants, who protest loudly at any threat to raise rents from A_1 to A.

These flaws are well known. They have not stopped politicians from maintaining, and often extending, controls. In Britain controls were first introduced in the First World War, relaxed for twenty years, and then tightened in 1939. The 1965 Rent Act introduced the idea of a 'fair rent', determined by local authority bureaucrats, while the 1974 Act extended security of tenure to all tenants. As the supply of new housing began, predictably, to shrink, governments have relaxed these provisions.

Repurchase agreements. Colloquially known as 'repos', they are a deal done between the FEDERAL RESERVE and financial institutions like

BANKS and SECURITIES firms. If the institutions are short of LIQUIDITY, they can exchange some of their ASSETS (for example, government bonds) with the Fed for cash. If the shortage is thought to be temporary – or the Fed does not want to boost liquidity permanently – the exchange will be given a limited life. The Fed buys the securities, agreeing to sell them back to the institutions on a specified day (usually within a fortnight). If the Fed wants to drain liquidity out of the system, it does the opposite – known as 'reverse repos'.

Resale price maintenance. British practice where a manufacturer could make retailers sell his product at a given price, or at not less than a minimum price – thus eliminating price competition in the distributive and retail trades. After years of agonizing, resale price maintenance was first curtailed by the Restrictive Trade Practices Act of 1956 and later abolished by the Resale Prices Act of 1964 – except in a limited range of trades, notably publishing. Most manufacturers switched to 'recommended retail prices' or similar guide prices.

Rescheduling. Of DEBT: much in vogue in the early 1980s. The road to rescheduling runs as follows. A country or a company borrows so much that its lenders grow nervous. They start lending for shorter and shorter maturities. Eventually the borrower, though still paying INTEREST on its debt, is unable to repay capital as it falls due. It therefore asks to reschedule – that is, to escape its immediate repayment commitments by converting short-term loans into longer-term ones.

BANKS have grown used to the idea, as long as only the capital element in their loans is being rescheduled. They object violently to suggestions that interest should be rescheduled – because that means that their loans would not be earning anything for a while, and a 'non-performing asset' is hardly different from a liability.

Countries wishing to reschedule their official debt should apply to the PARIS CLUB; if their commercial debt is the problem, they should talk to their biggest bankers. These will bring together the huge number of banks who have lent something to the would-be rescheduler (1,400 banks, in the case of Mexico); spend expensive hours in hotels and on telexes; and finally come up with a rescheduling package that saves their collective face, but does nothing to persuade them that the rescheduler deserves to be lent any more. By stopping 'new money', however, they only bring closer the day when their borrower will ask for another rescheduling or will DEFAULT.

Reserve currencies. Term commonly used to describe the form in which CENTRAL BANKS hold their countries' foreign reserves. In 1981, the split among industrial countries was 59 per cent in gold, 35 per cent in foreign currencies (including ECUs) and 6 per cent in SPECIAL DRAWING RIGHTS available at the INTERNATIONAL MONETARY FUND. Among foreign currencies, if ECUs issued against gold are excluded, the dollar accounted for 79 per cent, with the D-Mark 11 per cent, yen 3 per cent and sterling $\frac{1}{2}$ per cent. Including ECUs, the dollar accounted for 56 per cent. The D-Mark (9 per cent) and yen ($2\frac{1}{2}$ per cent) have become more significant as the years pass and the mighty dollar looks more volatile.

Restrictive practices. Generic term for anything that inhibits COM-PETITION and prevents the output of a firm or industry from being as large as it could be relative to its inputs. Examples abound, in blue-, white- and striped-collar jobs. TRADE UNIONS and management may agree that five people will be employed on a job that needs only four; those five will be members of three different unions; the electrician cannot turn his hand to a spot of maintenance if the engineer happens to be in the loo. In the professions, the number of new professionals is often restricted by the arcane rules of self-regulating institutes, or by unnecessarily long periods of study and apprenticeship.

Take one particularly British example of a professional restrictive practice – the law, where practitioners are divided into barristers and solicitors. In England and Wales (Scotland is different) nobody can become a barrister who has not studied law at university, joined one of four inns of court, and eaten twenty-four dinners in his or her inn (all in London). If they survive and want to practise as a barrister, they must then serve as a 'pupil' to another barrister for a year or more. They can then join a set of chambers – the *sine qua non* of professional practice – though vacancies are rare. The prize at the end: only barristers can appear in the high court or above, and by tradition only barristers are appointed to the judiciary.

Restrictive practices flourish, though those that involve collusion between firms are formally governed by various types of ANTI-TRUST law.

Retail banking. BANKS that have their 'shops' in the high street, taking deposits from all and sundry and offering the full range of personal banking services – loans, overdrafts and so on. In most European countries, the biggest banks derive their strength from their retailing base. In the United States, however, some of the biggest banks in the world do virtually no retail business. Their deposits come from corporations plus their borrowing in the INTERBANK MARKET; they lend almost exclusively to companies and countries.

Retail price index. Most common measure of INFLATION in Britain. In the United States, West Germany and other countries, a consumer price index serves the same purpose. The index (see INDEX NUMBERS) reflects prices of a basket of goods and services, weighted according to the spending patterns of a 'typical' family. In Britain, for example, food has a weight of 20.6 per cent, compared with only 6.2 per cent for fuel and light. Weights are changed periodically, and new items inserted. This often gives rise to charges of cooking the index; most people are, by definition, not average, so feel that the index does not reflect their cost of living. Accepting this, some governments collect other indexes – for example, for pensioners in Britain, for consumers by geographical area in America. However it is calculated, the retail price index usually rises.

Returns to scale. How does output vary as the amount of inputs – labour, raw materials, capital and so on – change? If those inputs are doubled and output more than doubles, returns to scale increase; if doubled inputs produce doubled output, returns are constant; if doubled inputs fail to double output, returns decrease. Note, though, that *all* inputs must vary: contrast this with the 'law' of DIMINISHING RETURNS, when only one input is altered.

Revaluation. Literally, a change in the value of something, whether it be an EXCHANGE RATE or a company's ASSETS. Though formally a neutral word, revaluation is usually taken to mean an upward change in value, the opposite of DEVALUATION. See also J-CURVE for the effects such a change can have.

Reverse yield gap. See YIELD GAP.

Ricardo, David. During a short life (1772–1823), he made a fortune as a British STOCKBROKER, owned Gatcombe Park (now better known as the horsey home of Princess Anne), was a member of parliament, and achieved lasting fame by writing *The Principles of Political Economy and Taxation*. It was first published in 1817, and holds an important place in both CLASSICAL and MARXIST economic theory. Ricardo analysed the distribution of national income between wages and profits, arguing that 'there can be no rise in the value of labour without a fall of profits'.

Rights issues. A company wanting to raise more capital can offer extra shares to its existing shareholders. They can choose whether or not to buy them. The offer is proportional to their stakes – for example, one new share for each ten held. Compare with SCRIP ISSUES, NEW ISSUES.

Risk. Means more or less what the man in the street understands it to mean, and then crops up in various forms of jargon. A 'risk-averse' individual or company plays safe, spreading ASSETS widely and safely. The returns on those assets are correspondingly smaller, whereas some investments need to offer a 'risk premium' above the normal rate of return if they are to attract money. 'Risk capital', sometimes also known as VENTURE CAPITAL, is provided on the tacit understanding that it may all be lost if a scheme or company goes bust.

Risk depends on the probability of certain things – failure or success, big or small losses, big or small profits – happening. And PROBABILITY in economics has a special meaning.

Rooker–Wise amendment. Two otherwise obscure members of Britain's parliament passed into the annals of tax law in 1977, when they sponsored a successful amendment to the Finance Bill, introducing a form of INDEXATION. Their amendment required the government in its spring BUDGET to raise the tax-free threshold for all personal INCOME TAX by the percentage increase in retail prices in the previous year. There was one let-out: the government could avoid this change if it obtained parliament's permission to do so.

Royalties. A reward for cleverness, whether it be for the inventor of a superior mousetrap or the author of a best seller. Also a reward for ownership – for example, mining royalties paid to the landowner on whose property minerals have been found. Royalty agreements are drawn up in advance between the inventor or landowner, and a company he is allowing to exploit the discovery. They typically provide the inventor or landowner with a certain percentage of the receipts from sales by the company.

S

Sales tax. Generic term for indirect TAXATION. Sales taxes can be levied only on the final consumer (for example, purchase taxes) or at different stages of production (for example, VALUE ADDED TAX). They can be *ad valorem* taxes – that is, expressed as a percentage of the price – or SPECIFIC DUTIES, which have a particular value, such as £1 per bottle of whisky.

Satisficing. Businessmen's goals have long absorbed economists. Standard NEO-CLASSICAL ECONOMIC theory has them aiming to maximize profits. An alternative view, coined by Nobel prize winner H. A. Simon, sees businessmen wanting to 'satisfice' – that is, achieve certain targets for sales, profits, market share, that may not coincide with maximum profits but will inflate boardroom egos and keep shareholders happy.

Savings. By definition, the difference between income and expenditure. In theory, all three chunks of the economy – households, firms and government – could save, but in practice households usually provide the savings which firms and government then borrow. (To complete the picture, foreigners also participate in this FLOW OF FUNDS between savers and borrowers.)

Personal savings vary enormously between age groups and countries, but much less between income groups. The notion that as people get richer they will save a higher proportion of their income has no empirical backing. But people do vary their savings behaviour over their lifetime, saving heavily in their early working years, then spending a lot while bringing up children, saving again for retirement, and then living off their nest eggs in old age. Average PROPENSITIES to save can therefore swing between being negative (that is, spending more than your income, by borrowing or running down savings) to perhaps a positive 0.5 – saving half your income – at your most thrifty.

Table 11 *Personal savings as a percentage of personal disposable income, 1981*

United States	6.4
Japan	19.2
West Germany	13.8
France	14.8
Britain	13.7
Canada	11.9

Source: OECD; US Department of Commerce.

Savings also depend on such things as the level of INTEREST rates (real, rather than nominal), the desired level of liquid assets (see WEALTH EFFECT), and the tax advantages of savings. In the United States, the taxman favours borrowers: interest payments on all borrowing for 'capital' spending (any number of houses, hi-fis or hot tips in the stock market) are tax deductible. By contrast, interest rate ceilings – to prevent usury – have been only cautiously abolished, long after INFLATION had made a nonsense of all of them. These American peculiarities help to explain the figures in Table 11.

Savings and loan associations. American financial institutions that lend mainly for house purchase: the equivalent of Britain's BUILDING SOCIETIES. They began life in the 1850s, as building and loan associations. Today, S & Ls are the biggest deposit taking institutions for small savers: at the end of 1981, they held $525 billion of deposits, compared with $155 billion for savings banks (the two types of institutions are collectively known as 'thrifts').

Like most financial institutions, S & Ls borrow short term to lend long: a risky business, but not too bad provided interest rates on loans can be adjusted whenever deposit rates are. Unfortunately for the S & Ls, the United States has a long history of fixed rate mortgages. In the 1970s, S & Ls therefore found themselves having to raise interest rates to attract deposits while the bulk of their mortgages provided unchanging interest payments. Their margins were badly squeezed; worse, interest rate ceilings made it hard for them to offer market rates to depositors (see REGULATION Q), so they started losing custom to competitors like MONEY MARKET FUNDS. Many S & Ls either closed down or were merged into BANKS and other financial institutions.

Savings bank. See BANK.

Say's law. Supply creates its own demand, according to the French economist Jean Baptiste Say (1767–1832). Nonsense, think KEYNESIANS who want DEMAND to be strong enough to bring forth all supplies (especially of labour). SUPPLY SIDE ECONOMICS has only a tenuous link with Say's law.

Scrip issues. An issue of extra shares to existing shareholders for which they do not have to pay: for example, one new share is granted for each ten held. Compare with RIGHTS ISSUES.

Seasonality. Almost all economic activity has some kind of seasonal pattern – for example, less construction work in winter, more demand for bank notes in the run-up to Christmas. To reveal underlying trends, statistics are seasonally adjusted to eliminate these quirks.

Secondary bank. Term used to describe second-rung (and often second-rate) banks that flourished in Britain in the early 1970s. They came under the supervision of the Department of Trade rather than the BANK OF ENGLAND. They borrowed heavily by offering higher interest rates than the clearing banks did, and lent heavily to property companies during the property boom of 1971–73. When the boom went bust, many secondary banks had to be saved from collapse by the clearing banks and other City institutions, directed by the Bank of England.

Securities. Originally documents proving ownership of property or rights to income that could be used as collateral for a bank loan, now more narrowly applied to STOCKS, shares (see EQUITIES), bonds (BOND MARKET) and gilts (GILT-EDGED STOCK) – that is, all interest-bearing paper traded on STOCK EXCHANGES or CAPITAL MARKETS.

Securities and Exchange Commission. The watchdog of the American SECURITIES industry, established in 1934. The SEC has five members, appointed by the President; its job is to prevent fraud, insider dealing and other financial hanky-panky to which STOCK EXCHANGES are prone to degenerate. Companies quoted on a stock exchange, or with assets of $1 million plus and 500 or more shareholders, are required to file information on their activities. These disclosure requirements are far more stringent than those of other stock exchanges.

Seignorage. Origins lie in the levy claimed by rulers for allowing metals to be turned into coins. The word has come to have modern connotations, describing the power of a country whose CURRENCY is held by other countries as a RESERVE (CURRENCY) asset. Only the United States has real seignorage powers today: it can pay for its IMPORTS with its own currency, whereas everybody else has to use FOREIGN EXCHANGE.

Selective employment tax. One of many experiments intended to raise Britain's dismally slow GROWTH rate. Introduced by a Labour government in 1966, abolished by a Tory one in 1973, the SET was a PAYROLL TAX levied on all firms, but then returned to some. The net effect was to tax service industries in order to subsidize (supposedly faster-growing) manufacturing.

Services. Those fruits of economic activity which you can't drop on your foot – anything from hairdressing to restaurants to transport to insurance and accountancy. As economies develop, they pass from being predominantly agricultural to predominantly industrial; they then become steadily more dependent on service 'industries' for both

Table 12 *Services as a percentage of output and employment*

	Output		Employment	
	1950	1980	1950	1980
United States	54.6	62.6	52.4	65.9
Japan	42.2	52.8	29.4	54.2
W. Germany	40.2	49.1	30.2	49.2
France	38.0	51.0	34.7*	55.3
Britain	46.1	57.5	46.7	59.2
Canada	46.5	43.7	41.6	66.0

*1954.
Source: OECD; UN; ILO; national sources.

output and employment. Table 12 shows how that has happened in a sample of countries.

As services loom larger in national economic life, so their importance grows in international trade (see INVISIBLE TRADE) as well. By 1980 they accounted for an estimated \$620 billion, roughly one quarter of the value of world trade. This total was shared in 1980 into four main categories: transport (22 per cent), tourism (16 per cent), miscellaneous goods and services (25 per cent) and interest, profits and dividends (37 per cent).

Shadow pricing. Economists have long recognized that prices of many goods and services either do not exist or are not set in free markets. Examples abound in CENTRALLY PLANNED ECONOMIES, where prices are decreed by bureaucrats; large firms, too, may transfer goods from one division to another at prices that do not obtain in outside markets. Shadow pricing is designed to get over this problem, by attaching imputed prices to the elusive products, treating them 'as if' they were being priced in free markets. Shadow pricing is commonly used in COST–BENEFIT ANALYSIS, where the whole purpose is to capture all the variables involved in an INVESTMENT decision, not simply those where market prices exist.

Shareholders' funds. Accounting term for sums that ultimately 'belong' to a company's shareholders – that is, issued capital (the face value of shares), retained profits or other reserves. But shareholders should not start counting their cash – these funds are not normally paid to shareholders unless the business goes bust.

Shares. See EQUITIES.

Sherman Anti-trust Act. See ANTI-TRUST.

Short term. Interchangeable with short run. Phrase frequently voiced by economists, and practised by politicians. If it has any literal meaning, it measures periods between one day ('short-term changes in share prices') and ten years ('the short-term effects of nuclear energy may be good, but what about the long-term?'). Contrast with KEYNES's undeniable dictum – 'In the long run, we are all dead' – which was intended to divert attention from what he saw as the damaging assumption of orthodox economists that, in the long term, economies would gravitate back to FULL EMPLOYMENT.

Sinking fund. Sink to swim. Way to repay debt in a lump sum when a loan matures, by making regular repayments of principal into a fund. See AMORTIZATION.

Slump. Another word for DEPRESSION; both are an extreme form of RECESSION. Worst slump in American history was 1930–33, when GNP fell 30 per cent in four years. In Britain, GDP fell 7 per cent in the two years 1930–31; in 1980–81, it fell $5\frac{1}{2}$ per cent over 18 months.

Small business. Much in vogue among politicians and economists, having been largely disregarded by them in the 1950s and 1960s. Definitions of 'small' vary from country to country, but all show that small companies account for a large proportion of output and employment. For example, almost 60 per cent of all manufacturing workers in Japan are in companies with fewer than 100 employees. For the United States and Britain, the comparable figure is below 20 per cent (which is one reason why Japan is so much more productive, say small-is-beautiful fans).

Within each country, small firms certainly appear to have been more dynamic than big ones. During the 1970s, the giant American companies in the *Fortune* 500 list did not increase their workforces at all, while American employment rose by 20 million. That suggests that all the growth came from medium and small firms: what is less clear is (1) how far existing small companies expanded ('acorns into oak trees'), or whether it was more a matter of new companies starting up; and (2) how far small firms depend on the giants to provide them with sub-contracting work. The answers to (1) influence the kind of tax incentives that governments provide to small companies, while (2) would determine whether small companies are autonomous springs of growth or merely derivative. If the latter, then the health of big companies is still as important as yesterday's fashion decreed.

Smith, Adam (1723–90). Father of modern economics, his book *Inquiry into the Nature and Causes of the Wealth of Nations* (1776) is still regarded as a bible of CLASSICAL ECONOMICS. He emphasized the importance of specialization (which he called the DIVISION OF

LABOUR), TECHNICAL PROGRESS and capital INVESTMENT as the main motors of economic growth. Above all, he believed in the INVISIBLE HAND – the idea that free markets would ensure that the pursuit of self-interest produced benefits for all.

Smithsonian Agreement. The final phase of fixed EXCHANGE RATES. The GROUP OF TEN countries met at the Smithsonian Institute, Washington, DC, in December 1971 to agree on a realignment of CURRENCIES. The dollar was devalued against gold (from $35 an ounce to $38) and against most other currencies by a trade weighted 8 per cent.

The agreement was a 'victory' for the United States, which had wanted other currencies – notably the D-Mark and yen – to raise their exchange rates to offset worsening American competitiveness. The Nixon administration had bullied other governments, by ceasing in August 1971 to convert dollars into gold and by imposing a 10 per cent surcharge on all dutiable imports. Within a few months, the Smithsonian changes became irrelevant. The pound was floated in June 1972, and others soon followed. None the less, the date of Smithsonian lingers on: many indexes of EFFECTIVE EXCHANGE RATES use December 1971 as the base for their calculations.

Snake. Colloquial name for the exchange rate system used to link some European currencies: the 'mini-snake' from 1972 until 1979, followed by the 'boa' – the EUROPEAN MONETARY SYSTEM.

Social contract. Originates in the work of French philosopher Jean-Jacques Rousseau (1712–1778), but has come to be part of the jargon of British INCOMES POLICY. The 1974–79 Labour government in Britain claimed to have a social contract with the TRADE UNIONS. In return for favourable labour legislation, PRICE CONTROLS, DIVIDEND controls and higher PUBLIC EXPENDITURE, trade unionists were supposed to demand smaller wage increases. As with all incomes policies, it worked for a time. INFLATION fell from a peak of 27 per cent in 1975 to only $7\frac{1}{2}$ per cent in 1978. But the third year of income restraint proved too much. Strikes and disruption in the winter of 1978–79 led to Labour's defeat in the May 1979 election. The social contract was rejected as being neither social, nor a contract.

Social security. Safety net for the poor, the old and the unemployed. Typically, employees pay a contribution (a fixed proportion of their wages) to the government's social security fund, matched by a similar (normally larger) contribution by the employer (see NATIONAL INSURANCE). Out of this fund are paid unemployment benefits and other welfare payments. In the 1980–82 recession, many countries found their social security funds swamped by high UNEMPLOYMENT.

Soft currencies. Phrase with a somewhat old-fashioned ring to it, since no currency can claim to have been really 'hard' (that is, retained its value) during the inflationary 1970s. But soft currencies are unmistakably the wall flowers at the FOREIGN EXCHANGE dealers' ball. They are not held as RESERVE (CURRENCY) assets; even for short periods, most foreigners can be persuaded to hold them only in return for usurious INTEREST rates. Examples (in ascending order of softness): the Italian lira, the Icelandic Króna, the Mexican peso.

Soft loans. Money lent on favourable terms that could not be obtained in the market. Most subsidies come as lower INTEREST rates and longer maturities. Governments give soft loans to domestic industries they wish to encourage. Also common in overseas aid programmes; see, for example, the International Development Association, part of the WORLD BANK.

Special deposits. Method of MONETARY CONTROL, used by BANK OF ENGLAND and several other CENTRAL BANKS. COMMERCIAL BANKS are required to place a (variable) proportion of their DEPOSITS with the central bank, earning interest (usually the rate offered on TREASURY BILLS) but effectively debarred from being lent. They therefore supplement requirements like cash ratios, liquid asset ratios and reserve asset ratios through which banks are prevented from lending out all their deposits in any way they choose. Special deposits were introduced by Bank of England in 1958. They were abolished in 1981, when the Bank reformed its system of MONETARY CONTROL.

Special drawing rights (SDRs). The nearest thing to 'world money', though of a specialized and somewhat arcane kind. SDRs were conceived in 1967 at the annual meeting of the INTERNATIONAL MONETARY FUND held in Rio de Janeiro. They were introduced in 1970, as an international RESERVE (CURRENCY) asset intended partially to replace gold and national CURRENCIES in settling international transactions. The SDR would, it was thought, have the virtues of stability (it was first fixed in terms of gold, then of a basket of currencies) and of taking the reserve burden off the dollar's increasingly wobbly shoulders. The IMF uses SDRs for all its book-keeping purposes. It also issues SDRs periodically to all its member countries, as a way of boosting international LIQUIDITY.

The valuation of the SDR has altered over time. Initially it was intended to be worth 1/35 of an ounce of gold – that is, $1 in the days when the gold price was fixed. When the dollar devalued against gold in 1971, the SDR was worth $1.0857 (still 1/35 of an ounce of gold). Floating currencies became the norm in 1973, so in 1974 the SDR was valued by a weighted basket of sixteen currencies (weights being determined by each country's share in world GNP, world trade and international reserves). This still gave the SDR an unwieldy, artificial persona. In 1981 it was slimmed down to just five currencies – the dollar (with a weight of 42 per cent), yen (13 per cent), D-Mark (19 per cent), French franc (13 per cent) and sterling (13 per cent). Their weights are to be reviewed at least once every five years, beginning 1 January 1986.

The slimming of the SDR coincided with it starting to offer market INTEREST rates. Initially the SDR carried a dollar interest rate of $1\frac{1}{2}$ per cent. After the SDR became a basket of sixteen currencies, it was allowed to offer interest equal to 60 per cent of the market rates of the five main currencies. In 1979, this was increased to 80 per cent. Finally, in 1981, the IMF switched to paying full market rates – again a weighted average of the market rates in the five main currencies. In each case, the rate chosen has usually been three-month TREASURY BILLS.

For the first ten years of its life, the SDR was doomed to be understood only by CENTRAL BANKERS and used only by the IMF for denominating its ASSETS and liabilities. Since it became based on market realities – only five currencies, paying market interest rates – the SDR has acquired a private life of its own. COMMERCIAL BANKS increasingly accept deposits and make loans denominated in SDRs. Some MULTINATIONAL companies have started using SDRs for their own accounting purposes. A sliver of international trade is now being settled in SDRs. This increased activity shows the SDRs' merits for risk-averse businesses who feel their real purpose is to make things, not speculate on the currency markets. By using the SDR, they expect to avoid the big losses and gains that can come from exclusive exposure to a single currency.

SDR fans say that it will gradually supersede the dollar as the dominant reserve asset. To try and force that change, in the late 1970s the IMF proposed opening a 'substitution account' through which central banks could swap unwanted dollars for SDRs, at a predetermined exchange rate. The plan was rejected in 1980, largely because the Americans did not like the idea of dethroning the dollar and replacing it with the SDR hybrid. The dollar anyway began strengthening at about that time; central banks no longer wanted to get rid of their dollars; the idea of a substitution account was shelved – until, some say, the next bout of dollar weakness.

Specific duties. Indirect taxes (see TAXATION) that are not directly linked to the value of what is being taxed. Example: £1 on a bottle of whisky, £0.50 per lb of tobacco, irrespective of whether the factory gate prices of whisky and tobacco rise or fall. Contrast with *ad valorem* taxes, like VALUE ADDED TAX, which are levied as a percentage of the product price. Failure to raise specific duties in line with inflation results in 'negative FISCAL DRAG'. British budgets have effectively indexed specific duties since the mid-1970s. In the United States, some duties – for example, on tobacco – have not been changed for twenty years.

Speculation. Much abused term, largely because it has become a convenient term of abuse. Strictly speaking, speculators are confined to COMMODITY and CURRENCY markets – where they are usually outnumbered by people who are not speculators. Instead most are traders, who need, for example, copper or Canadian dollars to make widgets and finance their business. Traders know that prices can fluctuate: to protect themselves against such fluctuations, they can match their purchase or sale in the SPOT MARKET with a contract in the FUTURES market (see HEDGING for how this is done).

Speculators also know that prices fluctuate; unlike traders, however, they do not hedge. They deal for the simple purpose of making money. Fluctuations, and informed gambling about their direction, are the essence of their business, which takes various forms. Examples:

● They buy at price x in the spot market, hoping to sell later at a profit.

● They sell a commodity in the futures market, hoping its spot price will have fallen below their contracted futures price by the time they have to deliver on their contract.

The key characteristic of speculation is therefore that it does not match a spot contract with a futures one. Speculators leave themselves 'uncovered', believing that they know better than the market. This is helpful for hedgers; they are insulated from risk only because speculators are prepared to expose themselves to it.

EQUITY and BOND MARKETS are not fertile ground for speculation, because they lack a futures market. However, speculators can take advantage of the accounting system which does not require buyers and sellers of shares to settle their accounts immediately (see STOCK EXCHANGE). At the beginning of one account they may buy 1,000 shares in a company without intending to take delivery of them and actually have to pay. If the share price rises during the account, the speculator will then sell and take his profit. See also STAG for a way of speculating on share prices while barely writing a cheque.

Spot markets. Currency and commodity markets where transactions are for immediate delivery ('on the spot', though that derivation of the term is not the only one). Compare with FORWARD MARKETS or FUTURES markets, where delivery is scheduled at some specified point in the future.

Spread. Any difference between buying and selling rates, but particularly the interest rate margin above LIBOR, the LONDON INTERBANK OFFER RATE paid by Euromarket borrowers. The spread demanded by banks on loans effectively indicates their profit; higher risks demand bigger spread.

Stag. Somebody who profits from a fixed price sale of shares (see EQUITIES) or bonds (see BOND MARKET), by selling his allocation immediately at more than he paid for it. Arouses feelings of outrage and envy in others: better approach is to end opportunities for stagging by using TENDERS for issuing new stock.

Stagflation. Origins of term unclear. Meaning very familiar: a combination of stagnation in economic activity plus INFLATION. Sometimes expressed as a 'misery index', the sum of unemployment and inflation rates. The index rose during the 1970s: see Table 13.

Table 13 *Misery indices*

	USA	Japan	West Germany	France	Britain	Canada
1971	10.1	7.3	6.2	8.1	13.4	9.0
1972	8.8	5.9	6.3	8.9	11.3	11.0
1973	11.0	13.0	7.8	9.9	12.4	13.1
1974	16.5	25.9	8.6	16.5	19.1	16.1
1975	17.4	18.7	9.7	15.9	28.9	17.7
1976	13.3	11.3	8.2	14.0	22.6	14.6
1977	15.4	10.1	7.4	14.1	22.3	16.0
1978	13.6	6.0	6.2	14.3	14.7	17.3
1979	17.0	5.7	7.3	16.7	19.1	16.5
1980	20.5	10.0	8.6	19.9	25.3	17.6
1981	17.0	7.1	10.2	21.0	23.1	19.9

Source: OECD.

Statistics. Prompted one of Benjamin Disraeli's best-known put-downs: 'There are three kinds of lies: lies, damned lies and statistics.' Pity the poor statistician, engaged in the essential task of collecting figures, 'cleaning' them for reliability and comparability, and then publishing them in accessible form. Disraeli's jibe was really directed at those who use statistics speciously, to prove any point they like. Main culprits: politicians and economists, about whom many ruder things have been said.

Sterling area. Once the cornerstone of world finance, now a museum piece. The sterling area included all countries whose EXCHANGE RATES were usually pegged to sterling and who held their FOREIGN EXCHANGE reserves (see RESERVE CURRENCY) in sterling. That meant Commonwealth countries (except Canada), plus places as diverse as Ireland and Kuwait.

Until the First World War, sterling was the world's main currency. It then started losing its shine, and sterling balances held abroad became an awkward embarassment for Britain. Any CENTRAL BANK deciding to convert some of its reserves from sterling into dollars – the new favourite reserve currency – could start a run on the pound.

After the Second World War, membership of the sterling area depended on a country maintaining more or less the same EXCHANGE CONTROLS as Britain did. Countries gradually diversified their reserves out of sterling: the 'area' ceased to have any meaning.

Stockbrokers. Dealers in STOCKS and shares (see EQUITIES) that act as an intermediary between the purchaser and (in Britain) the JOBBERS in the STOCK EXCHANGES. Stockbrokers typically earn a fee for their services.

Stock exchange. A market where shares (see EQUITIES), bonds (see BOND MARKET) and other kinds of SECURITIES are traded, and where fresh CAPITAL can be raised. Taking EQUITIES alone, the league table of markets is as in Table 14.

Movements in share prices are expressed in terms of an index of

Table 14   *Stock markets*

	Capitalization ($ billion)	No. of quoted companies (end 1982)
New York	1,290	1,600
Tokyo	380	1,440
London	185	2,800
Toronto	100	830
Frankfurt	65	450

representative shares. The best known are the DOW JONES INDEX in New York and the FINANCIAL TIMES INDEX in London.

Stock exchanges are sometimes known by the generic term BOURSES. Originally that referred to the principal place in a country where trade between that nation and others was settled by exchanging bills, and where merchants made deals for goods. In Britain this foreign bill business was, until 1921, conducted at the Royal Exchange.

Transactions on a stock exchange seldom have to be settled instantaneously. In London, for example, there are twenty-four ACCOUNT PERIODS in a year. At the end of each period, on 'settlement day', buyers have to pay for what they have bought during the period while sellers receive their cash. The New York Stock Exchange has a different approach: settlement is required within five working days of the transaction. See also BEARS, BULLS, NEW ISSUES, RIGHTS ISSUES, OPTION DEALING.

Stock–output ratio. Self-evident definition: the size of STOCKS (INVENTORIES) relative to output in a given firm, industry or economy. The ratio can indicate the future prospects for output: if stocks are low by historical standards then restocking should soon boost demand.

Stocks. Two meanings:

● Colloquialism for EQUITIES (as in STOCK EXCHANGE); more accurately, paper issued by companies or governments in consolidated form, so that it can be transacted in any amount. Shares, by contrast, cannot be bought or sold in fractions of a share.

● English for what Americans call INVENTORIES – goods held by companies in warehouses, so they are not caught short by unexpected needs. The stock cycle has a powerful effect on economic activity. If companies are adding to stocks, they are producing more than they are selling, and vice versa. Note that changes in stocks can give a boost to output even without companies actually adding to their stocks. It is enough for them simply to slow down their rate of destocking. Example:

		Year 1	Year 2	Year 3	Year 4
A	Factory output (£m)	110	90	90	95
B	Consumer demand (£m)	100	100	100	100
C	Change in stocks (= A − B) (£m)	+10	−10	−10	−5
D	Factory output (% change)		−18	0	$+5\frac{1}{2}$

Note that changes in the value of stocks can distort company profits (see CURRENT COST ACCOUNTING).

Stop–go. Colloquialism for the policies of economic management followed in the 1950s and 1960s. When governments saw activity flagging and UNEMPLOYMENT rising, they expanded demand by raising PUBLIC EXPENDITURE and/or cutting taxes (see TAXATION) ('go'); when INFLATIONARY signs of overheating appeared, they reduced spending and/or raised taxes ('stop'). As inflation accelerated, disillusion with KEYNESIAN FISCAL POLICIES spread during the 1970s; stop–go became stop–stop. See FINE TUNING.

Structural unemployment. The most difficult kind of UNEMPLOYMENT to solve, where dole queues are caused by basic problems: old-fashioned firms going bust in areas that are unlikely to be quickly revived by new firms or jobs. Contrast with FRICTIONAL UNEMPLOYMENT, caused by workers simply moving between jobs, and taking their time over it.

Subsidies. Money paid to keep prices below what they would be in a free market (see PRICE CONTROLS). Usually come from governments, to subsidize food, or fuel, or loans for particular purposes.

Substitution effect. When the price of petrol falls, people buy more of it: the ubiquitous law of supply and demand. But the extra gallons bought are influenced by two forces:
• The fact that petrol becomes cheaper relative to everything else, so people switch to it.
• Since the price of something has fallen, purchasing power (real income) rises – so people have more to spend on everything, including petrol.
The first of these two is called the substitution effect; the second is the 'income effect'. The first is always positive – lower price, more bought. The second could be negative, if the good is so inferior that people use their extra income to buy other things. Economists have long been intrigued by the possibility that a negative income effect may outweigh the positive substitution effect. If it did, then a lower price would mean fewer sales – that is, the demand curve would slope up from left to right instead of down from left to right. One Victorian economist named Giffen claimed that this happened to potatoes; today, nobody really believes that a 'Giffen good' is more than an intellectual teaser.

Supernormal profits. The extra profits that are earned by companies beyond the minimum they need to remain in business. Under PERFECT COMPETITION, profits are normal; in any other kind of market – OLIGOPOLY, MONOPOLISTIC COMPETITION, MONOPOLY, firms move into the supernormal league. Figures 4, 5 and 6 (under COMPETITION) show what this means.

Supply side economics. Common sense elevated into contentious theory. Economists have long recognized the importance of an economy's productive capacity – its stock of capital and labour, and the incentives needed to get the best out of them. However, these elemental points may have been obscured by the KEYNESIAN emphasis on managing DEMAND. As part of the reaction to Keynesianism, some politicians and economists began stressing the need to encourage supply instead. This became trivialized by the belief that cutting taxes would release new energy into the economy. The *reductio ad absurdum* of this view was the LAFFER CURVE – cutting tax rates would raise tax revenues.

Swaps. The term used for a transaction between CENTRAL BANKS (and sometimes national treasuries) as part of their intervention in CURRENCY markets. If central bank A wants to support its EXCHANGE RATE, it may borrow a foreign currency (usually dollars) from central bank B, lending its own currency in return. The swap is for a limited period – typically six months – and the borrowing bank is obliged to return the same amount of dollars. If its own currency depreciates in the meantime, therefore, it will lose on the transaction.

Swaps were developed in the 1960s, and were used by the United States in the late 1970s. It borrowed D-Marks, Swiss francs and yen to prop up the dollar. The support was ineffectual: the United States lost an estimated $70m on the deal.

T

Tap stocks. A gradualist method of selling SECURITIES widely used by the BANK OF ENGLAND for marketing GILT-EDGED STOCKS. A fixed price is put on a stock, and it is then offered for sale. Whatever is not bought immediately will be held 'on tap', and released ('trickled') to buyers as and when they want it. If the price chosen is too high to ensure a sell-out, the seller may subsequently have to cut it. That is understandably unpopular with the original buyers.

Compare taps with TENDERS, where the securities are put up for auction to the highest bidders, thus guaranteeing an immediate sale. This is the method employed by the United States Treasury for marketing its securities. The Bank of England has been moving in this direction since the mid-1970s, developing a tender–tap hybrid. A minimum price is put on a tender; if bids above this minimum do not buy out the whole issue, the rest is treated like a conventional tap stock.

Tariffs. A tax on IMPORTS, usually expressed as a percentage of the delivered price. Originally intended as a method of raising revenue for the government, they are now commonly used as a form of PROTECTIONISM – to restrict imports and shield domestic producers from foreign competition. A succession of negotiated reductions under the GENERAL AGREEMENT ON TARIFFS AND TRADE has reduced the importance of tariffs in many countries (though on particular products they can still be very high). Note, though, that the level of a tariff may not be an accurate guide to how far a domestic producer is being protected – see EFFECTIVE PROTECTION.

Tâtonnement. Literally, groping. It describes how buyers and sellers bargain themselves into a market-clearing EQUILIBRIUM, as seen through the eyes of the French economist, Léon Walras (1834–1910). To aid groping, Walras also employed the illustrative image of an auctioneer, who received bids and offered information until buyers and sellers were satisfied.

Taxation. First law of all taxmen: 'Shear the sheep, don't skin them'. For details of how they do it, see CORPORATION TAX, INCOME TAX, POLL TAX, RATES, SALES TAX, TURNOVER TAX, VALUE ADDED TAX, WEALTH TAX. For an idea of how successful they have been, see Table 15.

Table 15   *Taxation* as percentage of GDP*

	1960	1970	1980
United States	26.3	30.1	30.0
Japan	19.1	19.7	26.5
W. Germany	31.3	32.8	37.4
France	33.9†	35.6	42.5
Britain	28.5	37.5	35.9
Canada	24.2	32.0	33.6

* including SOCIAL SECURITY contributions.
† 1962.
Source: OECD.

Taxes are sometimes categorized according to whether they are proportional, progressive or regressive.
● A proportional tax is 'income blind', taking exactly the same proportion of Lord Bigbucks' income as of Miss Pauper's.
● A progressive tax takes proportionately more the higher up the income scale it bites. Example: most income tax systems have a basic rate – say 15 per cent – which applies to incomes in a certain band but then increases in stages as incomes rise.
● A regressive tax, by contrast, takes disproportionately more from the poor than the rich. Some indirect taxes are regressive – SPECIFIC DUTIES, for example, because £1 on a bottle of booze is a higher percentage of a poor drinker's income than a rich one's.

Note, though, that the simple formula direct equals progressive, indirect equals regressive is often misleading. Income tax allowances, especially on INTEREST payments, can sharply reduce the average tax rate of the highly paid. And exemptions from indirect tax – for example, food and fuel are usually free of VAT – can mean that the poorest pay little tax, because their budgets are biased towards exempt items.

Tax haven. Palm trees and brass plates, the formal home of companies and individuals who do business elsewhere but are taxed in their havens at between 0 and 5 per cent. The caricature is not wholly false, but tax authorities in the rest of the world are always keen to change it. They impose certain residency requirements on firms and individuals: it is almost impossible to live in New York or London for more than a few months a year without being legally required to pay American or British taxes. Taxmen have also become better at checking the accounts of MULTINATIONALS to make sure they are not TRANS-FER PRICING – arranging their affairs so that their tax liabilities accrue in some far-off, low-taxed spot.

The havens themselves hope to benefit from some of the money they attract being spent there. The more mature of them have no wish to be used purely as a post-box; they are also keen to improve their image, so have become a bit sniffy about who they allow in. The best known havens are Monaco, Jersey, Liechtenstein, the Cayman Islands and the Bahamas.

Technical progress. The critical link in the chain of economic GROWTH. Strictly, the element which ensures that a given quantity of inputs – land, labour, capital, raw materials – produces a growing output of goods and services. Economists have classified technical progress by whether it increases or reduces the ratio of capital to labour; ditto for the ratio of capital to output.

Tenders. Method of selling anything, but especially SECURITIES by auction to the highest bidder. Compare with TAP STOCKS.

Terms of trade. The ratio of EXPORT prices to IMPORT prices, expressed as an index because it is movements in the terms of trade that matter. Example:

	Year 1	Year 2	Year 3
Export prices	100	110	110
Import prices	100	100	105
Terms of trade index	100	110	104.8
Change in index (%)	—	+10	−4.7

When the index rises, the terms of trade improve; when it falls, they deteriorate.

The index measures the purchasing power of a country's exports in terms of the imports it must buy. If the terms of trade improve, a given quantity of exports will earn enough FOREIGN EXCHANGE to buy a larger quantity of imports than before. This happened most dramatically in the case of oil exporters after the OPEC price rises of 1973–74. Without increasing the volume of their exports, they were able to increase the volume of their imports by 21 per cent between 1973 and 1978, and still run a surplus on their current account (see BALANCE OF PAYMENTS).

Big shifts like that will distort the meaning of constant price figures for GNP. They measure the volume of output, not income, so they would not have revealed how much better off the oil exporters were as a result of higher oil prices. GNP can therefore be adjusted for changes in the terms of trade, giving a figure commonly known as gross national income (GNY).

Thresholds. Usually refers to TAXATION allowances and bands. In the United States in 1982, the first tax threshold for a single man was at $2,300; below that, income is tax-free (and the threshold will be higher if other kinds of tax breaks are claimed). In Britain in 1983–84, the first threshold occurs at £1,785.

If thresholds are not raised to offset inflation, the result will be FISCAL DRAG or what is known in the United States as 'bracket creep' – more and more people being brought into the tax net at lower and lower levels of real INCOME. Semi-automatic adjustment of thresholds has been in operation in Britain since 1977 (see ROOKER–WISE AMENDMENT); in the United States, it is promised for 1985.

Time deposits. Money placed in a DEPOSIT (ACCOUNT) for a period fixed in advance, in return for a relatively high rate of INTEREST.

Time lags. Usually refers to the gap between cause and effect. Plays a central role in economics, and is sometimes an invaluable scapegoat. Milton FRIEDMAN has described the link between monetary growth and inflation as being characterized by 'long and variable lags', which could mean just about anything. George Shultz, economics professor, treasury secretary under President Nixon and secretary of state under President Reagan, has produced an even more telling line: 'An economist's lag can be a politician's catastrophe.'

Time series. Figures for one variable – for example, industrial production, money supply – linked over time. Depending on the frequency with which the statistics are collected, a time series might show how American GNP moved over a period of twenty years. It could be combined with another time series on, say, consumer prices which provides information but no analysis; or one on, say, productivity, which implies that there is a causal connection between GNP and productivity.

Tokyo round. See GENERAL AGREEMENT ON TARIFFS AND TRADE.

Trade cycles. In extreme form, the swings from boom to bust; most economists think that such extremes can be moderated, though not entirely eliminated. See BUSINESS CYCLE, KONDRATIEFF.

Trade unions. Devils to some, saviours to others. Workers join trade unions for an annual subscription, and in return are represented in COLLECTIVE BARGAINING with a firm's management over pay, hours of work, conditions, and anything else that concerns workers. Their main weapons are disruptive ones: strikes, sit-ins, non-cooperation. So drastic action to get their way can make trade unions unpopular, especially with ordinary citizens not directly involved.

In Britain, for historical reasons there can often be more than one trade union in a factory, forcing competition between the unions for members, and necessitating several separate negotiations with the management. In West Germany, by contrast, trade unions are organized with just one main union per industry (for example, I. G. Metall, the metalworkers' union). This makes negotiation easier and minimises competitive, leapfrogging wage claims. Paradox: the West German unions were actually organized with British union advice after 1945. Reason: the British union leaders knew how their system should ideally be organized, but were unable to reorganize it because of history and vested interests. In Germany, the unions had been banned after Hitler's rise to power in 1933.

Trade war. Dramatic term for MERCANTILISM – the scramble to increase exports while reducing imports. The war has two main fronts – PROTECTIONISM (quotas, tariffs, and so on) and competitive DEVALU-ATION. The peacemaker is the GENERAL AGREEMENT ON TARIFFS AND TRADE.

Trade weighted. Commonly used with reference to exchange rates, where currency movements are weighted according to their importance in a country's trade and then expressed in an index. See EFFEC-TIVE EXCHANGE RATE.

Transfer payments. Money collected by governments through TAXA-TION, NATIONAL INSURANCE contributions and so on, and passed on directly to beneficiaries. See PUBLIC EXPENDITURE.

Transfer pricing. A tax avoiding practice commonly associated with MULTINATIONAL companies. A subsidiary in highly taxed country A sells components to another subsidiary in tax haven B for an artificially low price. This means that profits recorded in country A are themselves artificially low, while being correspondingly boosted in country B. Governments try to stop this by legislation, careful scrutiny of company accounts and international codes of conduct. As a result, transfer pricing is probably on the wane.

Treasury bills. Short-term paper issued by governments in many countries. They typically carry a three-month maturity and a fixed rate of INTEREST. They are invaluable for meeting the residual financing needs of governments during periods when revenues and receipts may be low. But excessive reliance on them creates problems for management. Treasury bills usually qualify as reserve assets for banks on which they can expand their lending. By contrast, selling bonds (see BOND MARKET) to the non-bank private sector, though more difficult to do in certain circumstances, actually contracts the money supply.

Trust-busting. Ever since economic theory demonstrated the evils of MONOPOLY – higher prices, lower output, bigger profits – compared with COMPETITION, governments have made more or less serious efforts to prevent monopolistic abuse. Official agencies are charged with trust-busting duties. For details, see ANTI-TRUST.

Turnkey contracts. Increasingly common construction and engineering deal where the contractor builds and equips a factory, power station or whatever right up to the point where the purchaser can turn a key and production starts. Third World countries are especially keen on turnkey deals as they reduce risk and make the main contractor directly responsible for subcontractors.

Turnover tax. One form of indirect TAXATION, it taxes a firm's sales revenue. This can lead to peculiar distortions, however, because a product that passes through several firms will be taxed more heavily than one that is entirely made within a single company. That is why turnover taxes are less common than SALES TAXES (levied only on retail values) and VALUE ADDED TAX (which is based on the difference between the value of a firm's purchases and of its revenues).

U

UNCTAD, UNDP, UNIDO. Ugly acronyms for international institutions. See UNITED NATIONS.

Unearned income. Words guaranteed to rile those in receipt of INTEREST and DIVIDENDS, who retort that the INCOME comes from hard earned, prudently saved capital. The slur is seldom intended; the phrase is merely a convenient way of distinguishing income from employment (EARNED INCOME) and income from capital. Having drawn that distinction, the taxman sometimes takes the opportunity to tax unearned income more heavily (see TAXATION). In Britain, there is a 15 per cent surcharge on investment income (but note that the first £7,100 is exempt); the United States has no surcharge. For a single person, the first $200 of dividend income is tax free. Thereafter, it is taxed at 'earned income' rates.

Unemployment. Conceptually simple, the number of workers without a job, usually expressed as a percentage of the workforce. In practice, the statistics are complicated, partly because definitions vary. In the United States, the unemployed are counted on the basis of a sample survey asking how many people are actively seeking work. Britain measures its unemployment by how many people choose to register for unemployment benefit. This is known to understate the true picture, because census figures show that many people (particularly married women) who would like a job have not bothered to register. In 1978, when the official figures showed 1.3 million adults out of work, an estimated 0.3 million more claimed to be keen to work. West Germany, like Britain, relies on the unemployed to register at a labour office before they are officially unemployed. See also FRICTIONAL UNEMPLOYMENT and STRUCTURAL UNEMPLOYMENT for some conceptual distinctions.

These differences make it very hard to compare unemployment rates between countries. Periodically the OECD helps by standardizing the published figures. Table 16 shows what they looked like for some of the main industrial countries in September 1982.

Table 16 *Unemployed as a percentage of labour force*

	Unstandardized	Standardized
United States	10.1	9.9
Britain	12.7	13.1
France	8.6	8.5
Japan	2.4	2.5
West Germany	8.3	6.9
Canada	12.2	12.1

Source: OECD.

Underwriter. Guarantor. When a company raises money from the STOCK EXCHANGE, either as a NEW ISSUE or as a RIGHTS ISSUE, it wants to be sure it will get all the money it expects. Its merchant bankers usually oblige: in return for an underwriting fee (about 1 per cent of the issue's value), they promise to make good any shortfall. Underwriting is also a term used interchangeably with insurers – especially as in LLOYD's of London underwriters.

Unit costs. Arithmetically, total COSTS divided by the quantity of production. Can be used to analyze company performance. Example: two companies making identical widgets but on very different scales can sensibly compare their efficiency by looking at their unit costs:

			Unit costs	
	A	B	A	B
Output (widgets)	1,000	10,000		
Total costs (£)	1m	10m	1,000	1,000
Wage costs (£)	500,000	6m	500	600
Labour costs* (£)	600,000	5.5m	600	550
Overhead costs (£)	200,000	1.5m	200	150

* Wage bill, plus pension payments, subsidized canteen, etc.

Company A ought to be able to economize on its non-wage benefits, though its smaller scale may prevent it cutting overheads. Company B seems to be employing too many people, or paying them too much.

Unit of account. One of the three stylized requirements of MONEY (the others being that it acts as a store of value and as a medium of exchange). See also the EUROPEAN CURRENCY UNIT.

United Nations. Has several economic agencies:
United Nations Conference on Trade and Development (UNCTAD). It began life as a conference in 1964, and promptly became a permanent agency of the UN general assembly. It holds periodic full-scale conferences – in 1968, 1973, 1976, 1979 and 1983, when rich and poor countries discuss everything from COMMODITY trade to shipping to debt. The most productive of these was the 1968 conference, which resulted in the generalized system of preferences, a scheme of preferentially low TARIFFS for poor countries. Between these formal sessions UNCTAD organizes numerous working groups; its secretariat, based in Geneva, is generally regarded as a spokesman for the developing world.
United Nations Development Programme (UNDP). Headquartered in New York, and formed in 1965 through the marriage of the UN Expanded Programme of Technical Assistance and the UN Special Fund. UNDP is principally concerned with technical assistance on a

wide variety of projects in the developing world. Its budget ($670 million in 1980) comes largely from voluntary contributions from UN member governments.

United Nations Industrial Development Organization (UNIDO). It was established in 1967 and is based in Vienna. Its purpose is to promote industrialization in the developing world, largely through project evaluation and advice on industrial strategy. It is committed to the so-called Lima Declaration of 1975, which aims at the developing countries having a 25 per cent share of world industrial production by the end of the century.

Universal bank. A form of banking peculiar to West Germany and Switzerland, where banks provide their customers (which range from individuals to companies to countries) with all kinds of services that in other countries might be the preserve of stockbrokers and merchant banks: investment advice; share dealing; bond issues; straight loans to companies and so on. Universal banks even get involved in company rescue plans, taking a slice of a sick company's equity and gaining representation on the board of directors.

Utility. Sometimes confused with utilitarianism ('the greatest happiness of the greatest number'), utility has a much more mundane meaning in economics: simply that if a person buys a good or service, it must have some utility – usefulness, but in a neutral sense. See CONSUMERS' SURPLUS.

V

Vacancies. The number of job openings counted by government statisticians, and thus invariably a poor guide to the demand for labour. In Britain, unfilled vacancies registered with the Department of Employment's Job Centres are estimated to be only one third of the total vacancies available. In the United States, vacancies are defined as job openings reported to state employment offices. Despite these statistical shortcomings, vacancy figures have one important use: the way they change is an accurate guide to the changing demand for labour.

Value added. Usually applied to firms, where it is defined as the value of the firm's output minus the value of all its inputs bought from other firms. This means it measures the wages paid, and profits earned, by a particular company. As a rough rule, the more value a firm can add to a product, the more successful it will be. The same analysis is sometimes applied to whole economies; those that act only as packagers or shop windows will not derive as much benefit as those who produce the bulk of the value added.

Value added tax. The most broadly based form of indirect TAXATION, it is used by all member governments of the EEC but has been shunned by other major economies – the United States, Japan and Canada. The principle of VAT is simple: though levied on the value added at each stage of production, it is intended to tax only the final consumer. Producers should therefore pay none of it; the VAT they pay on the inputs they buy from other companies is recouped when they sell their output. Take the example of a table that starts as a tree and then passes through two firms before being sold in a furniture store, and assume a VAT rate of 10 per cent. Table 17 shows the stages in VAT calculations.

Table 17   *Stages in VAT calculations*

	Pre-tax price (£)	VAT (£)	Selling price (£)	Tax payable (£)	Paid to customs by
1. Lumberjack sells tree	450	45	495	45	Lumberjack
2. Manufacturer sells table to wholesaler	600	60	660	15 (60 − 45)	Manufacturer
3. Wholesaler sells table to retailer	830	83	913	23 (83 − 60)	Wholesaler
4. Retailer sells to consumer	970	97	1,067	14 (97 − 83)	Retailer
Tax borne by consumer but collected in 4 stages £97					

Variable costs. In the short term, firms have two kinds of COSTS:
- Fixed, which include a large chunk of the wages bill, the cost of land, buildings and machinery, and so on.
- Variable, which depend on how much it is producing. Purchases of raw materials are one obvious example; overtime and shift payments often vary as well.

The size of a firm's variable costs help to hone its survival instincts, because it is wrong to assume that a loss-maker should automatically stop production. If revenues cover variable costs and make some contribution to fixed costs, a firm should stay open until it can either reduce its fixed costs or, if that really proves impossible, eliminate them altogether through liquidation. This yardstick underlines the general conclusion that, in the long run, all costs can be varied.

Velocity of circulation. Colloquially, the turnover rate of money; measured as nominal GROSS DOMESTIC PRODUCT (or GNP) divided by the MONEY SUPPLY (on any of its various definitions). The implications of the velocity of circulation are far reaching: see the QUANTITY THEORY OF MONEY.

Venture capital. Vague term for money invested in high-risk, start-up companies. MERCHANT BANKS have traditionally been looked to for venture capital, but other institutions such as pension funds have started earmarking a small proportion of their portfolios to the business. In the United States, specialized venture capital funds have become quite common, backed by BANKS, STOCKBROKERS and wealthy individuals. See RISK.

Vertical integration. When firms buy up companies in the same line of business but at a different stage in the production process. Example: oil companies are vertically integrated, often owning everything from oil wells through refineries to chains of filling stations. Contrast with horizontal integration, where companies expand by mergers or take-overs with companies in the same line of business and stage in the production process, so increasing their share of the market. Others buy up unrelated businesses to form CONGLOMERATES. Oil companies sometimes do that too: Gulf Oil even bought a circus during the late 1970s, when it was fashionable for oil men to reduce their dependence on the black gold.

Visible trade. Exports and imports that you can drop on your foot: cars, copper and Concorde. Known as merchandise trade in America. Contrast with INVISIBLE TRADE (and see also BALANCE OF PAYMENTS).

Voluntary unemployment. In neutral language, those who could find a job at the going wage but prefer to be unemployed than employed for a variety of reasons: they may be searching for the right job, or taking an extended break before taking up a new job. Pejoratively known as workshy, scroungers, and so on.

W

Wage drift. The difference between basic pay and actual EARNINGS. It is made up of overtime, bonus payments, shift pay, and so on, and is usually considerable. In the United States, average basic pay was $286 a week in 1981; average earnings were $318 a week. In Britain, the gap was even wider (despite a deeper recession) because overtime is more common. Basic pay was £120 a week in 1981, while average earnings were £141. During a cyclical upswing, wage drift increases – and then falls in the downturn.

Wage round. Shorthand for the sequence of bargaining over pay. In countries like Britain and Italy, with a tradition of annual pay awards, the wage round follows a regular pattern from one industry or firm to the next. Some other countries with annual pay awards tend to compress their bargaining into a shorter period – for example, Japan's shinto, the 'spring offensive' when all the major deals are decided within little more than a month. In the United States, where some industries habitually agree contracts lasting several years, it is harder to talk of a well-defined wage round.

Wages councils. British institutions, first established in 1909 to set pay and conditions in industries where normal bargaining between TRADE UNIONS and employers was thought impossible, largely because the industries were too fragmented. Wages councils were reformed in 1945, but their basic wage fixing function remains. Some people see them as a thin line of defence against sweat-shop employers; others argue that they contribute to unemployment by setting minimum wages above market clearing levels.

The councils are made up of three groups: representatives of employers and of trade unions, plus independent members (often academics) appointed by the government. In 1982, there were twenty-seven wages councils operating, covering some 2.7 million workers.

Wall Street. The symbol of CAPITALISM, 'the Street' runs for a third of a mile in lower Manhattan. It is New York's financial heart, with plenty of skyscrapers tall enough for bankrupt financiers to end it all after a stock market crash. Air conditioning has changed all that. The world's biggest and oldest STOCK EXCHANGE, the New York stock exchange (founded in 1792) is located on Wall Street; the much smaller American stock exchange, which is just around the corner, operates principally as a nursery for younger companies. The Street serves as home to the keenest watchers and influencers of the Fed's MONETARY CONTROLS – so the Fed annoys Street dwellers at its own risk.

Wealth effect. The process by which falling INTEREST rates and slowing INFLATION produces a rise in spending. Also known as the real balance effect and the Pigou effect (after the English economist, A. C. Pigou, 1877–1959). Whatever you call it, its implications are profound. The wealth effect is central to the question of whether, in a RECESSION, DEMAND can recover spontaneously, or whether it needs a KEYNESIAN fiscal stimulus. Wealth effect theorists maintain that falling interest rates boost capital values (of equities, bonds, and so on), while slowing inflation means that individuals need to save a smaller proportion of their income in order to maintain the real value of their liquid assets. As a result of being (and feeling) richer, people will spend more. How much more is a critical question, which has yet to be satisfactorily resolved. Reluctant to rekindle inflation by a Keynesian stimulus, many governments are relying implicitly on a wealth effect for recovery in the 1980s.

Wealth tax. Extolled by some, maligned by others, levied hardly at all. In the abstract, a straightforward idea: personal wealth above a certain level would be taxed, probably once a year. The levy could be large enough to reduce wealth holdings (a penal tax), or small enough to ensure that only the idle rich need to sell the silver to pay the taxman (an efficiency tax). In practice, problems abound: lobbies point to the special circumstances of farmers, small businessmen, old houses, old masters, and demand that they should be exempt.

This debate rambles on in countries without a wealth tax (with the exception of the United States, perhaps because there is not enough old money to irritate new rulers). But where wealth taxes are already in force, there is much less fuss. Countries with wealth taxes include West Germany, Switzerland, Norway, Sweden and Denmark.

Windfall profits. Controversial phrase, especially as the word 'tax' is usually tagged on to the end. To some, windfall profits are, if not ill-gotten, at least unexpected and unintended, the result of circumstances beyond the control of the companies concerned. To others, they are part of the ebb and flow of ENTREPRENEURIAL RISK taking, and should not be singled out for special treatment.

Example: the quadrupling of oil prices in 1973–74, which turned profitable oil wells into gold mines. The issue of how to tax this windfall came to a head in the United States in 1979, when the Carter administration lifted price controls on 'old' oil. This was presumed to be an unpopular (and certainly unpopulist) move; as a quid pro quo, the administration introduced a tax on the windfall, to raise an estimated $228 billion over 8–11 years. In Britain, Mrs Thatcher's Tory government followed much the same approach in its 1981 budget when it brought in a special tax on bank profits. These were artificially swollen, said the government, by the high interest rates of 1980–81. The banks squealed (partly because the tax was applied retrospectively); the Inland Revenue collected £360 million.

Withholding tax. A tax on DIVIDENDS sent abroad, thereby designed to encourage companies (particularly local subsidiaries of foreign parents) to retain profits at home. Increasingly common; since it is recognized in most double-tax treaties, however, its ultimate impact on the recipient of the dividend is not penal.

World Bank. Colloquial name for the International Bank for Reconstruction and Development (IBRD). Established at the 1944 BRETTON WOODS Conference, it opened for business in 1946, with 38 members. By 1960, their numbers had risen to 68, and to 143 in 1982. Originally intended to finance Europe's post-war reconstruction – the Bank's first loans were to France, Holland and Denmark – it quickly started to concentrate on loans to poor countries. It is now the largest single source of development aid.

The World Bank Group has three components:

• The IBRD, which raises all its money on commercial terms (enjoying triple A status in the BOND MARKET) and then lends it out a little more expensively. It lends largely to the better-off developing countries, with per capita incomes exceeding $730 in 1980. In 1981–82 it made loan commitments of $10.3 billion.

• The International Development Association (IDA), the soft loan agency. Set up in 1960, IDA is financed by contributions from rich country governments. It has been replenished six times, each time after controversy over the size and distribution of the replenishment. It lends on very concessional terms (no interest; fifty-year maturity, with repayments starting after ten years; a small disbursement fee) to the poorest countries. In 1981–82, it made loan commitments of $2.7 billion.

• The International Finance Corporation (IFC), established in 1956 to invest in the private sector of developing countries. It makes loans and also takes equity stakes.

The World Bank has its headquarters in Washington, DC. All its six presidents have been American – Meyer (1946), McCloy (1947–49), Black (1949–62), Woods (1963–68), McNamara (1968–81) and Clausen (appointed in 1981).

Y

Yaoundé convention. The first formal trade and aid agreement between the rich EEC and some poor countries, it was signed in Yaoundé (capital of Cameroon) in 1963. The poor countries were former colonies (mostly of France), known as the Associated African and Malagasy States. They received largely unimpeded access to EEC markets for most of their exports, plus increased aid and investment. In return, the EEC countries were assured of reciprocal treatment. A second (and similar) Yaoundé convention was signed in 1969; it was succeeded by the wider-ranging LOMÉ CONVENTION in 1975.

Yield curve. Shorthand for comparisons of INTEREST rates on, for example, bonds (see BOND MARKET) carrying different maturities. If investors consider it riskier to buy bonds with fifteen-year lives than with five, they will demand a higher interest rate; the yield curve will therefore slope up from left to right (also known as a 'positive' curve). If a CENTRAL BANK is keeping short-term money very scarce, that will bid up short rates – perhaps above the level of long rates, in which case the yield curve will slope down from left to right. See Figure 25.

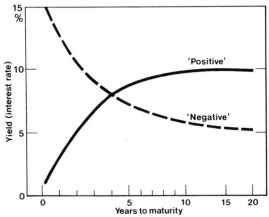

Figure 25 *Yield curve*

Yield gap. A way of comparing the performance of bonds (see BOND MARKET) and EQUITIES; the gap is defined as the average yield on equities minus the average yield on bonds. In the days of low INFLATION, equities yielded more than bonds – a reflection of their greater riskiness. The tables turned in 1959 (in both the United States and Britain), when a reverse yield gap opened up. Rising inflation was bad for bonds, depressing their capital values and therefore raising their yields, while equity prices rose (in nominal terms anyway) and so equity yields fell. Since the late 1950s, the reverse yield gap has fluctuated between 1.5 and 9.6 percentage points in Britain, 1.0 and 9.0 percentage points in the United States.

Z

Zero-coupon bond. To eliminate INCOME and therefore INCOME TAX, many investors are happy to buy bonds (see BOND MARKET) that offer no COUPON (INTEREST) at all. Instead they buy a $100 bond for, say, $35 with the promise that it will be redeemed at $100 when it matures in ten years time. The extra $65 – the equivalent of an annual interest rate of 9.6 per cent at redemption – will be treated as a capital gain and therefore subject to low or no tax. For this reason, some governments prohibit the issue of zero-coupon bonds (or even their less brazen sisters, DEEP DISCOUNT BONDS).

Zero-sum game. Notion that winners from economic transactions are counterbalanced by losers. Strenuously denied (and disproved) by virtually all economists. Examples of the zero-sum mentality: 'profits are earned at the expense of wages'; 'investment abroad means less investment at home'; 'overseas aid is a waste of money'.

Notes for further reading

All books on economic policy and institutions become quickly dated. To plug the gap between books and fast-moving events, try *The Economist* briefs, especially:

'Money and finance' (1982)
'Britain's economy under strain' (1982)
'The EEC' (1983)
'The world economy' (1979)
'Europe's economies' (1978)

For general economics textbooks:

R. G. Lipsey *Introduction to Positive Economics*
Paul Samuelson *Economics* (now in its 11th edition)
P. Wonnacott and R. Wonnacott *Economics*
Robert Heilbroner and Lester Thurow *Economics Explained*

On money and finance:

Lawrence Ritter and William Silber *Money* (especially good on American monetary policy)
J. Niehaus *The Theory of Money*
Brian Tew *The Evolution of the International Monetary System 1945–77*
Andrew Crockett *International Money*
Tim Congdon *Monetary Policy in the UK*
Joe Irving *The City at Work*

For a lighter read, try:

Anthony Sampson *The Money Lenders: Bankers in a Dangerous World*
Charles Kindleberger *Manias, Panics and Crashes*

On business and microeconomics:

M. L. Wachter and J. L. Wachter (eds) *Toward a New US Industrial Policy*
James Bates and J. R. Parkinson *Business Economics*
H. Gravelle and R. Rees *Microeconomics*

On accountancy:

W. Reid and D. R. Myddleton *The Meaning of Company Accounts*

Country studies:
Derek Morris (ed.) *The Economic System in the UK*
R. E. Caves and L. B. Krause (eds) *Britain's Economic Performance*
Martin Feldstein (ed.) *The American Economy in Transition*
Andrea Boltho (ed.) *The European Economy*
Ralf Dahrendorf (ed.) *Europe's Economy in Crisis*
Andrea Boltho *Japan, an Economic Survey*